T0224429

Lecture Notes in Computer Science 4620

Commenced Publication in 1973
Founding and Former Series Editors:
Gerhard Goos, Juris Hartmanis, and Jan van Leeuwen

Editorial Board

Awais Rashid   Mehmet Aksit (Eds.)

Transactions on Aspect-Oriented Software Development III

 Springer

Volume Editors

Awais Rashid
Lancaster University
Computing Department
Lancaster LA1 4WA, UK
E-mail: awais@comp.lancs.ac.uk

Mehmet Aksit
University of Twente
Department of Computer Science
Enschede, The Netherlands
E-mail: aksit@ewi.utwente.nl

Library of Congress Control Number: 2007939176

CR Subject Classification (1998): D.2, D.3, I.6, H.4, K.6

LNCS Sublibrary: SL 2 – Programming and Software Engineering

ISSN	1861-3027
ISBN-10	3-540-75161-0 Springer Berlin Heidelberg New York
ISBN-13	978-3-540-75161-8 Springer Berlin Heidelberg New York

Springer is a part of Springer Science+Business Media

springer.com

© Springer-Verlag Berlin Heidelberg 2007
Printed in Germany

Typesetting: Camera-ready by author, data conversion by Scientific Publishing Services, Chennai, India
Printed on acid-free paper   SPIN: 12162321   06/3180   5 4 3 2 1 0

Editorial

Welcome to Volume III of Transactions on Aspect-Oriented Software Development. Since its launch in 2006 the journal has attracted a steady stream of submissions, both to its indefinitely open call for papers and to calls pertaining to special issues focusing on key topics in AOSD. At the time of writing this editorial, the total number of submissions to the journal stands at 78. This is very healthy given that it is only the second year of the journal.

The journal aims to maintain the highest standards expected of an archival work in AOSD while ensuring timely feedback and notification to the authors. Each paper is handled by an associate editor, appointed by the co-editors-in-chief, who is a specialist on the specific topic. We ensure that the associate editor does not have a conflict of interest relating to the paper assigned to him/her. If the associate editor deems the paper to be worthy of a review, s/he solicits reviews from at least three reviewers on the quality of the work. On the basis of these reviews, s/he then makes a recommendation to reject the paper; ask the authors to resubmit the paper with major revisions; accept the paper with minor revisions or accept it without any further changes. We aim to notify the authors about the outcome of the reviews within 12 weeks. In a small number of cases, either unforeseen circumstances or other commitments of reviewers may lead to some further delay but we are pleased to say that such cases remain a minority.

In cases where major or minor revisions are recommended, the authors are expected to address the reviewers' comments. Papers with major changes are passed on to the reviewers again for a second review. If, even after the second review, a paper cannot be accepted as it is or subject to minor changes, then the paper is rejected. This is to avoid an endless review cycle. The procedure is applied pragmatically in that where there is a significant difference of opinion amongst the reviewers and, provided the associate editor recommends so, the authors are given a third and final opportunity to address the reviewers' comments.

Each special issue is handled by one of the co-editors-in-chief who works closely with the guest editors to ensure that the journal's review process is followed and quality standards are maintained. Given that aspect-oriented software development is a young discipline it was decided at the editorial board meeting in March 2006 that the co-editor-in-chief not handling a special issue should be locked out of the review process completely. This allows such a co-editor-in-chief to author a paper for the special issue as normally co-editors-in-chief cannot submit a paper to the journal.

This volume constitutes the first part of the special issue on Early Aspects guest edited by João Araújo and Elisa Baniassad. The handling co-editor-in-chief was Mehmet Aksit. The special issue was very successful in attracting high quality submissions and, as a result, had to be split over two volumes of the journal. The papers in this volume focus on analysis, visualisation, conflict identification and composition of Early Aspects. The papers in volume IV focus on mapping of Early Aspects across the software lifecycle.

We wish to thank the editorial board for their continued guidance, commitment and input on the policies of the journal, the choice of special issues as well as associate-editorship of submitted articles. We also thank the guest editors, João Araújo and Elisa Baniassad, for the excellent job they did with the special issue—the proposal they prepared is now used as a model for all special issue proposals to Transactions on AOSD. Thanks are also due to the reviewers who volunteered time amidst their busy schedules to help realize this volume. Most importantly, we wish to thank the authors who have submitted papers to the journal so far, for their contributions maintain the high quality of Transactions on AOSD.

Awais Rashid and Mehmet Aksit
Co-editors-in-chief

Organization

Editorial Board

List of Reviewers

Table of Contents

Guest Editors' Introduction: Early Aspects—Analysis, Visualization, Conflicts and Composition

João Araújo[1] and Elisa Baniassad[2]

[1] Universidade Nova de Lisboa, Portugal
ja@di.fct.unl.pt
[2] Chinese University of Hong Kong, China
elisa@cse.cuhk.edu.hk

Early Aspects are aspects found in the early life cycle phases of software development, including requirements elicitation and analysis, domain analysis and architecture design activities. Aspects at these stages crosscut the modular units appropriate for their lifecycle activity; traditional requirements documentation, domain knowledge capture and architectural artifacts do not afford separate description of early aspects. As such, early aspects necessitate new modularizations to be effectively captured and maintained. Without new tools and techniques, early aspects remain tangled and scattered in lifecycle artifacts, and may lead to development, maintenance and evolution difficulties.

The Early Aspects community has grown significantly since its inception as a workshop at the first conference on Aspect Oriented Software Development in 2001. Since then, the workshop series has flourished, becoming a regular feature of several conferences, and papers presenting and studying new Early Aspects techniques have been published in many major venues. Early aspects research groups now span the globe, and bridge industry and academia.

The level of maturity reached by the Early Aspects work prompted us to edit this special issue on Early Aspects. We believe that this issue will support the cross-fertilization of ideas between those focused on research throughout all phases of the software lifecycle, and will help researchers identify new questions in the world of Early Aspects.

Overview of the Articles and the Evaluation Process: This special issue consists of eight articles, selected out of ten submissions. Each were evaluated by three reviewers and revised at least twice over a period of seven months.

The Early Aspects special issue covers three main areas of research, and is split over two volumes of the journal. This volume presents papers in the areas of Analysis and Visualization, and Conflicts and Composition. Volume. IV contains papers on mapping early aspects throughout the lifecycle.

1 Analysis and Visualization

Early aspects research often involves examination of existing, traditionally organized, artifacts, and refactoring them into an aspect-oriented organization. This process might encompass identification of aspects in early requirements documents, examination of the relevance of early aspects in a certain type of artifact, how early

A. Rashid and M. Aksit (Eds.): Transactions on AOSD III, LNCS 4620, pp. 1–3, 2007.
© Springer-Verlag Berlin Heidelberg 2007

aspects can be used to better represent certain early lifecycle documents, or how to more effectively capture aspects for the sake of development activities in the early lifecycle. Early aspects also require new approaches for formation and visualizing lifecycle artifacts. For example, new techniques are required for elicitation and capture of requirements, the maintenance of domain information, and the formation and presentation of architectural information. In this issue, we present four papers which span this area, and touch upon its salient research questions.

EA-Miner: Towards Automation in Aspect-Oriented Requirements Engineering *by Américo Sampaio, Awais Rashid, Ruzanna Chitchyan, and Paul Rayson*
This paper describes the EA-Miner tool-based approach, which provides automated support for mining various types of concerns from a variety of early stage requirements documents and how these concepts can be structured into specific aspect-oriented requirements models. The automation consists of natural language processing, to reason about properties of the requirements as well as the utilization of semantics revealed by the natural language analysis in building the models.

Analysis of Early Aspects in Requirements Goal Models: A Concept-Driven Approach *by Nan Niu and Steve Easterbrook*
This paper presents a rigorous approach to conceptual analysis of stakeholder concerns. The authors use the repertory grid technique to identify terminological interference between stakeholders' descriptions of their goals, and formal concept analysis to uncover conflicts and trade-offs between these goals. The approach is applied to the goal models, commonly used in requirements analysis.

Analysis of Crosscutting in Early Software Development Phases based on Traceability *by Klaas van den Berg, José María Conejero, and Juan Hernández*
This paper proposes a conceptual framework for crosscutting where crosscutting is defined in terms of trace relations. The definition of crosscutting is formalized using linear algebra, and represented with matrices and matrix operations. Thus, crosscutting can be clearly distinguished from scattering and tangling. With this definition and transitivity of trace relations, crosscutting can be identified and traced through software development, also in early phases.

Visualizing Early Aspects with Use Case Maps *by Gunter Mussbacher, Daniel Amyot and Michael Weiss*
This paper describes how scenario-based aspects can be modelled at the requirements level unobtrusively and with the same techniques as for non-aspectual systems, with the help of Use Case Maps. These are a visual scenario notation under standardization by the International Telecommunication Union. With Use Case Maps, aspects as well as pointcut expressions are modelled in a visual way which is generally considered the preferred choice for models of a high level of abstraction.

2   Conflicts and Composition

With Early Aspect separation of concerns comes the need for composition of concerns. Early aspects composition is present in all early lifecycle phases.

Mechanisms for weaving early aspects into traditional artifacts are needed. In the requirements phase, composition means both the recombination of separately described requirements, and also the consideration of clashes between the semantics of those requirements. Here we present two papers in this area: one dealing with weaving aspects in design, and the other presenting an approach for handling conflicts in aspectual requirements.

Handling Conflicts in Aspectual Requirements Compositions *by Isabel Sofia Brito, Filipe Vieira, Ana Moreira, and Rita A. Ribeiro*
This paper discusses the use of Multiple Criteria Decision Making methods to support aspectual conflict management in the context of Aspect-Oriented Requirements Engineering. A conflict is detected whenever two or more concerns that contribute negatively to each other and have the same importance need to be composed together. The presented solution relies on the use of the obtained concern rankings to handle unresolved conflicts.

Weaving Multiple Aspects in Models *by Jacques Klein, Franck Fleurey, and Jean-Marc Jézéquel*
This paper presents an approach to statically weave behavioral aspects into sequence diagrams. The weaving process is automated, and takes into account the semantics of the model used, i.e., the partial order that a SD induces. To enable the weaving of multiple aspects, a new interpretation for pointcuts to allow join points to match them more flexibly is proposed.

EA-Miner: Towards Automation in Aspect-Oriented Requirements Engineering

Américo Sampaio, Awais Rashid, Ruzanna Chitchyan, and Paul Rayson

Computing Department, InfoLab 21, Lancaster University, Lancaster LA1 4WA, UK
{a.sampaio, awais, rouza, paul}@comp.lancs.ac.uk

Abstract. Aspect-oriented requirements engineering (AORE) provides separation of concerns at the requirements level. In order to cope with concern identification and structuring into different requirements models, tool support is vital to effectively reduce the burden of performing various AORE tasks. This paper describes how the EA-Miner tool-based approach provides automated support for mining various types of concerns from a variety of early stage requirements documents and how these concepts can be structured into specific aspect-oriented requirements models (e.g., viewpoints-based, use-case-based). The key insight for early-stage requirements automation is the use of natural language processing to reason about properties of the requirements as well as the utilization of semantics revealed by the natural language analysis in building the models. Evaluation of EA-Miner shows promising results concerning time-effectiveness and accuracy of undertaking AORE activities and building requirements models. Moreover, an industrial case study conducted at Siemens AG investigated how the tool performs in a real-world setting by analysing what benefits it brings and challenges it faces during AORE analysis. The EA-Miner analysis enabled to find concerns that were considered relevant by a research team at Siemens that is re-implementing the investigated system with aspect-oriented languages. Moreover, the exposure of the tool to industrial requirements written by different developers also revealed some challenges imposed by the structure of the documentation and the different use of vocabulary terms hence providing new paths to explore and improve the tool in the future such as better pre-processing support, "domain synonym" identification and detection of poorly written requirements.

1 Introduction

Requirements engineering (RE) is considered to be a fundamental part of the software engineering lifecycle [1–3] as poor requirements can have a significant impact in later stages of the life cycle and can often be a critical factor in the failure of a project.

One of the initial tasks in RE is gathering the requirements from the end users, managers, and other stakeholders. This is a challenging task since requirements engineers and stakeholders normally have different backgrounds and knowledge about the system under investigation that complicates their communication and understanding of the system goals and uses. Generally, during this process, the requirements engineer somehow records these requirements (e.g., creating a report, generating interview transcripts) to use them later for creating a more detailed specification of the system.

A. Rashid and M. Aksit (Eds.): Transactions on AOSD III, LNCS 4620, pp. 4–39, 2007.

However, in some real scenarios the requirements engineers do not have the opportunity to have much contact with the stakeholders, for example, in mass market application development (e.g., web and off-the-shelf software) [4] where the number and diversity of users can be extremely high. In these cases the requirements engineers have to elicit the requirements based on previous knowledge about the domain or based on available documentation such as marketing studies, legacy specifications and user manuals.

In both cases the goal of the requirements engineers is to make a transition from understanding the "problem world" and creating a requirements specification that represents the system under investigation and that will help developers to build the system in the "solution world" [2, 5]. During this transition process several documents with various structures (e.g., interview transcripts, user manuals, marketing analysis and legacy specifications) can be used to inform the requirements engineer.

Generally this transition process is done manually which can be very time-consuming depending on the size and complexity of the system. For example, consider that the input to the requirements specification and analysis task is a 60 page contract document and a 50 page legacy user manual. Given that the standard average rate of reading is between 250 and 350 words per minute, it is not difficult to realize that reading all the information and transforming it into a more structured RE model demands a huge effort. Therefore, in order to reduce this effort, it is vital to provide automated support.

As most documents used in RE are written in natural language, some researchers [6–14] have found promising results in automating RE tasks by building tools that apply natural language processing (NLP) techniques with requirements-related documents as input in order to automatically identify concepts and build RE models. Applying NLP in requirements interpretation is also challenging as natural language is not as precise as design and implementation languages containing lots of ambiguities and complex semantics.

Regarding structuring of requirements, recently, some researchers [15–19] have proposed the adoption of aspect-oriented requirements engineering (AORE) as an effective approach to achieve separation of concerns. AORE is based on the observation that, similar to what was evidenced by the AOP community, requirements artifacts can contain tangling and scattering that need special treatment. This treatment is provided by adapting current RE approaches with new abstractions (called early aspects) that modularize crosscutting concerns at RE level, thus bringing the following benefits [15–19]:

- Facilitate detection of conflicts between broadly-scoped requirements;
- Simplify analysis of interactions between early aspects (e.g., the impact that security can have on response time);
- Facilitate mapping to later stages (e.g., architecture, design and code) thus providing homogeneity in an aspect-oriented development process.

Even though separation of crosscutting concerns provides benefits, building an AORE specification with existing AORE approaches suffers from the same problems as for classical RE techniques mentioned above. In the case of AORE it is even more challenging since the identification and structuring of requirements level aspects, base abstractions and crosscutting relationships is harder due to these concepts being scattered and tangled across the documents. Moreover, the fact that AORE is a novel approach complicates the analysis since many system analysts do not have good understanding of early aspects.

This is where the EA-Miner tool-based approach comes into play by offering automated support for identifying the abstractions of different AORE techniques (e.g., viewpoints [20] based, use case [21] based) and helping to build the models. The tool's automated support helps to reduce the time spent to:

- **Identify model abstractions:** For example concepts such as use cases, viewpoints, and early aspects that belong to a specific requirements technique (e.g., Use Case based AORE [22], Viewpoints based AORE [16, 17]) can be automatically mined from different elicitation documents;
- **Structure abstractions into various models:** The tool offers features to edit the identified abstractions (add, remove, filter) as well as to map them into a chosen model (e.g., a structured AORE specification based on viewpoints or use cases).

It is important to mention that EA-Miner's automated support does not replace the work of the requirements engineer but only helps him/her to save time by focusing on key information. The key insight for early-stage requirements automation is the use of natural language processing (NLP) to reason about properties of the requirements as well as the utilization of semantics revealed by the natural language analysis in building the models. The use of NLP techniques to help with AORE automation was initially investigated by our previous work [23, 24] and provided some insights (e.g., which NLP techniques could be used for identifying model concepts) that helped us to reach the current state of the tool's implementation. After this, we have added several features on the tool such as synonym and stemming filtering, frequency analysis, and support for functional crosscutting as well as made several improvements on the identification mechanisms. Moreover, we have conducted several case studies including an industrial case study to evaluate the tool.

Most AORE approaches [16–19, 25] do not provide tool support for the identification of early aspects from requirements documents with the exception of Theme/Doc [15]. Therefore, EA-Miner offers a key contribution to complement these approaches by automating the identification task for them. Moreover, our NLP-based mining analysis and techniques used (Sects. 3,4) offer a higher degree of automation when compared to other mining approaches (Sect. 7) as the input requested from the user is minimal.

The remainder of this paper is structured as follows. Section 2 explains how EA-Miner can be utilized in an AORE process. Section 3 gives an overview of the utilization of natural language techniques for requirements model automation. Section 4 shows how EA-Miner uses these NLP techniques to automate the identification of concepts and mapping of models. Section 5 evaluates the tool showing its time-effectiveness and also presents data regarding the quality of the produced models. Moreover, an industrial case study shows how the tool can perform in a real-world setting and what benefits it can bring for the development process such as identifying relevant concerns that were missed by domain experts. Section 6 provides further discussion of EA-Miner and its features. Section 7 presents an overview of existing related work while Sect. 8 concludes the paper.

2 EA-Miner and the AORE Process

Recently, several researchers have worked on creating new approaches [15, 25, 26] or adapting contemporary requirements engineering approaches (e.g., viewpoints [3], scenarios [21], goals [27]) to what have been called AORE approaches such as Viewpoint-based AORE [16, 17], Scenario-based AORE [18] and goal-based AORE [19].

The common goal of all these AORE approaches is to provide an appropriate separation of concerns at the requirements level modularizing crosscutting properties in early aspects. While some approaches, often categorized as asymmetric, provide a clear separation of what are the base and crosscutting abstractions (e.g., in [16, 17] viewpoints are base abstractions while early aspects[1] are broadly scoped properties, such as security, availability, response time, that crosscut several viewpoints) other approaches, categorized as symmetric, give a uniform treatment to the decomposition units considering everything to be a concern [25].

It is not our intention to get into details of the advantages and disadvantages of each of the AORE approaches as our goal for EA-Miner is to offer a framework (tool + guidelines) that can be used with any AORE approach. In Fig. 1 we show a "general AORE process" which contains a set of activities that are common to most AORE approaches as described in [16–18].

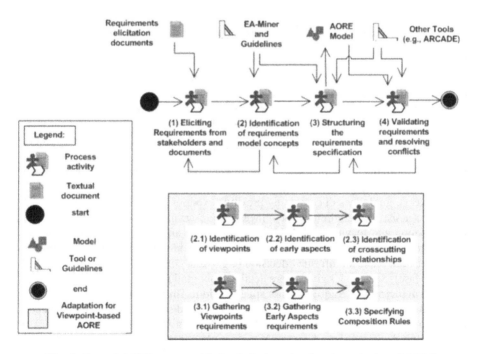

Fig. 1. General AORE process with detailed adaptation for viewpoint-based AORE

---

[1] Early aspects are also called concerns in this approach.

The top of Fig. 1 shows the general activities (1–4) common to most AORE processes while the bottom shows an adaptation of activities 2 and 3 based on viewpoint-based AORE. Depending on the AORE approach used, each activity is adapted accordingly (e.g., had we considered [18] we would identify scenarios instead of viewpoints in activity 2.1).

The reason we highlighted activities 2 and 3 is that these are the ones that represent the core focus of EA-Miner and also where it significantly contributes to existing AORE approaches, as current tool support for most AORE approaches does not address identification of concepts from requirement elicitation documents and mapping into an AORE model. We use Viewpoint-based AORE to discuss the features of EA-Miner. An overview of each activity, the artifacts involved and the role of EA-Miner is discussed below:

(1) **Eliciting requirements from stakeholders and documents:** As discussed in Sect. 1 elicitation can be partly done by interacting with stakeholders or, when they are not available, by reading available documentation or both. In this sense EA-Miner can help providing quick feedback while identifying the concepts in the next activity by offering views that show key information on the documents provided as input.

(2) **Identification of requirements model concepts:** EA-Miner helps in automating activity 2, using the documents produced in activity 1 as input, of identifying model concepts (e.g., viewpoints, early aspects, use cases and others) and presenting them to the user. Some characteristics about the identification are:

- **Rule-based and NLP-based:** For each AORE model considered, the mining technique utilized can be different. For example, for the Viewpoint model, part-of-speech NLP technique is used to identify nouns as viewpoint candidates while for a use case approach we can consider action verbs as candidate use cases. Section 3 explains this in detail while Sect. 4 shows how this is realized in EA-Miner.
- **Every concept identified is a candidate:** EA-Miner identifies the model concepts and considers them to be candidates. The tool offers several features to show information about the candidates (e.g., their frequency of occurrence in the text, their meaning) as well as process guidelines to help the requirements engineer accept or reject that concept.
- **Process guidelines can be used:** As mentioned before EA-Miner does not replace the work of the requirements engineer and is not aimed at 100% automation. For this reason, guidelines documenting previous experience and best practices can be used to assist the requirements engineer by prescribing some "tips" on how the information and features of EA-Miner can be used effectively. Guidelines can be customized according to AORE model to give an idea on how the requirements engineer can make an informed decision (e.g., what constitutes a "good" viewpoint or use case). Section 4.3 gives more details about guidelines.

(3) **Structuring the Requirements specification:** This activity constitutes editing the initial model produced in the previous activity by discarding irrelevant concepts, adding new ones not identified, and generating a structured model (e.g., a specification document based on the Viewpoint-based AORE approach). EA-Miner also provides features such as filtering (e.g., show the 10 most relevant viewpoints based on frequency) and process guidelines as discussed above to help the requirements engineer.

(4) **Validating requirements and resolving conflicts:** This step represents the validation of the specified requirements and also conflict detection and resolution. EA-Miner's output of step 3 can be easily used as input by other tools (e.g., Arcade [28]) that perform conflict identification. For example [16, 17] shows how the early aspects can contribute to each other (e.g., security and response time can both crosscut the same requirements of an ATM viewpoint and can contribute negatively to each other).

One important point to mention is that the previous activities are not necessarily conducted in a strict sequential order but in an iterative and incremental fashion providing forward and backward feedback cycles. The next section explains how NLP techniques can be used to address mining of concepts (activity 2) in different AORE approaches as well as structuring and filtering capabilities (activity 3).

3 Utilizing NLP Techniques for Automation

The cornerstone of EA-Miner's model automation are the natural language processing features provided by the WMATRIX NLP tool suite which have been shown to be effective in early phase requirements engineering [11, 28, 29]. WMATRIX implements NLP techniques such as frequency analysis, part-of-speech (with a precision of 97%) and semantic tagging (with a precision of 91%) that provide relevant information about the properties and semantics of a text in natural language. *Frequency analysis* shows statistical data about frequencies of words that help to find out which ones are more significant in the text.

WMATRIX takes a *corpus-based* NLP approach. Corpus Linguistics [30] can be understood as the study of language based on "real life" language use. A corpus is a collection of texts from different sources (e.g., newspapers, magazines, books, journals) that can be collected over several years and made available for researchers. For example, the British national corpus (BNC) [31], on which WMATRIX draws, is a 100 million word reference collection of samples of written and spoken English from a wide range of sources.

Part-of-speech (POS) tagging [11, 28] assigns to each word its grammatical function (part-of-speech) such as singular common noun, comparative adjective, infinitive verb and other categories such as the ones in Table 1. The tagging process in WMATRIX is based on a language model derived from the large reference corpus and uses surrounding context to decide the most likely tag for each word.

Table 1. Examples of POS and semantic tags from [11, 28]

POS TAG	WHAT IT REPRESENTS
NN1	singular common noun (e.g. book, girl)
VVI	infinitive (e.g. to give... It will work...)
SEM TAG	**WHAT IT REPRESENTS**
M	movement, location, travel and transport
S	social actions, states and processes
M3	vehicles and transport on land
S7.4	permission

Semantic tagging [11, 28] assigns a word or multiword expression to a specific class of meaning. The semantic tags are represented in a tagset arranged in 21 top-level categories (e.g., M and S in Table 1) that expand into 232 sub-categories (e.g., M3 and S7.4) [28]. Each of these categories groups words that are related via a specific meaning (e.g., M3 contains vehicle, car, bus, truck, automobile). The taxonomy originates from a corpus-based dictionary and has been comparatively evaluated against publicly available semantic hierarchies [32].

Moreover, the same word (e.g., performance) can contain different meanings (e.g., act of a dancer or artist; processing power of the computer) and thus be present in more than one semantic category. The semantic tagger deals with this by analyzing the context of the phrase in which the word is used and also by using POS tags for disambiguation in order to attribute the correct tag. It is important to highlight that both POS and semantic tagging are completely handled by WMATRIX and do not require any input neither from the requirements engineer nor from the EA-Miner tool. The semantic tagger makes its decisions based on a large coverage dictionary of single words and multiword expressions, currently containing 73,894 words and multiwords. These resources have been constructed manually by linguists for other corpus based projects over a number of years.

EA-Miner utilizes WMATRIX to pre-process a requirements document provided as input (Fig. 2). WMATRIX returns another file which consists of the same content as the input file but tagged with POS and SEM tags. Figure 2a shows an example of a toll collection system we will use throughout this paper. Figure 2b shows the first

a "In a road traffic pricing system, drivers of authorized vehicles are charged at toll gates automatically. The gates are placed at special lanes called green lanes. A driver has to install a device (a gizmo) in his/her vehicle. The registration of authorised vehicles includes the owner's personal data, bank account number and vehicle details. The gizmo is sent to the client to be activated using an ATM that informs the system upon gizmo activation. A gizmo is read by the toll gate sensors. The information read is stored by the system and used to debit the respective account. When an authorised vehicle passes through a green lane, a green light is turned on, and the amount being debited is displayed. If an unauthorised vehicle passes through it, a yellow light is turned on and a camera takes a photo of the plate (used to fine the owner of the vehicle). There are three types of toll gates: single toll, where the same type of vehicles pay a fixed amount, entry toll to enter a freeway and exit toll to leave it. The amount paid on motorways depends on the type of the vehicle and the distance traveled."

b
```
<?xml version='1.0' encoding='utf-8'?><file>
<s> <w id="2.1" pos="II" sem="Z5">In</w>
<w id="2.2" pos="AT1" sem="M3[i1.2.1">a</w>
<w id="2.3" pos="NN1" sem="M3[i1.2.2">road</w>
<w id="2.4" pos="NN1" sem="M3">traffic</w>
<w id="2.5" pos="NN1" sem="I1.3">pricing</w>
<w id="2.6" pos="NN1" sem="X4.2">system</w>
<w id="2.7" pos="." sem="PUNC">.</w>
<w id="2.8" pos="NN2" sem="M3/S2mf">drivers</w>
<w id="2.9" pos="IO" sem="Z5">of</w>
<w id="2.10" pos="JJ" sem="S7.4+">authorised</w>
<w id="2.11" pos="NN2" sem="M3fn">vehicles</w>
<w id="2.12" pos="VBR" sem="Z5">are</w>
<w id="2.13" pos="VVN" sem="I1.3">charged</w>
<w id="2.14" pos="II" sem="Z5">at</w>
<w id="2.15" pos="NN1" sem="I1.3">toll</w>
<w id="2.16" pos="NN2" sem="H5">gates</w>
<w id="2.17" pos="RR" sem="N3.8+">automatically</w>
<w id="2.18" pos="." sem="PUNC">.</w> </s>
```

Fig. 2. a Toll collection system adapted from [16, 17]. **b** First sentence of the toll system file with POS and SEM tags. The parsed file is structured in sentences <s> containing words <w>.

sentence of the file parsed by WMATRIX. One can notice, for example, that the word "road" has POS tag = NN1 which represents a singular noun and "traffic" has the SEM tag = M3 which represents the vehicles and transport on land semantic class.

Another important concept that is utilized in EA-Miner is *Stemming* [11, 28] which is the process of reducing similar words to the same canonical form. For example the words "availability" and "available" are stemmed to "avail". This makes it possible to recognize words that are not exactly equal and treat them as the same concept (e.g., for a requirements engineer the words "driver" and "drivers" are the same viewpoint).

3.1 Using NLP Techniques

The NLP techniques offered by WMATRIX are used by EA-Miner to automate construction and transformation of AORE models represented as different requirements artifacts. Fig. 3 presents an overview of the transformations that transform an initial set of elicitation level RE documents (e.g., user manuals, legacy specifications, interview transcripts) called model M0 into a structured AORE Model M1 and later into a filtered M2 model.

Fig. 3. Model transformations

The automation level discussed here focuses mainly on describing NLP-based mining analysis to identify the concepts (e.g., use cases, viewpoints, early aspects) (Sect. 3.1.1) within an AORE approach. Moreover, we also show how, after the model is created, some filtering techniques (Sect. 3.1.2) can be used to discard concepts that were improperly identified or to merge elements that represent the same concept but were identified as different concepts (e.g., "driver" and "drivers" as different viewpoints as mentioned above).

3.1.1 Identification of Model Concepts

The *identification* of **base concerns** in some AORE approaches (e.g., viewpoint-based [16, 17] or use case based [22]) can use the information produced by the POS tagging to list possible candidates. For example, **viewpoint** candidates can be words whose POS tag represents a noun (POS tag = NN1 or NN2). For example, Fig. 2b shows that "road", "drivers", "vehicles" and "gates" are viewpoint candidates since their POS tag represents a noun. Similarly, candidates for **use cases** can be words whose POS tag represents an action verb (auxiliary verbs can be ignored such as "are", "can") such as the word "charged" (POS = VVN) in Fig. 2b.

One problem with this approach, also mentioned in [33] that suggests looking at noun-phrases to identify objects during object-oriented analysis, is that the initial list can contain a lot of false positives especially when the input file is large. This is why it is important to provide tool support and methodological guidance so that the engineer can prune the list to arrive at a set of good candidates. Section 3.1.2 provides details on how some filters can be applied to narrow down the list, while Sect. 4.3 shows some guidelines that provide guidance on the use of the tool to support this task.

Another issue is related to the danger of restricting input: if the requirement engineer focuses exclusively on the available input documents, he/she will not be able to identify the important concerns that could arise from direct interaction with the stakeholders, but are not listed in the documents. Thus, our approach must not be used in isolation, but must be complemented with stakeholder feedback as well as domain knowledge and judgment of the requirements engineer for requirements refinement.

The *identification* of **early aspects** can be broken into two categories: non-functional and functional. **Non-functional** requirements (e.g., security, concurrency, persistence, parallelism and so forth) are generally natural candidates for crosscutting concerns at the RE level since they are broadly-scoped properties that tend to constrain many other requirements [16, 17]. One important NLP feature that can be used to identify these early aspects is the SEM tags produced by WMATRIX. For example the word "authorised" in Fig. 2b has the semantic tag SEM = "S7.4+" which means permission that is a natural candidate for a security early aspect (See Table 1. The "+" sign is just an extra annotation to mean that it is a positive type of permission. "unauthorised" would be tagged as "S7.4-").

As mentioned in Sect. 3 the semantic tags cluster words into classes of meaning and one word can be present in more than one category as its meaning might change depending on the context in which the word is used. For example, if we consider the context of the requirements of a system for a Ballet company it is likely that the semantic tagger will attribute the meaning of "performance" to be "act of a dancer". On the other hand, if we were dealing with a concurrent system specification it is likely that "performance" has the meaning of "processing power" that is a natural candidate for an early aspect.

Therefore, the NLP processor's semantic tagging can help to improve an automated mining analysis of early aspects by using contextual information and thus alert the user that, in the example above for the Ballet company system, that performance might be a quality of how well the actor did on the last show (an attribute of a class). On the other hand, for the distributed system, performance is related to how the system must respond in terms of throughput or response time (a non-functional concern that can have a large impact on the design of the system).

The identification of these broadly scoped non-functional early aspects (e.g., security, performance, concurrency, usability) both in a viewpoint-based or use-case based model can benefit from the NLP semantic tagging. In both approaches these broadly scoped concerns represent restrictions applied to other requirements and functionalities (the base abstractions such as viewpoints and use cases) and, therefore, are similar in nature and can be identified in a similar fashion. What is different between both approaches is the way these general non-functional requirements compose with the base concerns. In Sect. 4.1.3 we describe in more detail how NFR automation is handled in the context of EA-Miner and how we can benefit from existing NFR knowledge bases [27, 34, 35].

Regarding the analysis of **functional** early aspects, an adaptation of the Fan-in-based aspect mining code analysis technique [36] can be used. Fan-in analysis considers the fan-in of a node n in a method call graph as the number of incoming edges (represented by direct callers of *n*). To clarify, suppose, for example, that in some system there is a log method of the Logger class which is called by five other methods in different classes (the fan-in of the log method is 5). Methods with a high fan-in (such as log) represent behaviour that is likely to be crosscutting (as it is called from several places) and is a strong candidate for an aspect [36].

Considering the **viewpoint-based** model the same concept can be applied thinking about action verbs that are referenced by some viewpoints (the viewpoint contains the action verb in its requirements). An action verb can be automatically identified using POS tags and getting the verbs that represent an action. For each action verb (e.g., "log") its fan-in is analyzed (e.g., viewpoints X, Y, Z and W contain "log" in their requirements). In this example "log" has a high fan-in (fan-in = 4) and is likely to be a functional early aspect. Considering a **use case-based** model functional early aspects can also be thought of as use cases with a high fan in (e.g., a log use case can participate in an include relationship with several other use cases such as buy, sell, register).

3.1.2 Applying Filters
When the model is initially created it is likely to have lots of candidate concepts (e.g., listing all nouns as candidate viewpoints can generate many candidates depending on the size of the input document), therefore filtering options are important. Some filters are:

- Setting a threshold to get only the *N* most significant concepts (e.g., viewpoints). This information can be easily obtained from NLP tools such as WMATRIX as it returns data such as the frequency of occurrence of words. WMATRIX offers different types of frequencies (not only simple word counts) that enables to check what concepts are most relevant considering the context of the document;
- Stemmers make it possible to recognize words such as ("driver" and "drivers", "gate" and "gates", "vehicle" and "vehicles") present in the toll system example in Fig. 2a as the same concepts;
- Synonym list tools contain operations for returning the synonyms of a specific word. This makes it possible to identify, for example, that "freeway" and "motorways" in Fig.2a are synonyms and should be treated as the same concept.

4   EA-Miner

EA-Miner utilizes NLP-based techniques and mining analysis discussed in Sect. 3 to automate AORE tasks. Before detailing how EA-Miner works it is important to get a general understanding about its architecture (Fig. 4). The tool is now implemented as an Eclipse plug-in (the initial versions in [23, 24] were web-based) and offers several views (e.g., a Tree-based view of the Viewpoint model) of the underlying model built as Java objects. The Controller is responsible for checking the state of the tagging process in WMATRIX and instantiating the specific internal model parser (e.g., Viewpoint parser) which parses the requirements document and generates the specific internal model.

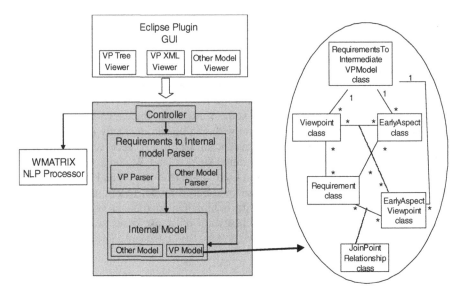

Fig. 4. EA-Miner architecture

The right hand side of Fig. 4 shows in more detail the classes that are contained in the Viewpoint model component. As the viewpoint parser parses the input file it builds the internal model represented by the "requirements to intermediate viewpoint model" class. This class contains collections representing the viewpoints identified, early aspects and the crosscutting relationships between viewpoints and early aspects. More details about the classes will be given later.

4.1 Identification and Presentation

Next we show in detail how EA-Miner works. The explanations are based on the viewpoint-based AORE model [16, 17] in the context of the toll system of Fig. 2a. First we show the identification and presentation of model concepts (Sect. 4.1). Afterwards we show how filtering is applied and how different specification documents can be generated (Sect. 4.2). An overview of the process is shown in Fig. 5 to aid comprehension.

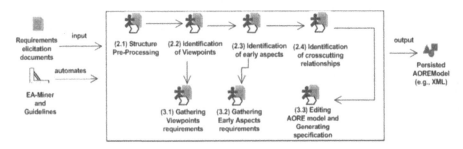

Fig. 5. Identification and Structuring activities in EA-Miner for viewpoint-based AORE model

4.1.1 Structure Pre-processing (Activity 2.1)

The first step to understand how the viewpoint model parser builds the underlying model and populates the objects is to understand the concept of a parsing unit. For EA-Miner a parsing unit is the minimal unit that represents a requirement, for instance, a sentence, paragraph, set of paragraphs, section in a document.

The parsing unit is used during EA-Miner's parsing to allocate requirements for the concepts as will be detailed in the following sections, for example grouping a set of sentences as requirements of a specific viewpoint. The reason why a parsing unit can vary is because input documents for the tool can have varied structured (e.g., a general description such as in Fig. 2a, an interview transcript, a legacy use-case specification, a user manual). Therefore, a sentence is not always a good parsing unit. For example, in structured legacy specifications, normally there is already a natural grouping of requirements in the document (e.g., organized by section).

The task of EA-Miner in this pre-processing can require a varied level of interaction with the requirements engineer. The default parsing unit assumed by EA-Miner is a sentence. If the user accepts this as the unit then no further pre-processing interaction is required as the file that comes back from WMATRIX is already tagged in sentences as shown in Fig. 2b. However, if the user wants a different parsing unit then the interaction is more active such as:

- The user is required to define patterns that represent parsing units, so EA-Miner can try to identify and flag them so that the user can accept or discard them. For example if one is mining a legacy document where requirements are grouped by Use Case ID followed by name (e.g., UC001: Register User) a pattern can be defined for that in a form of a regular expression.
- The user can also use some features that EA-Miner can offer such as selecting a chunk of text in the editor and clicking a button such as "tag as parsing unit".
- The output of the pre-processing activity is basically the same file shown in Fig. 2b with extra annotation in the form of parsing units (<parsingUnit> </parsingUnit>). If the user has selected the default sentence parsing unit, then no extra annotation is done. After the pre-processing process is complete the user moves on to the identification activity described below.

4.1.2 Viewpoint Identification, Presentation and Structuring (Activities 2.2 and 3.1)

After clarifying the concept of the parsing unit, now we explain how the viewpoint model parser builds the underlying model and populates the objects. For the examples in this section and the following ones we consider the parsing unit to be a sentence as it is more appropriate for the type of document shown in Fig. 2a. As shown in Fig. 2b each sentence of the input file is tagged with (<s> </s>) tags containing groups of tagged words (<w pos="value" sem="value"> word </w>). The basic algorithm of the parser is as follows:

- For each sentence in the tagged file, the parser identifies each sentence as a requirement;
- For each word contained in a sentence the parser identifies the viewpoints (and their related requirements) and early aspects (and their related requirements) based on some rules (e.g., nouns are candidates for viewpoints);

- After all sentences are parsed the collections of requirements of viewpoints and early aspects are compared to build the crosscutting relationships.

Figure 6 shows an overview of the features of EA-Miner as an eclipse plug-in. The top part of the figure shows the input file describing the toll system organized in numbered sentences. The view (bottom part) displays a list of viewpoints and early aspects (not shown) with their respective requirements. The goal of this view is to allow the user to quickly look and navigate through the requirements to aid understanding the requirements and identified elements.

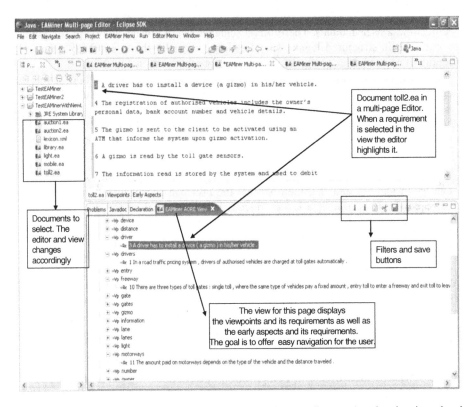

Fig. 6. EA-Miner screen shot. The mined file in shown in the editor (*top*) and a view is updated on the bottom according to the page the user navigates.

The current rule for identifying the viewpoints is based on the part-of-speech (POS) attributed to the word as explained in Sect. 3.1.1. EA-Miner identifies as viewpoint candidates words whose part-of-speech represents nouns. In Figs. 6 and 7 each viewpoint groups a collection of requirements (see the relationship between these classes in Fig. 4) that are added to it if the viewpoint appears in a specific requirements sentence. For example, in Fig. 6 driver appears in sentence "3", therefore this sentence is added to the collection of requirements for driver. The problems of identifying words with the same root (e.g., driver and drivers; gate and gates) and synonyms (freeway and motorways) as different concepts can be corrected by applying filters as explained later in Sect. 4.2.

Figure 7 shows the viewpoints details page with the list of viewpoints on the top left side. When the user selects a viewpoint, the requirements of this viewpoint are displayed on the right and its crosscutting relationships are displayed in the view on the bottom.

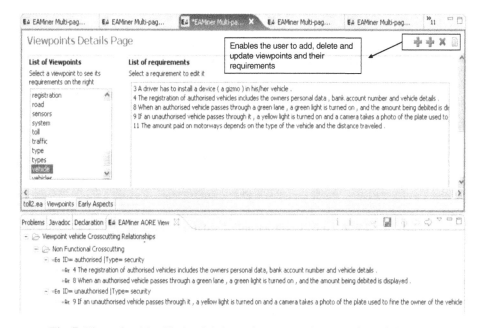

Fig. 7. Viewpoints identified and their requirements and crosscutting relationships

The user also has the option of adding/deleting/updating requirements or viewpoints. As mentioned before, EA-Miner lists candidate concepts and the requirements engineer is able to update the model built by the tool. Guidelines are available for informing the user to make a good decision. Section 4.3 discusses these guidelines.

4.1.3 Early Aspect Identification, Presentation and Structuring (Activities 2.3 and 3.2)

The rules used for identifying non-functional early aspects are based on the semantic tag attributed to a word as discussed in Sect. 3.1.1. The identification approach for the early aspects (see Figs. 8, 10) works similar to what was described for viewpoints. The tool looks for the semantic tag of each word in the sentences of the parsed input document and searches a lexicon[2] file to check if there is one entry of the same word with the same semantic tag. The word does not need to be exactly equal as a stemmer is used to reduce words to the base form when comparing the words (e.g., "authorised", "authorises" and "authorise" are reduced to the same base form).

---

[2] An excerpt of the lexicon file in shown in Fig. 8. It contains entries of NFR catalogue type words [14] along with their semantic tags.

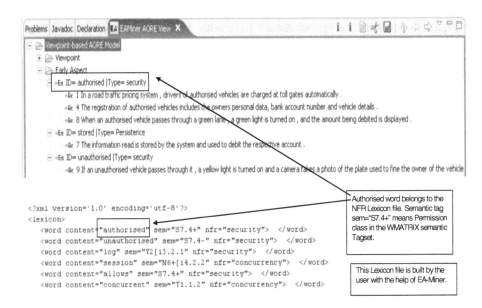

Fig. 8. Early Aspects identified and its requirements

If a match is found, the requirements sentences in which the word appears (e.g., sentences 1, 4 and 8 for "authorised") are included in the collection of the early aspect. This collection and the viewpoints collections are vital for identifying the crosscutting relationships as will be explained next.

Figure 9 helps to clarify how an automated process for building the lexicon file can be employed. The initial set of lexicon entries was built by requesting input from a wide set of domain experts. Close to ten faculty members and research staff of the Computing Department at Lancaster University provided input on their specific domains (e.g., networking, dependability, error handling). This set of entries was also complemented by the entries from NFR catalogues, as well as from elements identified from a number of completed case studies. This initial set of entries is used as a base, and is extended whenever a new requirements document is provided as input to EA-Miner in step 1. Afterwards, the following steps take place:

- In *step 2* EA-Miner searches for words that represent known non-functional requirements in existing NFR knowledge bases. Such knowledge bases already exist in the form of NFR type catalogues [27] and are constantly being updated and maintained by researchers in the field [35]. In our approach we can benefit from these catalogues by adapting them to fit our purposes by, for example, organizing a group of words (e.g., authorised, unauthorised, log on, encrypt, password) indexed by NFR type (e.g., security). Therefore, whenever EA-Miner finds an NFR that is present in the NFR knowledge base it includes it in the possible list of candidates that is shown in step 4 (described below).

- In *step 3* EA-Miner searches for words, that were not found in the previous step, and whose semantic category[3] belongs to semantic classes to which several NFRs belong (e.g., Permission related category such as S7.4, Time related category such as T1.1.2). Moreover, some NFRs can also be identified by analyzing the suffix of the words (e.g., words that end in "ilities" such as availability and "ness" such as correctness). At the end of this step the list of candidates identified is added to the list from step 2 and shown to the user.
- In *step 4* the user has the opportunity to see the list of candidates and then update the actual lexicon. The semantic tag enables the user to make an informed decision if it is appropriate to include that word in the lexicon (in Sect. 3.1.1 we explained that some words might have multiple meanings such as performance).

The process is repeated every time a new file is mined. From our experience the larger the lexicon gets the need to update it becomes rare. For the latest requirements documents on which we have used the tool recently, just two or three entries were added.

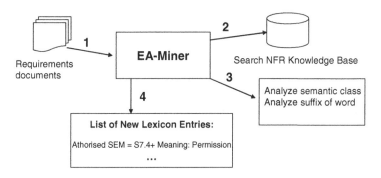

Fig. 9. Lexicon update process

Regarding the analysis of functional early aspects for the viewpoint-based model, EA-Miner utilizes the Fan-in based aspect mining code analysis technique [36] as explained before in Sect. 3.1.1. For each action verb word its fan-in is analyzed related to the viewpoints that make a reference to the word. If the word has a high fan-in (e.g., fan-in ≥ 4) then it is considered a candidate functional early aspect.

4.1.4 Crosscutting Relationship Identification (Activity 2.4)
As mentioned previously, the collection of requirements of viewpoints and early aspects are important for identifying the relationships. Each requirements sentence is understood as a join point and the collections of requirements are compared based on a set intersection operation. If the resulting set is empty it means that there is no crosscutting relationship between the viewpoint and the early aspect. If the resulting

---

[3] Remember that at this stage the file has already been tagged by WMATRIX and the semantic tag for each word has already been allocated.

set is non-empty then there is a crosscutting relationship between the viewpoint and the early aspect and the join points are the resulting set.

Figure 10 shows that the early aspect "authorised" of type security crosscuts the "vehicles" viewpoint at join points {1, 4}. It is not difficult to observe that these two sentences have both words ("authorised" and "vehicles") and that the set {1, 4} is the result of the intersection of the requirements of "authorised" {1, 4, 8} (Fig. 10) and "vehicle" {3, 4, 8, 9, 11} (Fig. 7). Section 4.2 will show that when filtering is applied the crosscutting relationships are updated and "vehicle" and "vehicles" would be understood as just one viewpoint and "authorised" will crosscut the union of their join point sets.

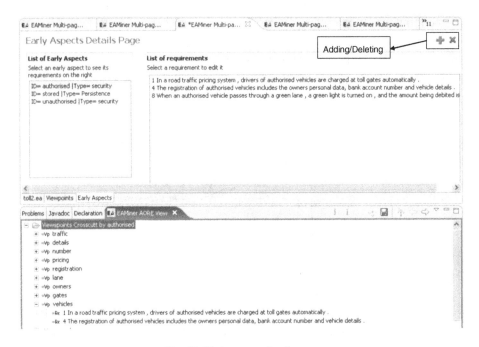

Fig. 10. Early aspect details page

4.2   Editing the AORE Model and Specification Generation (Activity 3.3)

After the model is built, filtering and editing features can be applied. The user is able to add/remove any of the identified concepts (e.g., viewpoints, early aspects, requirements) that s/he considers relevant/irrelevant, respectively. For example, considering the previous examples, it is common to discard lots of viewpoints as the tool lists as candidates all possible nouns. Another filter that helps to minimize the number of candidates (explained in Sect. 3.1.2) is setting a threshold to get only the N most significant concepts (e.g., viewpoints) based on the frequencies returned by WMATRIX. Two other important filters mentioned in Sect. 3.1.2 are the synonym list and stemmer that help to recognize different words as the same concept.

After the filters are applied, the crosscutting relationships are updated to reflect the changes. The early aspects start pointing to the new updated viewpoints. For example the "authorised" early aspect of Fig. 10 above instead of crosscutting "vehicle" and "vehicles" separately, crosscuts only "vehicle" at the join points set {1,4,8} after stemming filtering is applied.

After the user has finished screening out the information using the previous filters s/he has the option of generating part of the requirements specification document in different formats. This operation is very straightforward for EA-Miner and is just a matter of reading the previous concepts (which are represented in memory as Java Objects) and generating an output format (e.g., .XML file or .DOC file with similar structure as in Fig. 11).

Figure 11 shows part of the XML model that is generated. The first important point to consider is that the requirements {4, 8, 9} belonging to the "vehicle" viewpoint are a subset of all requirements first listed for this viewpoint. In this case using some guidelines (see next section) and EA-Miner features (e.g., filters, edition) the engineer decided to discard some requirements.

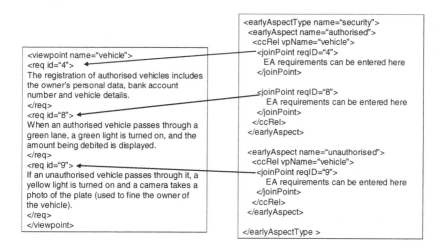

Fig. 11. Generated model. The *arrows* point where the early aspect crosscuts the viewpoint.

The requirements of the early aspects previously shown (e.g., "authorised" {1, 4, 8} in Fig. 10) in the specific case of this example are good only to indicate the crosscutting points, but not to indicate early aspects' requirements. Therefore, the engineer, based on his knowledge about the current system and the offered guidelines, can discard them as early aspects' requirements but leave them intact as viewpoints' requirements.

These requirements were previously replicated inside the early aspects before the user decided to discard them. They were a good indication for the automatic detection of crosscutting but do not necessarily need to remain everywhere they were detected in the final specification. Moreover, the user can also decide to add requirements specific to the authorization process in Fig. 11, for example, describing if an encryption algorithm needs to be used or if authentication is required.

Therefore, as mentioned before EA-Miner is not a "silver bullet" aimed at automating 100% of AORE tasks. However, EA-Miner is an extremely valuable tool in the sense of automating costly tasks and helping the requirements engineer to focus on key information, to improve understanding of the system as well as to generate the models in a specific AORE technique.

4.3 General Guidelines (Used in All Activities in Fig. 5)

The goal of the guidelines is to help requirements engineers to get the most of EA-Miner's features by offering guidance on how to make good decisions. Next we describe some guidelines that can be used in the previous activities for the Viewpoint-based AORE approach. If we had considered another AORE approach then another set of guidelines would be used.

Guidelines for Viewpoint Identification and Structuring:

- **Avoid viewpoints that are too general:** Viewpoints generally represent stakeholders or other systems that have a specific interest on the current system. Immediate candidates to discard are ones that represent a very general concept (e.g., system and type in Fig. 7);
- **Check the semantic tag:** Another good indication of the relevance of the viewpoint is to look at its semantic tag and check if it belongs to the most frequent categories. For example the most frequent semantic category in the previous example is "vehicle and transport on land" containing words such as vehicle, driver, lane, motorway and road which are good candidates as they represent entities from the problem domain under consideration (toll collection system);
- **Sort the viewpoints by relative frequency:** Generally important concepts are mentioned time and again in the document. Use EA-Miner filters to sort the relevant viewpoints. However, be aware that in some cases important viewpoints can contain a low frequency;
- **Apply the stemming and synonym filtering:** This enables to group viewpoints that have a slight variation (e.g., driver and drivers) or that are synonyms (e.g., freeway and motorway) as the same concept;

Guidelines for Early Aspects Identification and Structuring:

- **Edit the Requirements when appropriate:** As discussed before, the requirements assigned to the early aspects are a good indication for the crosscutting relationships but generally the requirements engineer has to enter new requirements for the early aspect. This should be done following discussion with relevant stakeholders;
- **Expand the lexicon:** Every time a new document is mined it is likely that new vocabulary has to be added to the lexicon representing new early aspects. The tool flags the candidates by showing their details (e.g., semantic tags). If the meaning represents a new broadly scoped property that is not in the lexicon then add it.

5 Evaluation

This section shows, in the context of two case studies, how EA-Miner can be a valuable approach for undertaking AORE activities. Evaluating software engineering methods and tools is always a challenging task [37–39] as one has to use subjects that participate actively in the study as well as have different backgrounds and experiences that can influence the results obtained.

The goal of our case first case study (Sect. 5.1) was to evaluate the *time-effectiveness* (Sect. 5.1.1) of using EA-Miner as well as its *accuracy* (measured by precision and recall – Sect. 5.1.2) for undertaking some AORE activities comparing it to a manual approach. Measuring accuracy in terms of precision and recall is commonly used in related works in order to assess the identification capabilities of tools [12, 36] (Sect. 7). The evaluation was conducted using two requirements documents and two different techniques (manual vs. EA-miner based) for identifying and structuring the concepts into an AORE model based on viewpoints.

Our second case study (Sect. 5.2) aimed at exposing EA-Miner to a real industrial exercise using the tool to conduct an AORE analysis on a set of documents, provided by Siemens, related to a toll collection system. The goal of this case study was not comparative as the one in Sect. 5.1 but was to investigate how the tool behaved, what benefits it brought and what challenges it faced in a real-world situation.

5.1 First Case Study: EA-Miner Versus Manual Approach

The two requirements documents used in the first case study are part of real world system specifications. The first is a well-known specification document of a light control system [40] that is commonly used in evaluating requirements approaches, as for example in [34]. The size of this file is approximately 11 pages (3,671 words). The second document is a description of a library system used in Lancaster University. In terms of structure the library document is different than the light system as it is structured in a "user manual" style highlighting in detail the use of the system. The size of this file is larger than the previous – approximately 29 pages (6,504 words).

The manual analysis conducted by one requirements engineer was compared against an EA-Miner based analysis done by a second requirements engineer. After both engineers finished their tasks they sent their results to a third senior requirements engineer who compared the results. The role of the senior engineer was to check the accuracy verifying what concepts were correctly identified by both engineers.

Different engineers performed the manual and EA-Miner based analysis because if the same engineer was used than s/he would learn about the document and the second analysis would be biased. We were also careful enough to select engineers with a similar level of expertise in AORE (both engineers are PhD students at the same group at Lancaster University and both have their research topics related to AORE). The evaluation shows very promising results about EA-Miner that highlight the contributions this tool offers for AORE.

5.1.1 Results of Time-Effectiveness

In order to clarify this variable it is important to explain what task each engineer conducted. The general task of both was to mine a requirements document (such as the one in Fig. 2a) in order to:

- *Identify* the AORE abstractions (such as viewpoints and early aspects); and
- *Structure* the requirements according to the viewpoint-based AORE model (e.g., creating a model such as the one in Fig. 11).

In the case of the tool the identification part considers the time to parse the input and show the results on the screen which is a fully automated task. The structuring considers the time to apply some filters (following the guidelines in Sect. 4.3 which are very straightforward) and generate the final specification. The results are shown in Table 2.

Table 2. Time spent In minutes

	Light Control		Library	
	Manual	EA-Miner	Manual	EA-Miner
Identification	49	1.03	81	1.48
Structuring	833	6	1377	10.67

The results about the total time spent show that the EA-Miner approach was approximately 130 times faster for the light control system and 120 times faster for the library system. The explanation for the fact that the manual approach took so long is that the engineer doing the tasks manually had to read the whole document to identify the concepts. Moreover, this engineer also wasted precious time to structure the final specification document since s/he read, several times, parts of the document again and again to copy and paste text. On the other hand the engineer doing the task with EA-Miner had the concepts identification as well as a suggested structure fully automated, therefore s/he had just to apply some filters and guidelines (e.g., filtering viewpoints by their relative frequency, and grouping viewpoints synonyms and with same root form—stemming) and then automatically generate the specification document.

One important issue to point out about EA-Miner's structuring time spent on Table 2 is that the filtering operations offered by the tool (e.g., frequency filtering for listing the 10 or 20 most relevant viewpoints) only takes a few seconds. Therefore the times shown also include a bit of interaction with the user to discard and requirements viewpoints (using the guidelines in Sect. 4.3) and generate the specification.

Another important clarification relates to the time spent to update the lexicon file used for early aspect identification. Before running the tool with both examples (Light control and library system) we had already an initial version of the lexicon previously built manually while the tool was developed and tested. The time spent to build this initial lexicon was not taken into account in our evaluation as our goal was to measure identification and structuring activities. We do not consider this a problem as the lexicon update process can be automated and reuse existing knowledge (e.g., NFR catalogues) as we explained in Sect. 4.1.3.

5.1.2 Results of Accuracy

Accuracy is measured by precision and recall as below:

- The precision for a technique Pt = (number of correct candidates identified by *t*) / (total number of candidates identified by t).
- The recall for a technique Rt = (number of correct candidates identified by *t*) / (total known correct candidates).

Considering the accuracy results we gathered data related to the identification of viewpoints and early aspects. The data is shown in Table 3, 4 and 5 and represent different comparison approaches which are explained next. First we give general explanations to help understand the tables:

- As explained before the total list of correct abstractions was assumed to be the list of the senior engineer who compared the results given to him/her. This number is used in the recall calculation in all tables and is assumed to be:
  - **Total correct viewpoints:** 11 for light control system and 8 for library system;
  - **Total correct early aspects:** Seven for light control and eight for library.
- For EA-Miner's viewpoint's precision and recall it is important to mention that the threshold filter (i.e., selecting the n most significant viewpoints based on frequency) defines the number of candidate viewpoints. This is done because in large documents the number of candidate viewpoints can be very long (Sect. 3) and yields a direct impact on the results. Another reason we set a threshold is because we wanted the accuracy results to remain consistent with the time analysis done previously that considered the identification to be fully automated (frequency filtering is an operation offered by EA-Miner). Therefore for Tables 3 and 4 we consider:
  - **Total number of viewpoint candidates for EA-Miner: 10** for both light control and library in Table 3 (highlighted in bold).
  - **Total number of viewpoint candidates for EA-Miner: 20** for both light control and library in Table 4 (highlighted in bold).
- In Table 5 we considered that the engineer using EA-Miner spent some more time using the tool (e.g., observing different thresholds), the guidelines shown in Sect. 4.3 as well as his/her personal experience. We did not record the exact time (even though it was still significantly less than the manual approach) spent for this, therefore it does not comply with the data on Sect. 5.1. The reason we present this data is to investigate the results of the combination of EA-Miner with user knowledge and process guidance.
- The only data that varies in all tables are precision and recall of viewpoints (highlighted in all tables) as they are influenced by the threshold.

Tables 3 and 4 shows the results with a threshold of 10 and 20 viewpoints respectively. For the identified viewpoints, recall tends to improve with the threshold size since EA-Miner tends to list more correct viewpoints. For example in the light control system the correct viewpoints listed increases from two (Table 3) to seven (Table 4) which means that five correct viewpoints are between the 11th and 20th most significant. This improves the recall from 18.2 to 63.6% which is superior than the manual approach.

Precision data for EA-Miner's identified viewpoints is highly influenced by the threshold. If we increase the threshold too much (e.g., 100, 200) it is likely that precision will be low as the total number of viewpoints identified is much higher when compared with the total of correct identified. On the other hand, if we set the threshold too low (e.g., 5, 10) precision can vary depending if the small list is a "good" list. For example, in Table 3, precision of EA-Miner is 20% for the light control and 50% for the library system meaning that in the latter case even though the list was small, it was "good". Table 4 shows that increasing the threshold improves precision for the light control and decreases for the library system.

Table 3. Data on accuracy with viewpoint threshold = 10

	VP Threshold = 10			
	Light Control		Library	
	Manual	*EA-Miner*	*Manual*	*EA-Miner*
Precision VP	6/9 = 66.7%	2/10 = 20%	7/11 = 63.6%	5/10 = 50%
Recall VP	6/11 = 54.5%	2/11 = 18.2%	7/8 = 87.5%	5/8 = 62.5%
Precision EA	6/8 = 75%	6/6 = 100%	7/10 = 70%	4/4 = 100%
Recall EA	6/7 = 85.7%	6/7 = 85.7%	7/8 = 87.5%	4/8 = 50%

Regarding the precision and recall on early aspects identified, EA-Miner provided a slight advantage over the manual approach. This is justified by the fact that the tool's early aspect identification does not list many candidates and the ones listed are already based on a more efficient knowledge (lexicon + semantic tag). In some cases such as for example the recall of EA for library system the number can be low because the lexicon was not properly populated for that specific domain. As explained in Sect. 4 EA-Miner offers capabilities to update the lexicon minimizing this problem.

Table 4. Data on accuracy with viewpoint threshold = 20

	VP Threshold = 20			
	Light Control		Library	
	Manual	*EA-Miner*	*Manual*	*EA-Miner*
Precision VP	6/9 = 66.7%	7/20 = 35%	7/11 = 63.6%	6/20 = 30%
Recall VP	6/11 = 54.5%	7/11 = 63.6%	7/8 = 87.5%	6/8 = 75%
Precision EA	6/8 = 75%	6/6 = 100%	7/10 = 70%	4/4 = 100%
Recall EA	6/7 = 85.7%	6/7 = 85.7%	7/8 = 87.5%	4/8 = 50%

Table 5 shows data on the identified viewpoints by EA-Miner combined with the use of guidelines and the experience of the requirements engineer. In this case the precision and recall of viewpoints grows respectively to 90 and 81.8% for the light control and to 88.8 and 100% in the library system. We can see that in this case the accuracy of EA-Miner for viewpoint identification is much superior to the manual approach. As we mentioned before the time spent in identification for this was not exactly recorded but was still inferior than the manual approach (between 15–20 min for light control and 25–30 to library).

Table 5. Data on accuracy based on knowledge of the system

	VP influenced by knowledge of the system			
	Light Control		**Library**	
	Manual	*EA-Miner*	*Manual*	*EA-Miner*
Precision VP	6/9 = 66.7%	9/10 = 90%	7/11 = 63.6%	8/9 = 88.8%
Recall VP	6/11 = 54.5%	9/11 = 81.8%	7/8 = 87.5%	8/8 = 100%
Precision EA	6/8 = 75%	6/6 = 100%	7/10 = 70%	4/4 = 100%
Recall EA	6/7 = 85.7%	6/7 = 85.7%	7/8 = 87.5%	4/8 = 50%

Therefore, when compared to a manual analysis, EA-Miner can offer superior precision and recall of viewpoints specially when combined with the engineer's knowledge. Moreover, analyzing the list provided by EA-Miner in the two examples, in several cases the important viewpoints are listed first. For example, for the library system, four out of the eight correct viewpoints were among the first six listed.

Therefore, we can conclude by both time-effectiveness and accuracy results that EA-Miner shows promising results for addressing AORE activities in a time-efficient manner without compromising the accuracy of the produced output. The examples showed that EA-Miner analysis was significantly faster than a manual analysis and that the quality of the outcome can also be higher when combined with the knowledge of the engineer without having a significant impact on time. Moreover, the case studies showed that the tool was not influenced by the different structures of the requirements documents used and that the tool constantly lists the most important concepts first which helps with tasks such as attributing priorities to requirements.

5.1.3 Case Study Discussion

This first case study has addressed the issue of answering a *research question on how well does EA-Miner perform when compared to a manual approach*. In order to answer this question we collected data about a study conducted using two different engineers that had the same task of producing an AORE specification for two different systems (light system and library system). We collected data related to effort and accuracy (measured in precision and recall) of the models produced.

Sections 5.1.1 and 5.1.2 analysed the data collected showing positive results related to the use of EA-Miner, for example, that the tool helps to save time and the end result (the resulting model) was not worse than a model done manually.

One important point that we would like to further explain is the trade-off existing between the number of candidates listed by the tool with respect to scalability (in terms of time) and requirements completeness.

As the identification process considers viewpoints to be noun candidates, depending on the size of the document this number can be very high. One can think that because of size, the time spent on the analysis can be very high. However, the time spent to process the document and produce the initial version (with all viewpoints included) is not high even when one considers extremely large files.[4]

However, the main problem is not the size of the files. The main issue is how long it can take for the engineer to prune this large initial set of candidate viewpoints and arrive at a final list of the relevant ones. This is where the filters and guidelines are essential as explained in the previous sections. The tool offers the users the possibility of shrinking the candidate list for the N most relevant concepts based on statistical information of relative and absolute frequency. As shown in the examples above, it is likely that the most important concepts are listed first (e.g., with a threshold of 20 recall was high for both systems). Therefore, in the case of large documents these filters are essential for saving time.

On the other hand, one problem with using filters is that some important concepts might be left out of the list. However, by using the tool, the engineer also has the option to view the complete list if s/he wants. Moreover, other filters such as selecting only the viewpoints that appear as subjects in the requirements can help to prune the list of pertinent candidates. As mentioned before, the goal of the tool is to support and not to replace the requirements engineer. In addition, doing a manual analysis does not necessarily guarantee completeness (and is obviously not scalable in terms of time) with respect to concepts identification as the user can skip requirements and simply ignore important concepts due to lack of attention (see for example the next case study in Sect. 5.2 where developers missed relevant concerns).

5.2 Toll System Industrial Case Study at Siemens

The case study described in this section is related to a family of toll systems. Part of the real requirements is used as input to a prototypical implementation of the toll system family using AO technologies developed by Siemens AG. The documentation available for this system encompasses several requirements documents describing different features of the system and written by several Siemens' developers.

In this study we analyzed a fraction of the original requirements documents focused on communication. The size of all analyzed documents is around 4,000 words and they represent an interesting exercise for our analysis as they vary in structure and terminology and they were written by multiple authors. The requirements describe a real system that is a product line of toll systems that are used in several European countries containing several peculiarities each with its own country-specific variations.

Our goal with this case study was not to undertake a comparison like the previous one but to analyse how well does EA-Miner perform in an industrial setting. We discuss our findings in the next section, however we are unable to give much details about the requirements themselves as there are confidentiality issues involved.

5.2.1 Findings
Our task in this case study was to use the set of available documents as input to EA-Miner to perform an aspect-oriented requirements analysis on them. The idea was to

---

[4] In a recent test with a file of 56,031 words (237 pages), the time taken for identification was around 20 min.

have as an output a specification document describing which concerns were found by the tool (crosscutting or not) with their respective requirements and describe this information in a simple way that was easy to understand by Siemens' developers.

The aim of our case study was that, by the end of our analysis, we would have a document that Siemens' developers would be able to use as a guide to their implementation. When we conducted the case study there was already an ongoing implementation of the prototypical system with aspects and the developers already had an initial understanding about the requirements.

Siemens' main goal, on the other hand, was to check how our approach could contribute to what they had already done in terms of requirements analysis and implementation. More specifically they wanted to check if our approach could help them find relevant concerns that they hadn't already thought about that could impact their existing architecture and implementation.

Table 6 shows the concerns we identified using EA-Miner. The concerns are organised by type where base means the concerns that group requirements that are central to the functionalities of the system. The early aspects (functional and non-functional) constrain the base concerns by applying restrictions on requirements. Remember that for each type of concern the previous identification heuristics hold (use POS tags for noun-identification for base concerns; action verb identification along with fan-in analysis for functional early aspects; for the identification of non-functional early aspects the NFR lexicon and semantic tags are used).

The list of concerns presented in Table 6 was obtained after we used EA-Miner's editing, filtering and sorting features to cut down the initial list suggested by the tool. We also used the guidelines in sect. 4.3 discarding concerns that were too general and some concerns whose frequency was too low. While we were discarding some concerns we had to take care and check if they might be important concepts despite their low frequency. One example we found was related to the Back office concern (ETBO). Most documents used the term ETBO to refer to this concept while just one document referred to it as back office. The reason for this might be due to the fact that the documents were written by different developers, but what is important to highlight is that when we observed the requirements the tool allocated to back office we immediately realised that this term was the same as ETBO and we used a merging operation in EA-Miner to make the concepts synonyms.

Table 6. List of Identified Concerns

Type of Concern	List of Identified Concerns
Base Concern	Road, Vehicle, Driver, On-board Unit (OBU), Payment Back Office (ETBO), Enforcement Devices, Payment
Non-Functional Early Aspect	Scalability, Reliability, Security, Compatibility, Error-Handling, Persistence, Concurrency, *Legal Issues*
Functional Early Aspect	Charge Calculation, Monitoring, Logging, *Connect/Disconnect*, *Transaction Management*, *Communication Trigger*

After we created the final list in Table 6 we presented them to Siemens' developers in order to obtain their feedback. The concerns that are not highlighted represent concepts that were considered relevant by Siemens' developers but that they were already aware of their existence. These concerns were already addressed by their current architecture and developers already had an understanding about them from their previous knowledge about the system and the existing requirements.

Table 7. Details on some early aspects[5]

Concern Name: *Legal Issues*
Requirements: • communicate with enforcement equipment via DSRC interface according to the *standards* … • Limitations in using *standard* … **Rationale:** • This concern is likely to be implemented as an aspect as it may undergo frequent change (due to change in standards and legislations). It is also possible that it may require customisation (e.g., per various hardware).
Concern Name: *Connect/Disconnect*
Requirements: • The average *connection* time of the communication between the OBU and the background system shall be less that 16 seconds…. • … amount of data transmitted during one *connection*… • … CSD *connection* establishment …. • … data transmitted during one *connection* is 6 kByte … • The dialer tries to *re-connect* to GSM network in the hope … • … execute GPRS *disconnection* … • After receiving the response from ETBO the OBU application SW can *disconnect* the GPRS *connection*… • …establish and *disconnect* GPRS connection: API simulation... **Rationale:** • These concerns are likely to be implemented via aspects as otherwise they will be called from a number of locations as well as may have a number of variations (due to the variations in the types of OBU hardware making the calls). For instance, connect will be required at initialization, for periodic data transmission, possibly, as part of Error Handling. The disconnect will be required upon successful completion of the transmission, in case of reaching the max number of allowed connections.

---

[5] The highlighted words in table 7 are the ones that are identified by EA-Miner and the requirements in which they occur are grouped in the Concerns in Table 7.

Table 7. *(continued)*

Concern Name: *Transaction Management*

Requirements:
- data and file *transmission* from background system to OBU via different media: GSM CSD, GPRS, SMS
- ...include data overhead for *restart a transmission* ...
- ... no *retransmission*...

Rationale:
- In the documents there are references to *re-transmitting data*, which needs some sort of transaction management while transmitting data in order to detect errors and take proper action accordingly. Besides, the transaction management could be customised in aspects to be applied to the transmissions from ETBO only, from all ETBO and OBU transmissions, or to transmissions from a subset of OBU. Moreover, if there are more than one ETBO, the data synchronisation between these shall be transactional.

Concern Name: *Communication Trigger*

Requirements:
- ...the *trigger* method shall be configurable...
- ...at least the following *trigger* method should be implemented:
  - ... at one or more defined time...
  - ... at defined day of the week...
  - ... after defined period of time, e.g., 5 hours...
  - ... after journey...
  - ... when a defined geoobject is detected...
  - ... when available memory is used up to 70%...

Rationale:
- This concern is likely to be implemented as an aspect since it implies a wide set of possible options (candidates for advice) and their possible combinations which could be customised for each system instance.

The *highlighted* concerns in Table 6 represent concerns that were missed by Siemens' developers but they recognized them as highly relevant as, from their perspective, these concerns might have an important impact on the architecture and also might be implemented as aspects.

Table 7 shows details about the highlighted concerns such as excerpts of the source requirements identified by the tool (we cannot show the complete requirements for confidentiality reasons as explained before) as well as the rationale we used to explain to Siemens' developers why we understood them as crosscutting concerns that could influence their current architecture and implementation.

Regarding the mapping of early aspects we are not claiming that there is a direct mapping from them to code. In [16, 17] is suggested that early aspects mappings can be of various types such as utility functions, aspects and architectural decisions. In the case of Table 7 we found that these early aspects represent concerns that are likely to be implemented using aspects but it does not necessary mean a one-to-one mapping. Our suggestion was corroborated by Siemens' developers that found these concepts very relevant and recognized that they hadn't spotted them before.

While we conducted this case study we faced several challenges that we have not found for example when we conducted the first case study in Sect. 5.1. Some of the issues we found are as follows:

- The structure of the requirements was somewhat different than previous documents used. Each requirements document described specific features of the system and generally the requirements were logically grouped into sets of paragraphs or in a whole document section. We had to use our pre-processing tool support (Sect. 4.1.1) in order to deal with larger parsing units (e.g., paragraphs and sections) than sentences.

- Also, another challenge was when different terms were used as the same concepts in different requirements documents as we mentioned above for back office and ETBO. It also happened in other documents with OBU and (on-board equipment) OBE and we were also able to detect it while viewing the requirements and editing the AORE model.

- Another challenge was that since EA-Miner works with documents some times the input files might be incomplete or badly specified. To resolve this problem we sometimes had to communicate with the developers of the toll system prototype to gain a better understanding of the requirements.

All the above challenges are issues that we need to further explore in order to improve the tool by, for example, improving the pre-processing support in order to automatically identify larger chunks of text such as paragraphs and sections. Moreover, automation of "domain synonyms" identification such as ETBO and back office as well as poorly written and ambiguous requirements can also provide a great contribution for AORE.

In conclusion, we believe that this case study was an interesting exercise to study the effectiveness of our approach. The use of real industrial requirements written by different developers with various writing styles and vocabulary posed a real challenge to our approach. The EA-Miner analysis was invaluable by finding relevant concerns, such as the ones in Table 7 that were previously missed by Siemens' developers, but recognised as relevant. Moreover, the list of concerns found in Table 6 made it possible for us to verify with the developers that the end result of the EA-Miner-based analysis was similar to what they already had in mind about the requirements of the system (except for the missed ones).

The case study demonstrates that output from an EA-Miner-based analysis in an industrial setting is not only at least as good as the manual analysis by developers who were domain experts but is also capable of revealing concerns that may have been missed in analysis of large requirements sets.

6 Discussion

The main goal of EA-Miner is to offer automation for costly activities in the AORE process which are mainly done manually such as identification and structuring. The previous sections have clarified the role of EA-Miner in the process, its mining analysis techniques, how it works in practice as well as an evaluation showing its time-effectives and accuracy. Next we summarize some important issues about EA-Miner that can be misunderstood.

The *Degree of automation* provided by EA-Miner as we mentioned before is not provided with the intent of doing 100% of the work and replacing the requirements engineer. EA-Miner automates costly activities and provides several features and guidelines that help the users do their job efficiently and accurate as shown in our evaluation.

Some might think that because EA-Miner focuses the attention of the engineer in some identified abstractions and can offer filtering based on relevance (e.g., sort viewpoints by frequency) that *completeness* is compromised and that the engineer might miss relevant information and skip several requirements. This is not the case as EA-Miner can also offer the full information (e.g., complete list of viewpoints) showing, for example, a view that contains all the requirements originally obtained from the input document. The goal of the tool is always to preserve the information and offer functionalities that aid the user in visualizing and getting the best understanding of the requirements.

Another misconception might be that the *lexicon expansion* of the tool might be cumbersome. A mechanism for expanding the lexicon based on some known sources of common broadly-scoped properties can offer partial automation for this task. Moreover, when the lexicon gets populated with enough entries the need for other updates becomes rare and easier.

The *extensibility* of EA-Miner to incorporate other AORE approaches is addressed in two dimensions. In the *tool dimension* it is necessary to extend the tool's architecture to offer the specific parsers and views (Fig. 4). For example if a new AORE model (e.g., use-case based AORE) needs to be incorporated in the tool, the first thing is to think about the mining techniques (e.g., a use case candidate is an action verb—Sect. 3). After that, the specific parser for that model needs to be implemented (basically a new class with an overridden parse method—Fig. 4). Moreover, the internal representation of the model as java classes also needs to be built (e.g., a use case can have several requirements and relationships with other use cases).

Having a common meta-model to represent AORE models and a domain specific language enables a higher level extension (e.g., defining what is a concern, what is a crosscutting relationship, what are the general mining rules for that concern) of EA-Miner's architecture. From this perspective, the requirements engineers using EA-Miner can have some extension points in the plug-in where they are able to incorporate new AORE models without having to change the code directly.

This higher-level architectural extension is objective of our future work. In the *dimension of process extension* of EA-Miner the goal is to catalogue other guidelines, similar to those in Sect. 4.3, for other AORE approaches.

7 Related Work

The use of NLP techniques in automation of some tasks in RE has been discussed in [6, 9, 10, 12, 13, 41]. They also focus on using NLP at the requirements level to identify concepts and build models.

The Color-X approach [6] offers natural language processing to semi-automatically parse the input (e.g., a document in natural language) into an intermediate formal model based on the common representation language (CPL) [6]. The transformation is not a fully automated step and requires manual structuring from the user (some guidelines are offered) and some words need to be entered in a lexicon. After the CPL representation is built two models can be generated: One static object model, called CSOM, similar to a UML class diagram, and an event-based model, called CEM, similar to a state machine.

The Circe [9, 41] environment provides a tool that process natural language text as input and generates an intermediate model based on some rules called model, action and substitution rules. After the intermediate model is created, different analysis models can be generated such as entity relationship (E—R) models, data flow diagrams (DFDs) or OO models. Similar to what happens with Color-X, the user has to input some elements in the glossary along with some tags that refer to the semantics of the rules. This characteristic is a bit different from our approach since our NLP processor does not require any input from the user (apart from the natural language documents). Nor does it require that the user has detailed knowledge on how it works.

The Abstfinder [10] approach offers automation for the identification of abstractions in requirements documents described in natural language. Abstractions are considered to be relevant concepts that can be understood without having to know their details such as "booking" and "flight" in a reservation system. The process of concept identification is based on pattern matching between sentences in the text. The output of the tool is a list of abstractions and the knowledge on what to do with this information is left to the requirements engineer.

The NL-OOPS approach [12, 13] is based on a natural language processor, called LOLITA, and utilizes semantic networks produced by LOLITA to automate the production of object-oriented conceptual models (e.g., classes and their methods, attributes and relationships). The semantic networks are updated every time a file is provided as input to the NLP processor and represent concepts organized into hierarchies (entity nodes) as well as their relationships (event nodes). The NL-OOPS tool then applies some heuristics to filter out and classify the information contained in the semantic networks in order to produce the object-oriented conceptual models. Moreover, similar to what we have done in our evaluation this approach also utilized precision and recall measures to compare the quality of models produced by engineers using and not using the tool. LOLITA does not offer either POS or semantic tagging what could also be very helpful for identifying class candidates (e.g., nouns) or methods (e.g., action verbs) and attributes (e.g., adjectives). Moreover, the NL-OOPS approach does not clarify if there is some support for filtering the initial list of candidates in terms of the tool's features and guidelines.

Recently, some work has focused [7, 8] on using information retrieval techniques based on similarity measure for establishing links between requirements. In [8] a tool called ReqSimile offers support for automatically assigning links between marketing requirements (i.e., a customer wish) and business requirements (i.e., product requirements) based on a similarity analysis calculated on the basis of comparing the words contained in the requirements. The comparison is based on a technique called "vector space model" which represents each requirement as a vector of words that can be compared. The tool was evaluated using requirements of the Bann company showing encouraging results (51% of correct links could be identified and 66% of effort was saved).

Similar to [7, 8] the approach described in [42] shows successful results of applying "vector space model" based similarity analysis to establish links between source code and input documents such as user manuals.

Therefore, the previous approaches show that using NLP and information retrieval techniques can provide a great deal of contribution on automating requirements engineering. One problem that none of the previous approaches address is how to identify and deal with crosscutting concerns at the requirements level. Moreover, our approach is based on a precise and scalable NLP processor that offers part-of-speech and semantic tagging that are the base for our automation heuristics.

The work addressing crosscutting in requirements can be represented by Viewpoint-based AORE [16, 17], scenario-based AORE [18] as well as recent work on goals and aspects [19], Theme/Doc [15] and multidimensional separation of concerns [25]. Among these approaches the only one that supports automation for identification of requirements concepts is Theme/Doc that provides a tool for semi-automatic identification of crosscutting behaviours from requirements specification. In this approach the developer has to read through input documentation and manually provide a list of action words and their related entities as input to the Theme/Doc tool.

The advantage of EA-Miner over the above AORE mentioned approaches is the use of precise part-of-speech and semantic tagging that helps to improve the identification of concepts at the requirements level. Moreover, EA-Miner offers mining capabilities for different AORE models as well as handles requirements documents of varied structure (e.g., user manuals, interviews and others). Therefore, EA-Miner can be seen as complementary to current AORE approaches offering automation for their costly activities. For instance, we could implement a plug-in that facilitates mining for *themes* which are subsequently modelled and analyzed using Theme/Doc.

Regarding code level aspect mining approaches such as [36], what is important to consider is how some techniques such as Fan-in analysis can be adapted to be used at the requirements level. Aspect mining at RE level helps to achieve earlier separation of concerns that can minimize refactorings at later stages such as code. However, some crosscutting concerns (e.g., the code of a design pattern) can only be detected at code level since they don't make sense at the requirements level. Therefore, requirements and code aspect mining are complementary approaches that can be applied whenever it suits best the problem at hand.

Moreover, it is also important to mention work related to the issue of cataloguing and reusing non-functional requirements (NFR) knowledge in case tools as we use this in our lexicon-based approach for identifying NFRs. [35] proposes ways for structuring and cataloguing NFR framework [27] knowledge with the intention of reusing and querying this knowledge. [34] describes in detail an approach for eliciting and building NFR models as well as integrating the non-functional perspective with the functional one in scenarios as well as in class diagrams. This approach utilizes a lexicon (language extended lexicon—LEL) that contains information about the entities of the system as well as the non-functional requirements. We believe that our NLP-based approach could benefit [34] by enabling to automatically identify the entities and NFRs and suggest a list of candidates that could be added by the user in the LEL lexicon. We also believe that the reusable NFR knowledge bases described in [34, 35] can benefit our approach with regards to the automated lexicon update process as explained in Sect. 4.1.3 (See Fig. 9).

8 Conclusions

Aspect-oriented requirements engineering (AORE) techniques do not offer adequate tool support for costly tasks in early stages of requirements engineering such as identifying model concepts from different requirements documents as well as mapping these concepts to AORE models.

This paper described the EA-Miner tool and how it offers NLP-based support for automating AORE activities. We have presented some mining analysis approaches based on NLP techniques (e.g., identification of viewpoints, use cases, early aspects) and showed how the tool implements them in the context of one example (toll system). EA-Miner utilizes a precise NLP processor (Sect. 3) that offers several NLP techniques such as part-of-speech and semantic tagging and frequency of occurrence of words that are key to EA-Miner's mining features.

Our evaluation data shows encouraging results that suggest that EA-Miner is a much more time-effective approach when compared to the usual manual analysis conducted during AORE. Accuracy data on precision and recall also show that the models created by the tool do not suffer from poor quality and can even be superior (when combined with the experience of the engineer) than a pure manual analysis.

Moreover, an industrial case study conducted at Siemens AG investigated the effectiveness of EA-Miner to analyse real-world requirements written by different developers with various writing styles and vocabulary. Our analysis found relevant concerns that were previously missed by Siemens' developers in their aspect-oriented prototype implementation, but recognised as relevant by them. It also revealed some challenges imposed by the structure of the documentation and the different use of vocabulary terms hence providing new paths to explore and improve the tool in the future which are better pre-processing support, "domain synonym" identification and detection of poorly written requirements.

In addition to these paths other future work will focus on further investigating mining analysis considering other AORE techniques such as Scenario Modelling [18] and symmetric approaches such as [25]. Moreover, we plan to conduct evaluation with diverse types of requirements-related documents such as interview transcripts and legacy specifications.

Acknowledgments

This work is supported by European Commission grant IST-2-004349: AOSD-Europe project, 2004-2008. The authors also wish to thank Siemens AG researchers for providing us the requirements documents for our case study as well as invaluable feedback and discussions.

References

[1] Alexander, I., Stevens, R.: Writing Better Requirements, p. 159. Addison-Wesley, Reading (2002)

[2] Sommerville, I.: Software Engineering, 7th edn., p. 784. Addision-Wesley, Reading (2004)

[3] Sommerville, I., Sawyer, P.: Requirements Engineering– A Good Practice Guide. Wiley, Chichester (1997)

[4] Potts, C.: Invented Requirements and Imagined Customers. In: IEEE Requirements Engineering Conference (RE 95), York, UK. IEEE Press, Los Alamitos (1995)

[5] [5] Jackson, M.: Software Requirements and Specifications, p. 228. Addison Wesley, Reading (1995)

[6] Burg, F.M.: Linguistic Instruments in Requirements Engineering. IOS Press, Amsterdam (1997)

[7] Dag, J., Regnell, B., Carlshamre, P., Andersson, M.: A feasibility study of automated natural language requirements analysis in market-driven development. Requirements Engineering 7(1), 20 (2002)

[8] Dag, J.N.o., Gervasi, V., Brinkkemper, S., Regnell, B.: Speeding up Requirements Management in a Product Software Company: Linking Customer Wishes to Product Requirements through Linguistic Engineering. In: 12th IEEE International Requirements Engineering Conference, Kyoto, Japan. IEEE Press, New York (2004)

[9] Gervasi, V.: Environment Support for Requirements Writing and Analysis. Università Degli Studi de Pisa (1999)

[10] Goldin, L., Berry, D.: AbstFinder: A Prototype Natural Language Text Abstraction Finder for Use in Requirements Elicitation. Automated Software Engineering, 4 (1997)

[11] Sawyer, P., Rayson, P., Garside, R.: REVERE: Support for Requirements Synthesis from Documents. Information Systems Frontiers 4(3), 343–353 (2002)

[12] Mich, L., Garigliano, R.: NL-OOPS: A Requirements Analysis tool based on Natural Language Processing. In: 3rd International Conference On Data Mining, Bologna, Italy (2002)

[13] Mich, L., Mariangela, F., Pierluigi, N.I.: Market research for requirements analysis using linguistic tools. Requirements Engineering Journal 9(1) (2004)

[14] Kiyavitskaya, N., Zeni, N., Mich, L., Mylopoulos, J.: NLP-based Requirements Modeling: Experiments on the Quality of the Models, University of Trento, Trento, pp. 1–13 (2004)

[15] Baniassad, E., Clarke, S.: Finding Aspects in Requirements with Theme/Doc. In: Workshop on Early Aspects (held with AOSD 2004) Lancaster, UK (2004)

[16] Rashid, A., Moreira, A., Araujo, J.: Modularisation and Composition of Aspectual Requirements. In: 2nd International Conference on Aspect Oriented Software Development (AOSD), ACM Press, Boston, USA (2003)

[17] Rashid, A., Sawyer, P., Moreira, A., Araujo, J.: Early Aspects: a Model for Aspect-Oriented Requirements Engineering. In: International Conference on Requirements Engineering (RE), IEEE Press, Los Alamitos (2002)

[18] Whittle, J., Araujo, J.: Scenario Modeling with Aspects. IEE Proceedings–Software, (Special Issue on Early Aspects: Aspect-Oriented Requirements Engineering and Architecture Design). 151(4), 157–172 (2004)

[19] Yu, Y., Leite, J.C.S.d.P., Mylopoulos, J.: From Goals to Aspects: Discovering Aspects from Requirements Goal Models. In: International Conference on Requirements Engineering, IEEE Press, Los Alamitos (2004)

[20] Finkelstein, A., Sommerville, I.: The Viewpoints FAQ. BCS/IEE Software Engineering Journal 11(1) (1996)

[21] Jacobson, I., Chirsterson, M., Jonsson, P., Overgaard, G.: Object-Oriented Software Engineering: A Use Case Driven Approach, 4th edn. Addision-Wesley, Reading (1992)

[22] Jacobson, I., Ng, P.-W.: Aspect-Oriented Software Development with Use Cases, p. 464. Addison Wesley Professional, Reading (2005)

[23] Sampaio, A., Chitchyan, R., Rashid, A., Rayson, P.: EA-Miner: A tool for automating aspect-oriented requirements identification. In: 20th IEEE/ACM International Conference on Automated Software Engineering (ASE2005), Long Beach, California, USA (2005)

[24] Sampaio, A., Loughran, N., Rashid, A., Rayson, P.: Mining Aspects in Requirements. In: Early Aspects 2005: Aspect-Oriented Requirements Engineering and Architecture Design Workshop (held with AOSD 2005), Chicago, Illinois, USA (2005)

[25] Moreira, A., Rashid, A., Araujo, J.: Multi-Dimensional Separation of Concerns in Requirements Engineering. In: The 13th International Conference on Requirements Engineering (RE'05), IEEE Press, Los Alamitos (2005)

[26] Baniassad, E., Clarke, S.: Theme: An Approach for Aspect-Oriented Analysis and Design. In: International Conference on Software Engineering, Edinburgh, Scotland, UK (2004)

[27] Chung, L., Nixon, B.A., Yu, E., Mylopoulos, J.: Non-Functional Requirements in Software Engineering. In: Basili, V.R. (ed.) The Kluwer International Series in Software Egnieering, Kluwer Academic Publishers, Dordrecht (2000)

[28] Rayson, P.: UCREL Semantic Analysis System (USAS) (2005), http://www.comp.lancs. ac.uk/ucrel/usas/ [cited 2005].

[29] Sawyer, P., Rayson, P., Cosh, K.: Shallow Knowledge as an Aid to Deep Understanding in Early Phase Requirements Engineering. IEEE Transactions on Software Engineering 31(11), 969–981 (2005)

[30] McEnery, T., Wilson, A.: Corpus Linguistics. Edinburgh University Press, Edinburgh (1996)

[31] British National Corpus (BNC), Available from: http://www.natcorp.ox.ac.uk/

[32] Archer, D., Rayson, P., Pia, S., McEnery, T.: Comparing the UCREL Semantic Annotation Scheme with Lexicographical Taxonomies. In: 11th EURALEX (European Association for Lexicography) International Congress (Euralex 2004), Lorient, France (2004)

[33] Lubars, M.D., Potts, C., Richter, C.: Developing Initial OOA Models. In: ICSE (1993)

[34] Cysneiros, L.M., Leite, J.C.S.P.: Nonfunctional Requirements: From Elicitation to Conceptual Models. IEEE Transactions on Software Engineering 30(5), 328–349 (2004)

[35] Cysneiros, L.M., Yu, E., Leite, J.C.S.P.: Cataloguing Non-Functional Requirements as Softgoals Networks in Requirements Engineering for Adaptable Architectures. In: 11th International Requirements Engineering Conference (2003)

[36] Marius Marin, A.v.D., Moonen, L.: Identifying aspects using fan-in analysis. In: Working Conference on Reverse Engineering (2004)

[37] Basili, V., Selby, R.W., Hutchens, D.H.: Experimentation in Software Engineering. IEEE Transactions on Software Engineering 12(7) (1986)

[38] Pfleeger, S.L.: Design and Analysis in Software Engineering - Part1: The Language of Case Studies and Formal Experiments. Software Engineering Notes 19(1), 16–20 (1994)

[39] Wohlin, C., Runeson, P., Host, M., Ohlsson, M.C., Regnell, B., Wesslen, A.: Experimentation in Software Engineering: An Introduction. In: Basili, V.R. (ed.), Kluwer Academic Publishers, Dordrecht (2000)

[40] Queins, S., Zimmermann, G., Becker, M., Kronenburg, M., Peper, C., Merz, R., Schäfer, J.: The Light Control Case Study: Problem Description: Available from: http://wwwagss.informatik.uni-kl.de/Veroeffentl/jucs2000.pdf [cited 2005]

[41] Ambriola, V., Gervasi, V.: Processing natural language requirements. In: International Conference on Automated Software Engineering, IEEE Computer Society Press, Los Alamitos (1997)

[42] Marcus, A., Maletic, J.I.: Recovering documentation-to-source-code traceability links using latent semantic indexing. In: 25th International Conference on Software Engineering 2003, IEEE Computer Society, Los Alamitos (2003)

Analysis of Early Aspects in Requirements Goal Models: A Concept-Driven Approach

Nan Niu and Steve Easterbrook

Department of Computer Science, University of Toronto
Toronto, Ontario, Canada M5S 3G4
{nn,sme}@cs.toronto.edu

Abstract. *Early aspects* are stakeholder concerns that crosscut the problem domain, with the potential for a broad impact on questions of scoping, prioritization, and architectural design. Analyzing early aspects improves early stage decision-making, and helps trace stakeholder interests throughout the software development life cycle. However, analysis of early aspects is hard because stakeholders are often vague about the concepts involved, and may use different vocabularies to express their concerns. In this paper, we present a rigorous approach to conceptual analysis of stakeholder concerns. We make use of the repertory grid technique to identify terminological interference between stakeholders' descriptions of their goals, and formal concept analysis to uncover conflicts and trade-offs between these goals. We demonstrate how this approach can be applied to the goal models commonly used in requirements analysis, resulting in the clarification and elaboration of early aspects. Preliminary qualitative evaluation indicates that the approach can be readily adopted in existing requirements analysis processes, and can yield significant insights into crosscutting concerns in the problem domain.

Keywords: early aspects, goal-oriented requirements analysis, repertory grid technique, formal concept analysis.

1 Introduction

It has long been recognized that modular systems are easier to produce, maintain, and evolve [23, 32]. However, complex problems are hard to decompose cleanly, and any choice of decomposition will inevitably give rise to concerns that crosscut the resulting structure. Aspect-oriented software development (AOSD) provides explicit means to model concerns that crosscut multiple system components. Initially, much of AOSD research was focused on the solution domain: developers identify and capture aspects mainly in the source code. Recently, a considerable amount of work on *early aspects* [8] has been carried out to identify and model crosscutting properties in the early phases of software development, including the requirements engineering (RE), domain analysis, and architecture design activities.

A. Rashid and M. Aksit (Eds.): Transactions on AOSD III, LNCS 4620, pp. 40–72, 2007.

Early aspects focus on the problem domain, representing the goals and constraints of users, customers, and other constituencies affected by a software-intensive system. Current requirements techniques offer a variety of structures for organizing the requirements, such as (structured) natural languages, use cases, viewpoints, goal models, features, etc. [24, 29]. No matter how the requirements are structured, an early aspect crosscuts the dominant decomposition, and has an (implicit or explicit) impact on more than one requirements artifact. Research on early aspects can help to improve modularity in the requirements and architecture design and to detect conflicting concerns early, when trade-offs can be resolved more economically [1]. Analyzing early aspects also enables stakeholder interests to be traced throughout the software development life cycle.

We assume there exists a relatively well-organized set of requirements derived from some dominant decomposition criteria. Our task is to gain an early understanding of these requirements and the (crosscutting) concerns they address. This vision is influenced by the work on "weaving together requirements and architectures" [30], which suggests an agenda "from early aspects to late requirements" because identifying aspects too early is counterproductive [31]. This paper presents a rigorous approach to systematically capturing and analyzing crosscutting entities in requirements goal models.

1.1 Aspects and Goal-Oriented Requirements Analysis

Goal modeling has become a central activity in RE. It shifts the emphasis in requirements analysis to the actors within an organization, their goals, and the interdependencies between those goals, rather than focusing on processes and objects. This helps us understand *why* a new system is needed, and allows us to effectively link software solutions to business needs.

Requirements goal models use *goal* decomposition to support the description and analysis of stakeholder intentions that underlie the required software system. Some goal-oriented frameworks, such as i^* [53], also explicitly model the agents who hold these intentions. Goal modeling frameworks also distinguish between regular goals and *softgoals*. A regular goal has a clear criterion that determines whether it is satisfied. In contrast, softgoals are those goals for which there is no clear sense in which they can be fully satisfied. Softgoals therefore often capture non-functional requirements (NFRs) such as usability, reliability, maintainability [5]. In the design process, each softgoal can be used to induce a preference ordering over different design solutions.

The process of goal decomposition produces a goal hierarchy, which expresses how low-level, concrete goals and tasks contribute to (or detract from) the higher level goals. The most abstract goals, especially softgoals, tend to crosscut the goal model, connected by contribution links to many other lower level goals [1]. We treat such goals as *candidate early aspects*, and analyze the extent to which they capture key problem domain concepts that crosscut the structure of requirements and architectural designs. Candidate aspects are suited to be implemented as code aspects, but developers may choose other means to address these crosscutting concerns. Even in the latter case, it is desirable to keep candidate early aspects modularized so that one does not have to recover them from the code at a later date.

Our analysis focuses on clarifying the problem domain concepts that underlie the candidate early aspects. By investigating the meanings of the terms that stakeholders use to describe these high-level goals, we can determine whether they do indeed represent concerns that crosscut requirements and design artifacts. Not all high-level goals are crosscutting. For example, a softgoal might be relevant just to a single design decision, or it might impact a large number of design decisions. If the early aspect requires specific implementation steps to be taken, these may be contained in a single part of the program code, or may be code aspects that crosscut the program structure.

A key problem with goal models is the high level goals, which are candidate aspects, are often described by stakeholders using vague terms such as "reliable" and "user friendly". Hence, our approach includes a rigorous analysis of the stakeholder *concepts* relevant to their stated softgoals. Concepts are fundamental building blocks of human learning [28]. We use formal concept analysis (FCA), a mathematical technique that treats concepts as binary relations between objects and their properties [12]. We apply FCA to the contribution links between system tasks and softgoals in a goal model. The resulting concept lattice offers non-trivial insights into relationships between candidate aspects and various concerns appearing in the problem domain.

The development of any sizeable software system invariably involves many stakeholders, whose concerns may overlap, complement, or contradict each other. Models with built-in notions of agents or perspectives add another challenge to requirements' crosscutting structure: stakeholders may express their concerns using overlapping, yet incoherent, vocabularies. For example, what one calls "responsiveness" may correspond to "performance" in another person's description, thus the same concept is *scattered* over multiple terms. As another example, "usability" for software running in a cell phone may be interpreted as "easy to learn" by one stakeholder, and as "mobility" by another stakeholder, causing different concepts *tangled* in one expression. The challenge is to align concepts with respect to stakeholder vocabularies. We argue that an early aspects framework must provide mechanisms to avoid tangling of distinct concepts expressed using the same term, and to prevent scattering of one concept over dissimilar lexicons.

Analysis of conceptual and terminological interference is only possible if we are able to discover relationships between different stakeholders' mental models and the terms they use to describe them. Kelly's personal construct theory (PCT) [18] addresses this issue. It explains how an individual constructs a personal (i.e., idiosyncratic) view of his or her environment (e.g., artifacts, events). The theory has been used to develop techniques for exploring personal constructs, most notably the repertory grid technique (RGT) [10]. We present a novel use of RGT as a means of exploring how stakeholders interpret the labels attached to softgoals, thereby helping to build a vocabulary map to tackle early aspects' intertwinement in different viewpoints.

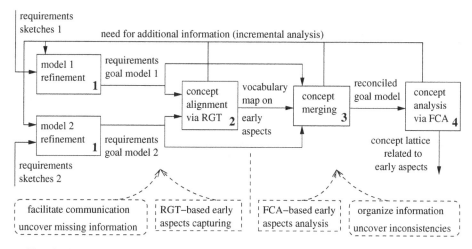

Note: Dashed parts are annotations, not IDEF0 notations.

Fig. 1. Process overview of the concept-driven framework in IDEF0 notations

A detailed analysis of candidate early aspects in requirements goal models offers a number of benefits:

- Explicit reasoning about interdependencies between stakeholder goals;
- Improving the modularity of requirements and architectural models;
- Identification of the impact of early aspects on design decisions can improve the quality of the overall design and implementation;
- Test cases can be derived from early aspects to enhance stakeholder satisfaction; and
- Tracing stakeholder interests becomes easier since crosscutting concerns are captured early on.

From the standpoint of aspect-oriented program analysis and evolution, early aspects provide a baseline to justify and validate code aspects against their purpose of existence: are they required by specific stakeholders or refactored based on particular implementations?

1.2   Approach Overview

Our objective is to leverage available and appropriate techniques to form a coherent early aspects analysis framework. Although they originated from separate disciplines, RGT and FCA share a common underlying structure: a crossreference table. This allows these two techniques to be incorporated seamlessly.

This paper presents a concept-driven framework for capturing and analyzing early aspects in goal models based on RGT and FCA. The process overview of our framework is depicted in Fig. 1 using the integration definition for function modeling (IDEF0) notations [14]. The indexed boxes in Fig. 1 represent the sequence of main actions. Incoming and outgoing arrows model inputs and outputs of each function, respectively.

The motivation to employ a composite (RGT + FCA) approach is to utilize each technique under proper conditions and for proper tasks. Having roots in the psychology of personal constructs makes RGT suitable for aligning and merging stakeholder softgoals (step 2 in Fig. 1). Being a mathematically rigorous technique, FCA provides a basis for conflict detection and trade-off analysis among various concerns addressed by goal models (step 4 in Fig. 1). Jointly, these two techniques offer a coherent early aspects framework, while facilitating communication, organizing information, and uncovering missing information and inconsistencies (dashed boxes in Fig. 1) [13].

Preliminary work on our use of repertory grid was published in [25, 26, 27]. The emphasis of [25] was to present RGT as a general method to support aspectual requirements identification, while the applicability of leveraging RGT to reconcile softgoals with respect to stakeholder vocabularies was further investigated in [26, 27]. This paper integrates the new FCA-based early aspects analysis to provide a more complete treatment of our framework. Throughout the paper, we demonstrate our approach using a media shop e-business example adapted from the literature [4, 54], where stakeholder goals and intentions are modeled using i^* notations [53].

This paper has mainly focused on analyzing stakeholder softgoals in the problem domain. However, we believe that our proposed concept-driven approach could also facilitate the analysis of aspects in the solution domain or pertinent to functional requirements, such as buffering and caching. Section 2 describes goal modeling of the media shop problem domain. A concept-driven approach is then introduced: Sect. 3 focuses on the RGT-based concept alignment method and Sect. 4 discusses the FCA-based early aspects analysis method. In Sect. 5, we report on the results of an initial qualitative study of the utility of our approach. Section 6 reviews related work. Section 7 draws some concluding remarks and outlines future work.

2   Goal Models for Media Shop

Media shop is a store selling different kinds of media items such as books, newspapers, magazines, audio CDs, and videotapes [4]. We assume that a goal-oriented analysis has been performed to investigate requirements for new on-line services, using i^* as the requirements modeling framework [54]. Early requirements analysis focuses on the intentions of stakeholders. In i^*, stakeholders are represented as (social) actors who depend on each other for goals to be achieved, tasks to be performed, and resources to be furnished [53].

The i^* framework emphasizes the analysis of strategic relationships among organizational actors. A strategic rationale (SR) model exposes the reasoning within each actor by identifying goals, tasks, softgoals, and their relationships. The SR models for two media shop stakeholder roles, customer and developer, are

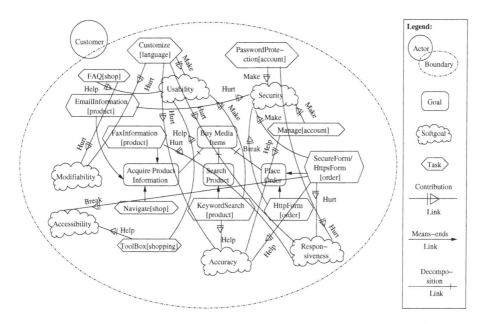

Fig. 2. Strategic rationale (SR) model for media shop customer

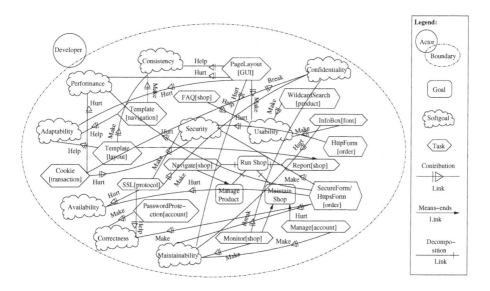

Fig. 3. Strategic rationale (SR) model for media shop developer

shown in Figs. 2 and 3, respectively. Goals are states of desires, such as customer wants to "buy media items" (Fig. 2). Goals can be hierarchically decomposed to subgoals, and can be achieved by various means-ends relations linking to tasks.

Tasks are actions with goals and commitments, such as customer receives "emails about product information" (Fig. 2). NFRs are expressed as softgoals, which can only be *satisficed* within acceptable limits, rather than satisfied absolutely [5]. The satisficing degree is labeled with "make", "help", "hurt", and "break" along the contribution links pointing to specific softgoals in Figs. 2 and 3.

Softgoals are candidate aspects because aspects are usually "units of system decomposition that are not functional" [19]. However, softgoals are often viewed as abstract concepts because they are difficult to express in a measurable way. Zave and Jackson [55] argued that goals by themselves do not make a good starting point for RE, as almost every goal is a subgoal with some higher purpose. Concrete operationalizations must be sought to ensure the satisfaction of goals.

Each goal model defines a particular context for requirements comprehension. Within this context, we identify concepts pertinent to softgoals. A *concept* [1] stands for the knowledge about objects having certain attributes or properties. In a given context, a concept has an extent and an intent. The *extent* is the set of objects in the context that are constituents of the concept, and the *intent* is the set of attributes that capture the essence of the concept. For example, the concept "country" has the extent of Canada and Portugal, but does not subsume Toronto or Europe. The intent may include "a territorial division", "a federation of communities", and the like.

In our approach, we treat each softgoal as a concept. The intent is the concern that a particular softgoal addresses, and the crosscutting nature or broad impact of that concern in the goal model. The extent is the set of model entities that are affected by the candidate aspect. We use tasks that contribute to the softgoal as a baseline to crystallize the concept. The reason is twofold. First, tasks are more concrete than softgoals. While people may have different criteria for determining whether the softgoal, for example, "usability" of the media shop is fulfilled, they generally tend to have a common interpretation of the task "keyword search of product" (Fig. 2). Second, to become true early aspects, not just candidate ones, softgoals need to have specific operationalizations, or advising tasks [54], to contribute to their satisfactions [25]. Concrete entities like tasks are what make softgoals understandable, operationalizable, localizable, and measurable.

In the following two sections, we introduce the concept-driven approach by discussing how contribution links between tasks and softgoals in a goal model can be used to align stakeholder softgoals and analyze candidate aspects' crosscutting properties. We use the media shop example to illustrate the proposed approach.

3   Early Aspects Alignment

When people observe a complex problem domain, their observations are inevitably incomplete. Personal values and experiences act as a filter, leading people to focus on aspects that are particularly salient to them personally. This gives rise to many partial conceptual structures. When asked to articulate these, people choose terms that are meaningful to them. Often, they find it necessary

---

[1] Formal definition of concept is given in Sect. 4.

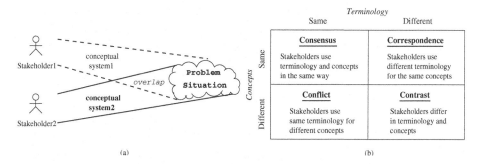

Fig. 4. Conceptual and terminological interference. **a** Overlap in two conceptual systems. **b** Relations between terminology and concepts.

to adapt or invent new terms to describe situations that they have not previously needed to articulate.

In a well-established scientific domain, experts develop a consensus over relevant distinctions and terms. Over time, they identify and test *objective knowledge* independent of individuals [34]. However, such objective knowledge is not yet available for most RE problem domains. If there is no pre-existing consensus over terminology, it is important to be able to compare the conceptual structures among multiple experts [11].

Figure 4a illustrates the situation. Two stakeholders, or more accurately, people playing particular stakeholder *roles*, have developed overlapping conceptual systems that they use to make sense of a problem situation. When these two stakeholders attach terms to their concepts, there are four possible conditions for the relationship between their concepts and terms, as summarized in Fig. 4b [43].

The challenge in knowledge elicitation is to discover which of the situations in Fig. 4b apply for a given set of stakeholder terms:

- *Consensus* is a desirable situation, since stakeholders then have a basis for communication using shared concepts and terminologies.
- *Conflict* (also known as *terminological inconsistency* [16]) can cause significant communication problems throughout the requirements process.
- Discovering *correspondence* is important because it lays the grounds for mutual understanding of differing terms through the availability of common concepts.
- Strictly speaking, *contrast* does not involve terminological interference, but the lack of shared concepts could make communication and understanding among stakeholders very difficult.

We interpret both conflict and correspondence as instances of *terminological interference*. Both have the potential to cause communication problems, if they are not identified and managed. We believe that terminological interference is both inevitable and useful in RE. It is inevitable because stakeholders have complementary perspectives, and are unlikely to have evolved a well-defined terminology for describing the problem situation. It is useful because it provides an opportunity to probe differences in the stakeholders' conceptual systems, to challenge ill-defined terms, and to identify new and productive distinctions for important concepts in the problem domain. However, this can only be achieved if terminological interference is identified and managed. Explicit consideration of terminological interference also helps to keep stakeholders from reaching a false, and often too early, consensus [43].

3.1 Personal Construct Theory and Repertory Grid Technique

George Kelly's PCT [18] presented a view of "man-the-scientist". From within this view, people were assumed to construct a model of the world (much as a scientist constructs a theory), act on the basis of their model (as the scientist creates an experiment to test the theory), and then alter their model in the light of feedback from the results of their actions (as the scientist uses data from the experiment to modify the theory). It is interesting to note that this view shares much of the spirit of the Inquiry Cycle presented in [35], in which requirements models are theories about the world, and designs are tests of those theories.

From the PCT perspective, the meaning we attach to events or objects defines our subjective reality, and thereby the way we interact with our environment. Constructs are ways of construing the world, enabling people to respond to what they experience in ways which are "explicitly formulated or implicitly acted out" [18]. For example, the way in which I interact with my desk is determined by the way I construe it — do I polish it carefully because I see it as something to be looked after or do I put my feet up on it because I see it as a convenient resting point? Thus, in Kelly's theory, the idea of the notion of "objectivity" disappears, and the best we can do along these lines is "inter-subjectivity", thinking rather of a dimension representing degree of agreement between construers and degree of certainty of judgment [42].

Kelly originally developed PCT in the context of psychotherapy and developed an associated methodology, the RGT, so as to explore patients' constructions of their social world. However, RGT has long been recognized as a content-free method for externalizing individuals' personal constructs, and has seen applications in a wide variety of situations, for example, education and market research, which are far removed from clinical psychology.

Underlying RGT is the notion that enables people to verbalize how they construe certain factors within the area of interest. These verbalizations are known as *constructs*, and the factors are called *elements*. A construct is hence a single dimension of meaning for a person allowing two phenomena to be seen as similar and thereby as different from a third [10]. A construct is bipolar in nature, where each pole represents the extreme of a particular view or observation. Kelly suggested RGT as a structured procedure for eliciting a repertoire of these conceptual constructs and for investigating and exploring their structures and interrelations [10].

Figure 5a shows a sample repertory grid for the media shop, in which rows represent constructs and columns represent elements. For a greater degree of differentiation, a five-point scale is used to indicate where an element lies with

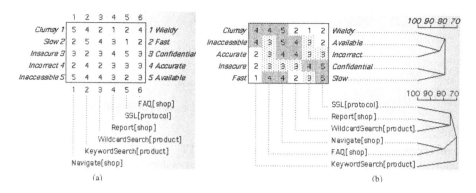

Fig. 5. A sample repertory grid for the media shop. **a** Display of repertory grid. **b** Cluster analysis of repertory grid.

respect to the poles of each construct. The construct poles to the left of the grid are the "1" end of the scale, and those to the right are the "5" end. The occurrence of the central point "3" in a grid can have two different interpretations: 1. **Neutral:** the element is at neither one pole nor the other of the construct. 2. **Not applicable or unknown:** the element is outside the range of convenience of the construct. For example, the element "Report[shop]" is not pertinent to the construct "Inaccessible-Available". Therefore, a rating of "3" appears in the fifth row and the fourth column of Fig. 5a.

The most interesting feature of RGT is the wide variety of different types of analyses that can be applied to the gathered personal constructs. In our approach, the FOCUS program [42] is used to perform a two-way hierarchical cluster analysis, and to reorder the grid so that similarly rated elements are adjacent and similarly used constructs are adjacent.

Figure 5b shows the reordered media shop sample grid. The upper and lower dendrograms illustrate the strength of association between constructs and between elements respectively. To highlight the clusters within the grid, ratings of four and five are given dark shading, ratings of three are given light shading, and ratings of one and two are left unshaded. This enables the easy identification of "blocks" within the grid [42]. For example, the top left cluster in Fig. 5b shows that keyword search, FAQ, and navigation are similar with respect to the "Clumsy–Wieldy" criterion in this particular context. Next, we show how to leverage RGT to align candidate aspects regarding to different stakeholder vocabularies.

3.2 Early Aspects Alignment Via Repertory Grid Technique

A competent early aspects framework shall provide mechanisms to avoid tangling of distinct concepts expressed in the same term, and to prevent scattering of one concept over dissimilar lexicons. We present a novel use of RGT with roots in PCT as a means of addressing terminological problems in different viewpoints

1 – break (strong negative)
2 – hurt (weak negative)
3 – neutral (unknown or don't care)
4 – help (weak positive)
5 – make (strong positive)

Fig. 6. Qualitative scale for measuring softgoal contributions

("correspondence" and "conflict" areas shown in Fig. 4b). We associate softgoals with stakeholders' personal constructs, and use the tasks that contribute to these goals as elements that stakeholders can rate using their constructs. The key idea is to compare the stakeholders' constructs by how they relate to a shared set of concrete entities, rather than by any terms the stakeholders use to describe them. In this way, we avoid making any assumptions about the meanings of individuals' constructs. Four highly iterative and interactive activities are involved in our framework: extraction, exchange, comparison, and assessment. We now describe each step in more detail using the media shop example described in Sect. 2.

Extraction: Given a set of goal models, we need to extract relevant information within some context to identify constructs and elements for grid analysis. A key underlying assumption of PCT and RGT is that elements define the context. Elements need to be carefully chosen to be within the range of convenience of the constructs we wish to study [10]. For instance, it bends our minds to consider "antique" or "modern" numbers and "prime" or "non-prime" furniture.

When analyzing goal models, we begin with some core agent or key activities in the system, and this generally provides a well-scoped area of interest. We carefully record the context of each grid so that sensible and relevant exchange and comparison can be performed.

Softgoals are candidate aspects and are often difficult to express in a measurable way, so it is hard to ensure that different stakeholders understand them in the same way. Softgoals within the context are selected as personal constructs, and each construct is identified as a pair of polar extremes corresponding to "make the goal" and "break the goal". Concrete entities of the same type (e.g., tasks), which are related to the chosen constructs, are selected as elements. The reason is twofold. First, empirical evidence suggests that people are better at comprehending and making analogies between concrete concepts rather than abstractions in RE [33]. Second, heterogeneous elements are likely to result in range of convenience problems as well as decreasing the validity of the grid [10].

Each element is then rated on each bipolar construct. For each grid, some ratings can be obtained from the goal models directly, some can be derived through label propagation algorithms [5], and the remainder need to be completed by the stakeholder. A five-point scale is defined in Fig. 6 to make such measures both subtle and specific. This multi-rating scale captures softgoals' satisficeability: softgoal fulfillment is relative and "good enough" rather than absolute [5].

The goal models shown in Figs. 2 and 3 share the media shop context, and the extracted tasks and softgoals from these strategic rationale models are listed

Tasks / Elements		Softgoals / Constructs	
Navigate[shop]	Customize[language]		
KeywordSearch[product]	WildcardSearch[product]		
ToolBox[shopping]	Report[shop]	Usability [C,D]	Consistency [D]
FAQ[shop]	PageLayout[GUI]	Responsiveness [C]	Availability [D]
PasswordProtection[account]	InfoBox[font]	Security [C,D]	Maintainability [D]
Manage[account]	SSL[protocol]	Modifiability [C]	Adaptability [D]
EmailInformation[product]	Cookie[transaction]	Accessibility [C]	Correctness [D]
FaxInformation[product]	Template[layout]	Accuracy [C]	Performance [D]
HttpForm[order]	Template[navigation]		Confidentiality [D]
SecureForm/HttpsForm[oder]	Monitor[shop]		

Fig. 7. List of elements and constructs for media shop

in Fig. 7. In our approach, the set of tasks determines the common ground and is shared among all analysts. In addition to its name, each task also contains the subject matter [55] shown in squared parentheses. Softgoals are treated as personal constructs, so we specify the owner(s) after each softgoal in Fig. 7. Where softgoals have the same name but different owners, we treat them as distinct constructs. The labeling convention — explicitly marking every softgoal's owner after it ("C" refers to "customer" and "D" represents "developer") — is adopted in this paper. This also addresses the traceability concern from the model management perspective [40].

The construction of a repertory grid is perhaps best regarded as a particular form of structured interview with each stakeholder. The answers to such questions as, "how does this task affect the system's maintainability?", may give us an understanding of the interweaving of the stakeholder's terminology and provide us with an understanding of her outlook that no dictionary could offer.

Exchange: Each grid expresses the way in which a particular stakeholder views the domain and in what terms she seeks to make sense of the underlying elements. Each of these dimensions is expressed in personally meaningful terms, and is significant to the person who used it.

In a shared context, each stakeholder's personal construct system overlaps to some degree with others, and this makes it possible for people to exchange their grids data to share their individual perceptions of the domain. Such exchange needs to be administered in a structured manner in order to reduce stakeholders' cognitive burdens, and at the same time, to achieve sensible results that are amenable to interference analysis.

We only exchange the extracted common set of tasks between stakeholders, and keep the use of softgoals inside each person's individual conceptual system. Structural exchange allows the tasks in the goal model derived from one stakeholder to be assessed by another in order to determine whether the two stakeholders have consensus or conflict in their use of terminology and concepts.

In our approach, only concrete entities, i.e., tasks, are exchanged, because at this stage, the abstract constructs only have meaning within each person's individual conceptual system. A construct is a discriminator, not a verbal label [10].

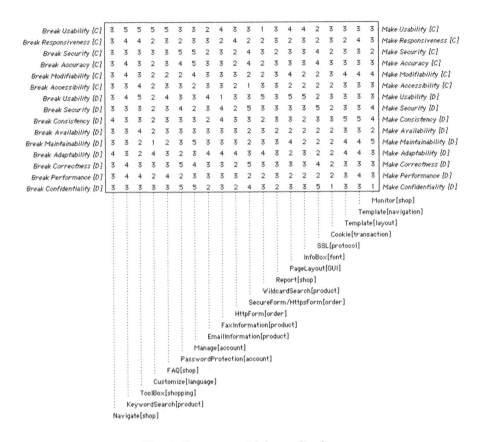

Fig. 8. Repertory grid for media shop

Construct names are merely convenient labels to remind the person of the thoughts and feelings that the construct provoked, and hence are not transferable to another person without discussion and negotiation [42].

On the other hand, the concrete entities *are* exchanged, because to make comparisons across individuals and investigate construct similarity requires that they each construe the same set of elements [22]. We assume that people focusing on similar topics would agree on the definition of a common set of concrete tasks within the area of interest, i.e., when presented with specific and relevant tasks that are devised by others, people are likely to grasp the essential meaning behind the notions.

In the media shop example, the tasks from different viewpoints are consolidated and shared. Then, each stakeholder rates all twenty tasks (elements) on his or her own softgoals (constructs) using the 5-point scale defined in Fig. 6. Figure 8 presents an integrated view of individual repertory grid filled up by the customer and the developer.

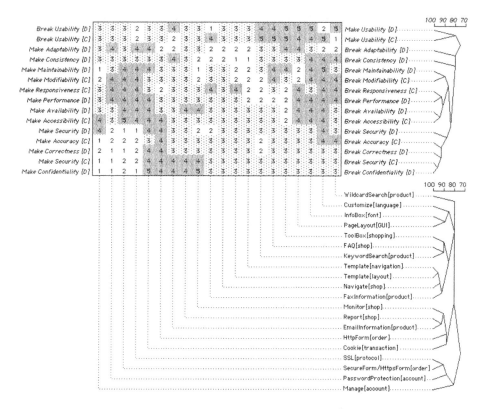

Fig. 9. Cluster analysis for the repertory grid in Fig. 8

Comparison: After focused extraction of repertory grids from goal models and structured exchange of tasks between stakeholders, stakeholders' softgoals can now be compared. The set of all tasks offers a common ground to evaluate softgoals in a particular context. We compare the softgoals according to the extent to which they array the set of tasks.

The relationship between any two constructs can be examined by seeing to what extent the ratings of all the elements on one of the constructs tend to match, or differ from, the ratings on the other construct [39]. If two softgoals orchestrate the tasks in the same or very similar way, "correspondence" (Fig. 4b) is established between these constructs even though they may be labeled differently. If two softgoals that have been labeled using the same terms align the tasks in a markedly dissimilar fashion, then "conflict" (Fig. 4b) is detected.

Figure 9 presents the cluster analysis result for the repertory grid shown in Fig. 8. It is apparent from Fig. 9 that the terms used to express softgoals interfered greatly. For example, what the customer meant by "Security" and the concern "Confidentiality" in the developer's viewpoint were associated at the 96.2% level. In terms of the tasks shown in the grid, these two softgoals differ only in the degrees, not in the poles' extremity, rated by three elements: one rated two on "Security [C]" and one on "Confidentiality [D]", and the other two rated four on "Security [C]" and five on "Confidentiality [D]". Thus, these two crosscutting concerns are considered to be very similar based on grid analysis. If they are indeed used interchangeably, correspondence would be established. Otherwise, further elicitation should be performed to distinguish these constructs.

Although the customer and the developer both used the term "Usability", they probably did not refer to the same concept. These two constructs were associated at the 80% level, one of the lowest matching scores between softgoals appeared in Fig. 9. From the developer's perspective, the task "wildcard search" affected "Usability" positively because people could do a fuzzy search and still retrieve useful information. But the customer thought the task actually broke "Usability" since using "wildcard" would involve a steep learning curve for a non-technical user. Exploring such an inconsistency could spark the discussion about what the concern "Usability" really meant to the media shop organization and whether "wildcard search" should be implemented.

The grid analysis results, such as the correspondence and conflict relationships identified above, not only enable us to gain insights into stakeholders' use of terminologies and concepts, but also allow us to generate specific and plausible hypotheses to be tested with subsequent efforts in eliciting and communicating requirements. This indeed characterizes part of incremental analysis depicted in Fig. 1, and leads us to assessing the RGT-based early aspects alignment method.

Assessment: Analogies can be drawn between RGT and structured interview. Stakeholders undergo the interview by completing extracted and exchanged grids. Analysis of resultant grids raises a plethora of new questions for further exploration. Essentially, a repertory grid is the start of a dialogue between analyst and stakeholders. For example, if we have identified a potential correspondence between two softgoals, we might ask the stakeholders to suggest further examples of concrete instances, to see if they confirm or refute the correspondence. If stakeholders suspect their softgoals do not correspond, they may be inspired to find tasks that disambiguate them. If they suspect two conflicting constructs really do mean the same thing, they might discuss the apparent discrepancy in their ratings of the concrete elements against this construct.

Assessment can thus be considered as a follow-up interview to address the newly generated questions, and for stakeholders to provide evaluation and feedback about the quality and usefulness of the obtained data. In our framework, there is no independent measurement since the collected data is context-laden and is open to interpretation in a number of ways. Our exploratory RGT-based approach is of practical value if our findings can provoke fruitful discussions and guide further RE activities to precisely comprehend stakeholders' terminologies and conceptual systems, thereby producing requirements that adequately reflect their desires and needs.

Our concept alignment approach is appealing, since PCT and RGT avoids the problems of imposition of terminology, and the meaning of a term is essentially treated as a relationship between signs and actions. One desired outcome of aligning concepts could be a vocabulary map between different viewpoints.

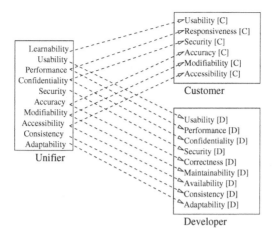

Fig. 10. An attempt to establish a unifier and vocabulary map for media shop

Figure 10 shows our initial attempt to build such a vocabulary map for the media shop example. This mapping is based on grid analysis of Fig. 9, and each attempt to establish a unifier and vocabulary connector can be seen as a hypothesis about how to put different viewpoints together, in which choices have to be made about which concepts overlap, and how the terms used by various stakeholders are related. If a particular set of choices yields an unacceptable result, it is better to perform the concept merge, investigate the resulting inconsistencies, and carry out the incremental analysis (Fig. 1), rather than restrict the available mapping choices. Detailed processes of exploratory vocabulary reconciliation are beyond the scope of this paper, and are considered as future work. We use Fig. 10 as the baseline mapping to facilitate discussion for the rest of the paper.

3.3   Discussion

We have presented a PCT- and RGT-based approach to systematic and effective concept alignment, and have illustrated the method by identifying synonyms and homonyms of candidate aspects in goal models. Our approach is lightweight in that both elements and constructs are extracted from well-organized models from goal-oriented RE [29], rather than being elicited from scratch. Currently, focused grid extraction based on key activities is used as a heuristic to reduce irrelevance between different views. Future work is planned for ensuring the range of convenience of repertory grids offered by different stakeholders.

Softgoals in goal models are a good starting point for analyzing early aspects, and candidate aspects can be seen as operationalizations of softgoals and the relations to functional goals [54]. Our RGT-based concept alignment approach is also applicable to the analysis of crosscutting functional requirements. In [25], dichotomized repertory grids are constructed as an impact analysis tool to reveal crosscutting properties of goal model entities. It is thus advantageous to align candidate aspects in goal models by using the tasks they crosscut, and RGT could provide support for doing so.

To investigate construct similarities and differences across individuals using RGT, we assume that concrete entities, such as tasks, in the given context can be mutually understood among stakeholders. It might not be the case that people can precisely and accurately interpret other people's elements, because the actual phrasing and labeling of elements will have crucial impact on our proposed method. Our overall perception is that people make good approximations when trying to understand concrete and pertinent concepts, so our assumption is "good enough" for applying RGT to deal with early aspects alignment in goal models. Besides, any comparison of conceptual systems necessarily involves approximation since a complete conceptual system may involve indefinitely complex relations and different concepts will never be identical in all respects [43].

Finally, like any process, the quality of the output of our RGT-based method is only as good as the quality of the inputs and the controls over the process. Our inputs rely on various stakeholders in the problem domain, on which early aspects research is based. And we believe that our approach not only has strong yet flexible controls over the extraction, exchange, comparison, and assessment process, but also has a profound and solid foundation, namely the PCT, of aligning concepts in different viewpoints. Our output, such as the clustering result shown in Fig. 9 and the vocabulary map in Fig. 10, can enable the requirements analyst to both gain insights into stakeholders' use of domain concepts and to generate plausible hypotheses to guide further early aspects analysis activities.

4   Early Aspects Analysis

This section describes the application of FCA to supporting trade-off analysis and conflict detection of early aspects in requirements goal models. We also discuss the seamless integration of FCA with RGT so as to form a coherent concept-driven framework. Before diving into the details of FCA, we examine the connection that "concept merging" (step 3 in Fig. 1) makes between candidate aspects alignment and analysis.

The early aspects alignment method introduced in Sect. 3 can assist in highlighting discrepancies over the terminology being used and the concepts being modeled. Concept merging in goal models can thus be considered as grid merging of consolidated tasks and reconciled softgoals. We assume that in the adapted merged view, there may only be one contribution relationship between a task and a softgoal: either being negative or being positive, but cannot be both, [2] i.e., the merged model exhibits an internal consistency with respect to softgoal contributions. For example, although both the customer and the developer expressed "Usability" in their original views (Figs. 2 and 3), a terminological

---

[2] We simplify the scale for measuring softgoal contributions to be "positive" and "negative". In Fig. 6, "break" and "hurt" are associated with "negative", "help" and "make" correspond to "positive", and "neutral" means there is no contribution relationship between the task and the softgoal.

conflict was detected between these two concepts (Fig. 9) and the customer's softgoal was aligned to the "Learnability" concern by grid analysis (Fig. 10). Thus, in the reconciled view, occurrences of terminological interference are identified and managed, and distinct early aspects are represented using distinct lexicons.

4.1   Formal Concept Analysis

Formal concept analysis (FCA) is a mathematical technique for analyzing binary relations. The mathematical foundation of concept analysis was laid by Birkhoff [3] in 1940. For more detailed information on FCA, we refer to [12], where the mathematical foundation is explored.

FCA deals with a relation $\mathcal{I} \subseteq \mathcal{O} \times \mathcal{A}$ between a set of objects $\mathcal{O}$ and a set of attributes $\mathcal{A}$. The tuple $C = (\mathcal{O}, \mathcal{A}, \mathcal{I})$ is called a *formal context*. For a set of objects $O \subseteq \mathcal{O}$, the set of common attributes $\sigma(O)$ is defined as:

$$\sigma(O) = \{a \in A \mid (o, a) \in \mathcal{I} \text{ for all } o \in O\}. \tag{1}$$

Analogously, the set of common objects $\tau(A)$ for a set of attributes $A \subseteq \mathcal{A}$ is defined as:

$$\tau(A) = \{o \in O \mid (o, a) \in \mathcal{I} \text{ for all } a \in A\}. \tag{2}$$

A formal context can be represented by a relation table, where columns hold the objects and the rows hold the attributes. An object o_i and attribute a_j are in the relation $\mathcal{I}$ if and only if the cell at column i and row j is marked by "×". As an example related to the media shop, a binary relation between a set of objects {CD, MAGAZINE, NEWSPAPER, VIDEOTAPE, BOOK} and a set of attributes {free-distribution, timely, paper, sound} is shown in Fig. 11a. For that formal context, we have:

$$\sigma(\{\text{CD}\}) = \{\text{free-distribution, sound}\},$$
$$\tau(\{\text{timely, paper}\}) = \{\text{MAGAZINE, NEWSPAPER}\}.$$

A tuple $c = (O, A)$ is called a *concept* if and only if $A = \sigma(O)$ and $O = \tau(A)$, i.e., all objects in c share all attributes in c. For a concept $c = (O, A)$, O is called the *extent* of c, denoted by $extent(c)$, and A is called the *intent* of c, denoted by $intent(c)$. Informally speaking, a concept corresponds to a maximal rectangle of filled table cells modulo row and column permutations. In Fig. 11b, all concepts for the relation in Fig. 11a are listed.

The set of all concepts of a given formal context forms a partial order via the superconcept-subconcept ordering $\leq$:

$$(O_1, A_1) \leq (O_2, A_2) \iff O_1 \subseteq O_2, \tag{3}$$

or, dually, with

$$(O_1, A_1) \leq (O_2, A_2) \iff A_1 \supseteq A_2. \tag{4}$$

MEDIA SHOP	free-distribution	timely	paper	sound
CD	X			X
MAGAZINE		X	X	
NEWSPAPER	X	X	X	
VIDEOTAPE				X
BOOK			X	

(a)

$\top$	({CD, MAGAZINE, NEWSPAPER, VIDEOTAPE, BOOK}, Φ)
c_1	({CD, VIDEOTAPE}, {sound})
c_2	({CD, NEWSPAPER}, {free-distribution})
c_3	({MAGAZINE, NEWSPAPER, BOOK}, {paper})
c_4	({MAGAZINE, NEWSPAPER}, {timely, paper})
c_5	({NEWSPAPER}, {free-distribution, timely, paper})
c_6	({CD}, {free-distribution, sound})
$\bot$	(Φ, {free-distribution, timely, paper, sound})

(b)

Fig. 11. An example relation between objects and attributes. **a** Formal context. **b** Concepts for the formal context.

Note that (3) and (4) imply each other by definition. If we have $c_1 \leq c_2$, then c_1 is called a *subconcept* of c_2 and c_2 is a *superconcept* of c_1. For instance, in Fig. 11b, we have $c_5 \leq c_3$.

The set $\mathcal{L}$ of all concepts of a given formal context and the partial order $\leq$ form a complete lattice, called *concept lattice*:

$$\mathcal{L}(C) = \{(O, A) \in 2^O \times 2^A \mid A = \sigma(O) \text{ and } O = \tau(A)\}. \tag{5}$$

The *infimum* ($\sqcap$) of two concepts in this lattice is computed by intersecting their extents as follows:

$$(O_1, A_1) \sqcap (O_2, A_2) = (O_1 \cap O_2, \sigma(O_1 \cap O_2)). \tag{6}$$

The infimum describes a set of common attributes of two sets of objects. Similarly, the *supremum* ($\sqcup$) is determined by intersecting the intents:

$$(O_1, A_1) \sqcup (O_2, A_2) = (\tau(A_1 \cup A_2), A_1 \cup A_2). \tag{7}$$

The supremum yields the set of common objects, which share all attributes in the intersection of two sets of attributes.

The concept lattice for the formal context in Fig. 11a can be depicted as a directed acyclic graph whose nodes represent the concepts and whose edges denote the superconcept-subconcept relation $\leq$ as shown in Fig. 12. Figure 12 is also called a *line diagram*, which consists the names of all objects and all attributes of the given context. The nodes represent the concepts and the information of the context can be read from the diagram by the following simple reading rule:

An object o has an attribute a if and only if there is an upwards

leading path from the node named by o to the node named by a,

or, dually, with

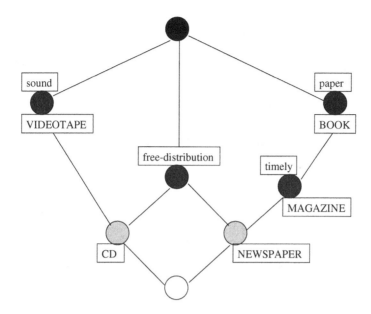

Fig. 12. Concept lattice for the example context in Fig. 11

An attribute a has an object o if and only if there is an downwards leading path from the node named by a to the node named by o.

Hence, we recognize from the line diagram in Fig. 12 that the node "MAGA-ZINE" has exactly the attributes "timely" and "paper", and the node "timely" has exactly the objects "MAGAZINE" and "NEWSPAPER". As a consequence of the reading rule, we can easily read from the line diagram the extent and the intent of each concept by collecting all objects below respectively all attributes above the node of the given concept. Hence, the object concept "MAGAZINE" has the extent "MAGAZINE" and "NEWSPAPER" and the intent "timely" and "paper". The extent of the top concept ($\top$) is always the set of all objects, and the intent of the bottom concept ($\bot$) is always the set of all attributes. While in the context of Fig. 11a, the intent of the most general concept ($\top$) does not contain any attribute. In other contexts, it may occur that the intent of $\top$ is not empty. For example, if we add to the given context the attribute "media" with crosses in each row in Fig. 11a, then the top concept would be the attribute concept of "media" and the intent of $\top$ would contain just the attribute "media".

4.2   Early Aspects Analysis Via Formal Concept Analysis

Although they originated from separate disciplines, RGT and FCA share a common underlying structure: a cross-reference table. This allows these two techniques to be incorporated seamlessly. In our approach, the consolidated and reconciled repertory grid provides the cross-reference table from which one can

MEDIA SHOP	1	2	3	4	5	6	7	8	9	10	11	12	13	14	15	16	17	18	19	20
Navigate[shop]																		X		X
KeywordSearch[product]		X		X		X						X								
ToolBox[shopping]		X		X		X										X		X		
Customize[language]		X	X		X			X		X			X		X		X			X
FAQ[shop]		X		X								X								
PasswordProtection[account]					X			X		X		X	X					X		
Manage[account]								X	X			X		X						
EmailInformation[product]	X			X			X			X						X				X
FaxInformation[product]		X	X		X												X			X
HttpForm[order]							X		X		X									X
SecureForm/HttpsForm[order]					X			X		X		X	X			X				
WildcardSearch[product]	X			X	X						X						X			
Report[shop]						X								X						
PageLayout[GUI]		X		X	X									X	X					X
InfoBox[font]		X		X									X	X						
SSL[protocol]	X			X		X		X		X		X	X		X				X	
Cookie[transaction]					X		X		X						X				X	
Template[layout]														X				X		X
Template[navigation]					X								X					X		X
Monitor[shop]							X		X					X				X		

Attributes:
  1 −Learnability 2 +Learnability 3 −Usability 4 +Usability 5 −Performance 6 +Performance
  7 −Confidentiality 8 +Confidentiality 9 −Security 10 +Security 11 −Accuracy 12 +Accuracy
  13 −Modifiability 14 +Modifiability 15 −Accessibility 16 +Accessibility 17 −Consistency
  18 +Consistency 19 −Adaptablity 20 +Adaptability

Fig. 13. Formal context for media shop derived from the repertory grid in Fig. 8 and the vocabulary map in Fig. 10. Elements in the repertory grid are transformed to objects for the context, and constructs in the grid, which are mapped to negatively (−) and positively (+) contributed softgoals, form attributes for the formal context.

derive the formal context and then identify sub-super relationships among the concepts in the line diagram to facilitate trade-off analysis on early aspects.

To transform a repertory grid to a formal context, we map elements in RGT (the tasks in goal models) to the set of objects $\mathcal{O}$ for the formal context. This can be seen as a direct translation since in our approach, the set of tasks offers a common ground to evaluate early aspects in a particular context and is shared among all stakeholders.

Constructs in RGT are associated with attributes in the formal context. We simplify the finer-grained scale for measuring softgoal contributions to be positive or negative, and assume that if there is a contribution relationship between a task and a softgoal, there can only be one: either negative or positive, but cannot be both. So, for each softgoal a, we have the labels "$-a$" (being negatively affected) and "$+a$" (being positively contributed) appear in the set of attributes $\mathcal{A}$ for the formal context. Note that FCA does have mechanisms for handling multi-valued formal context [12], but the discussion for that support is beyond the scope of this paper.

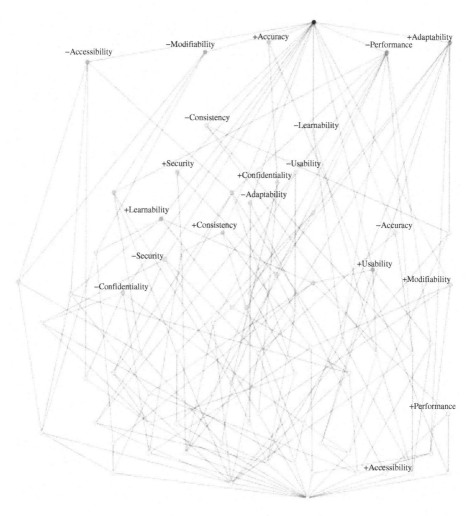

Fig. 14. Concept lattice for the media shop context in Fig. 13. To reduce the clutter of the figure, only the attribute concepts are labeled.

Figure 13 shows the formal context for media shop derived from the repertory grid in Fig. 8 and the vocabulary map in Fig. 10. The concept lattice of this context is shown in Fig. 14, in which only attribute concepts are labeled to reduce the clutter of the line diagram. For each concept c in the media shop example, $extent(c)$ is the set of tasks that have same contribution links to a set of softgoals, and $intent(c)$ is the set of softgoals that crosscut those tasks.

A line diagram provides a rich graphical representation of the information within a particular context, and is amenable to various analyses at the concept level. For example, between the concepts of any context, there is a natural hierarchical order — the subconcept–superconcept relation. This relation can be easily identified in the line diagram by path traversing [12], and can play an important

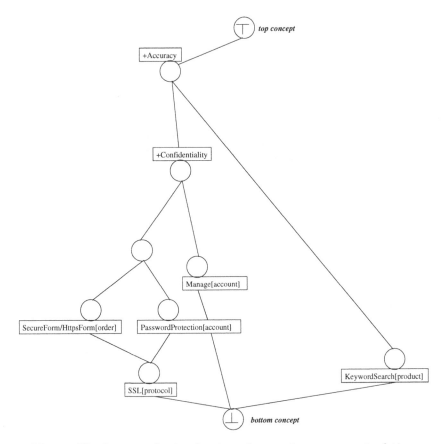

Fig. 15. Sliced concept lattice showing subconcept–superconcept relations

role in analyzing trade-offs, preferences, and priorities on various concepts presented in goal models. A useful technique is to have a slice of interested concepts, i.e., stakeholder concerns, projected from the whole context. Our heuristic is to analyze softgoal fulfillment in a bottom–up way (subconcept to superconcept), and to select concrete operationalizations top–down. This is because fulfillment of subconcept infers fulfillment of superconcept, and selection of superconcept infers selection of one or more subconcepts.

To illustrate subconcept-superconcept relations, a sliced concept lattice for media shop is shown in Fig. 15. By definition [cf. (3) and (4) in Sect. 4.1], the concept labeled with "+Confidentiality" is a subconcept of the one named "+Accuracy". This indicates that in the media shop context, all the tasks that positively contribute to the "Confidentiality" aspect will have positive contributions to "Accuracy". In another word, if the softgoal "Confidentiality" is achieved by the intended software, so is "Accuracy". However, if for some reason, e.g., due to conflicting requirements, "Confidentiality" cannot be satisfied, we still have a choice of implementing the task "KeywordSearch[product]" to address the "Accuracy" concern.

In a similar vein, identifying subconcept–superconcept relations in the concept lattice can help to perform trade-off analysis on concrete tasks. In the media shop case, for instance, the "SSL[protocol]"-labeled concept is a subconcept of the "PasswordProtection[account]"-labeled one, which implies that in addition to all the concerns that "PasswordProtection[account]" addresses, "SSL[protocol]" has (negative or positive) contributions to other softgoals. If these two are competitive tasks for the software system to implement, we may start analyzing the concerns that are uniquely linked to "SSL[protocol]", and neglecting the commonly shared, identically contributed softgoals by both tasks. If our goal is to satisfice as many softgoals as possible, [3] based on the context of Fig. 13, we may choose to include "PasswordProtection[account]" in our architectural design, because "SSL[protocol]" contributes "Learnability" and "Usability" negatively, and these two tasks have exactly the same contribution relationships to the rest of the softgoals in the context. Such analysis helps the analyst to specify preferences and priorities on (aspectual) requirements.

Conflicting candidate aspects in the context can be detected by using the concept lattice. In our setting, one way is to start with softgoals of stakeholder interests that form a subconcept-superconcept relationship. If they have different signs, i.e., one labeled with "−" and the other labeled with "+", then we note them as potential conflict. For example, in Fig. 14, "−Performance" is a superconcept of "+Confidentiality". We mark them as potential conflict since all the tasks that help to fulfill "Confidentiality" will negatively affect media shop's "Performance".

Another way of detecting conflicting concepts is to treat the formal context, such as the one in Fig. 13, as a distance matrix. If the distance between two softgoals is small with respect to some threshold, and they have different signs ("+" versus "−"), then there is a potential conflict between them. This conflict detection method has a similar flavor to the RGT-based hierarchical cluster analysis described in Sect. 3.2, in that both methods examine how different softgoals align a common set of tasks.

In order to perform the trade-off and conflict analyses mentioned above, a query language or some line diagram slicing algorithms shall be provided to facilitate the analyst to select and project interested (clustered) concepts in the concept lattice. However, these features are not yet available for most FCA-based analysis tools [2, 48]. Our early aspects analysis suggests the need for improvement in some areas of FCA tool support.

4.3 Discussion

We have applied FCA for conflict detection and trade-off analysis on early aspects in requirements goal models, and have seamlessly incorporated this FCA-based method with the PCT- and RGT-based early aspects alignment method

---

[3] This criterion is intuitive, since softgoals may contradict each other. We will show the FCA-based conflict detection method later in this section.

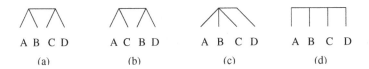

Fig. 16. Illustration of limitation of hierarchical clustering analysis. Even though the same information is presented, cognitions may vary among **a–d** due to different representational strategies: **a** cluster (AB) joins cluster (CD) **b** cluster (AC) joins cluster (BD) **c** cluster (ABC) joins D **d** single cluster (ABCD).

described in Sect. 3. A table of crosses represents a very simple and frequently used data type. We have showed how the reconciled and consolidated repertory grid can provide the cross-reference table from which the formal context of problem domain concepts can be derived: The set of elements in RGT are treated as objects in FCA, and personal constructs define the attributes in the formal context.

Although the translation from RGT to FCA is fairly straightforward and it seems that our composite approach replicates the same information in different formats: grid and table, we cannot replace one technique with the other. Firstly, each technique has an underlying theory and can only be applied under proper conditions and for proper tasks. Having roots in the psychology of personal constructs makes RGT suitable for concepts alignment among multiple stakeholder views; and with its origins in lattice theory, FCA offers mathematically rigorous analyses for a particular context.

Furthermore, these techniques are complementary to each other, and one of our purposes of employing a composite approach is to leverage the strengths of different approaches in overcoming each other's weaknesses. For example, the hierarchical clustering analysis of RGT is generally criticized because it can yield different inputs for the same data as in some instances several clusters are equidistant, leading to an arbitrary choice of the next clustering step [49]. This also increases analysts' cognitive overhead when they are in the process of identifying clustering potentials based on visual inspection, as illustrated in Fig. 16. FCA overcomes the problem since equidistant clusters are always grouped within one concept. Conversely, RGT helps to solve certain drawback of FCA. For instance, the constructs' reordering feature of FOCUS [42] addresses FCA's tool support limitation on analyzing trade-offs and detecting conflict, as pointed out by the media shop study in Sect. 4.2. The much needed slicing and projection features for FCA tools can be achieved by focusing on specific sub-clusters resulted from the FOCUS program. As a result, these techniques complement each other, and play appropriate roles in our coherent concept-driven framework.

Early aspects research in RE relies on stakeholders' inputs, and aims at presenting insightful analysis results to stakeholders for eliciting further information and feedback to better understand the problem world and the machine [15]. Thus, it is crucial for an early aspects framework to generate sensible analyses and plausible hypotheses to advance the RE process, and to guide system design and implementation. In that regard, our proposed approach is able to offer insights into early aspects' trade-offs and architectural solution rationale. For instance, in media shop, we analyzed the trade-offs between the aspects of "Accuracy" and "Confidentiality", and discussed the rationale for choosing particular implementations such as "SSL" and "PasswordProtection". Conflict detected in our approach can be used to drive negotiation strategies among stakeholders. The initial investigations into designing such a concept-driven framework also sharpen our understanding of the role modeling plays in RE: modeling is a way of telling people ideas, and like any telling, it clarifies; it also allows stakeholders to display and reflect on different ways of seeing the data.

5 Evaluation

An initial evaluation method for assessing the effectiveness of the concept-driven approach is defined on the basis of diffusion theory [38], which examines the rate and the motivations of adoption of a technological innovation by a group of potential users. Such an approach may also be fruitful for the evaluation of a novel conceptual framework (such as a design or requirements method), by assessing whether it is appreciated by a community of stakeholders [17].

The diffusion theory defines five perceived quality attributes of an innovative product. *Triability* is the degree by which the product can be tried on a limited basis before adoption. *Observability* refers to the observable results deriving from the use of the new product. *Relative advantage* is the perception of how much better the innovation is than the competing solutions currently adopted. *Complexity* refers to the fact that the innovative product should not be overly complex to understand and to use. *Compatibility* measures how the innovation is perceived as compatible and consistent with existing practices shared among the community of users [38].

On the basis of these attributes, a qualitative evaluation about the proposed approach was conducted, since we were still in the process of theory discovery and theory exploration, trying to reflectively learn something during the evaluation exercise rather than definitely test already known hypotheses. Qualitative data are records of observation or interaction that are complex and contexted, and they are not easily reduced immediately, or sometimes ever, to numbers. Qualitative research seeks to make sense of the way themes and meanings emerged and patterned in the data records built up from observations, interviews, document analysis, surveys and questionnaires, literature reviews, and other research media [37].

We used the media shop study described in this paper as an illustrative example to solicit feedback from seven requirements analysts, among whom five were computer science graduate students with some industrial RE experiences, and the other two were industry requirements engineers in small- and medium-sized companies.

Obviously, the number of sample users is not representative of the community of (goal-oriented) requirements modelers and analysts, and any quantitative data analysis will lack statistical significance and credibility. However, qualitative analysis methods, such as categorizing and coding used in our evaluation, can give an initial reaction to how such a systematic approach to early aspects is considered by requirements analysts.

Based on the quality criteria provided by diffusion theory, five free-form questions were designed. We collected data through interviews and questionnaires [21], and used coding (relating answer sections to proper quality attributes under testing) and categorizing (classifying answers to be positive or negative) [37] to perform qualitative data analysis. Requirements analysts' quotes are represented *italic* and cited in double quotation marks (" ") when analyzing the following five questions.

Question 1: According to your experience, do you think that this approach provides sufficient constructs and guidelines to be tested on a limited basis before adoption?

Quality Attribute: Triability.

The answer to this question was quite positive. Most requirements analysts were familiar with the notions of softgoals and tasks, and supported the idea of using contribution links to uncover and analyze goal models' crosscutting properties. To quote from feedback provided by an analysts: "*. . . (for one of our projects), we're currently conducting interviews (with multiple stakeholder roles), and would like to try out the (proposed) idea for separating concerns . . .*"

Question 2: Do you see preliminary observable results from the application of the proposed approach to the analysis of crosscutting concerns in goal-oriented requirements engineering?

Quality Attribute: Observability.

The response to this question was very positive. Analysts found the results in the given media shop example "*non-trivial*", "*insightful*", and "*useful*".

Question 3: Compared to relevant techniques you are aware of, do you think that the adoption of the proposed approach can better help you improve the quality of the goal-oriented requirements analysis?

Quality Attribute: Relative advantage.

Most analysts did not provide answers to this question. Instead, some mentioned that "*there's yet requirements method (that I'm aware of) that focuses on crosscutting concerns (explicitly).*"

Question 4: Do you think that the proposed approach is overly complex to be understood and used?

Quality Attribute: Complexity.

The answers to this question diverged. Some analysts regarded the approach proposed was easy to apply since no new modeling notations were introduced. Others admitted that even though the concept lattice offered interesting analyses, the line diagram produced for any sizeable model "*was somewhat too cluttered and complicated to understand.*" Tools that supported focused representations would be desirable.

Question 5: Do you perceive the proposed approach to be compatible and consistent with the existing practices, values, standards, and technologies shared in your organization or institution?

Quality Attribute: Compatibility.

"*Too early to tell*" was a representative response to this question. Some analysts expressed concerns to the proposed approach, such as scalability, tool support, and so on.

Although this initial evaluation was preliminary and much improvement was needed for the proposed approach, analysts felt that having a conceptually precise treatment for early aspects was necessary and important, and RGT and FCA were to be readily used in RE to tackle interesting problems.

6 Related Work

Baniassad et al. [1] presented an integrated approach to manipulating early aspects and exploiting them throughout the software development life cycle. The approach emphasizes the use of intuition, domain knowledge, and heuristics to facilitate the identification of aspects in requirements. In goal-based modeling, softgoals represent tangled and scattered concerns, and have been treated as candidate early aspects recurrently in the literature (e.g. [25, 54]). Niu and Easterbrook [25] argued that to become true early aspects, not just candidate ones, softgoals need to have specific operationalizations, or advising tasks [54], to contribute to their satisfactions. Yu et al. [54] also used the media shop example in their study, but no attempt was made to show how their process could be extended if multiple viewpoints and conflicting concerns were involved. Our approach extends previous work and existing knowledge, thoroughly analyzes the contribution links between tasks and softgoals in requirements goal models, and provides a conceptually rigorous framework for handling various concerns addressed in those models.

NFR catalogue [5] attempts to collate, from a wide range of sources, verifiable information on non-functional requirements in specific domains. One of the main motivations of catalogue or ontology building is the possibility of knowledge sharing and reuse: as soon as a particular domain (such as banking or meeting scheduling) is fixed, it seems reasonable to expect a large part of domain knowledge to be the same for a variety of applications, so that the high costs of knowledge acquisition can be better justified. Catalogue-based methods suggest that requirements analysts equip themselves with a glossary of standard terms to make communication easier and more precise. However, these methods can cause problems when stakeholders continue to use different interpretations of the terms codified in the catalogue. They also miss an important opportunity to explore differences in stakeholders' own categories so as to better understand their perspectives. Our approach takes the view based on personal constructs theory, which offers a mechanism to compare and contrast objects in the domain of interest. Our PCT- and RGT-based concepts alignment method avoids the problems of imposition of terminology when individuals construe and describe concepts in the problem domain, and the meaning of a term is essentially treated as a relationship between signs and actions in our framework. NFR or early aspects catalogue building could benefit from our approach since a well-categorized taxonomy is viewed as a catalogue of how constructs represented by linguistic symbols relate formally in a particular context.

Natural language processing (NLP) plays an important role in identifying aspects in requirements. Many early aspects frameworks (e.g. [6, 41, 46]) adapt certain steps in linguistic engineering (flatten, tokenize, stem, and remove stop words) so that aspect words (e.g. verbs that scattered in multiple requirements) can be extracted from requirements statements. Although NLP-based techniques could reach high recall and precision under certain circumstances, taking for granted that natural language-based requirements statements are an unproblematic starting point is a historical accident rather than a position grounded in the realities for RE [47]. We assume that there exists a relatively well-organized set of requirements models, and present a concept-driven framework that takes advantage of these models. Our approach complements existing NLP-based early aspects methods by providing mechanisms to capture and analyze overlapping, corresponding, conflicting, and crosscutting concerns addressed in fine-grained requirements models.

FCA has typically been applied in the field of software engineering to support software maintenance activities [49, 51], such as program understanding [52], object-oriented class identification [50], reengineering of class hierarchies [44], dynamic analysis [9], and software configurations [20]. In the analysis of software systems, especially source code exposing certain structural and behavioral properties, several relationships among the composing entities emerge. For this reason, FCA has found a very productive application area associated with static and dynamic analyses. Recent work, such as [36], has also reported the application of FCA in RE activities. The proposed approach exploits structural properties in requirements goal models, in particular, the binary contribution relations between tasks and softgoals in those models. Our novel application enhances the overall competence of FCA in exploring crosscutting properties in the early phases of software development.

The idea of translating RGT into FCA due to their common cross-reference data structure is not new. Much work has been carried out in the knowledge engineering field. For example, Delugach and Lampkin [7] presented a hybrid approach containing RGT and FCA to facilitate the knowledge acquisition process of transferring and transforming information from the domain experts to the expert system. In their approach, the traditional "triad" method [10] associated with RGT was applied to elicit knowledge from domain experts, and the translation from RGT to FCA was performed via an intermediate knowledge representation schema — conceptual graphs [45]. In contrast, our approach outlines a direct translation mechanism from RGT to FCA, thus seamlessly glues these two techniques together so that they complement each other's effectiveness. The coherent framework proposed in this paper is, to the best of our knowledge, the first attempt to employ a composite concept-driven approach to systematically characterize crosscutting concerns during RE activities.

7   Conclusions

Aspects provide the mechanism that enables the source code to be structured to facilitate the representation of multiple perceptions and to alleviate tangling and scattering concerns. Many of these concerns often arise in the problem domain [31], and, therefore, it is important to identify and represent concerns that arise during the early phases of software development, and to determine how these concerns interact.

In this paper, we have presented our initial investigations into designing a composite concept-driven framework for capturing and analyzing early aspects in requirements goal models based on RGT and FCA. We have illustrated the proposed approach on a simple, but not simplistic, example. The results obtained from a preliminary qualitative evaluation of the approach suggest that RGT and FCA can be readily used during RE activities. We have mainly focused on analyzing stakeholder softgoals in the problem domain in this paper. In the future, we plan to extend the proposed concept-driven approach to facilitate the analysis of aspects in the solution domain or pertinent to functional requirements, such as buffering and caching.

Our approach is considered as an integral part of goal-oriented RE, with an emphasis on in-depth analysis of interdependencies between stakeholder goals. Crosscutting concerns are clarified and elaborated early to guide architectural design and implementation of the system, and to trace stakeholder interests onward. The resulting goal structure is modularly improved, so that code aspects can have a baseline to justify and validate their existence: are they images of stakeholder needs or reflections of implementation decisions?

From our initial experience with the proposed approach, we feel that the combination of RGT and FCA has a rich value in helping analysts to externalize stakeholders' views of the problem world and the machine, explicate interrelationships among the entities appeared in requirements models, and uncover early aspects' conflicts and trade-offs. In-depth empirical studies are needed to lend strength to the preliminary findings reported here. A combination of qualitative and quantitative analyses is needed to examine more quality attributes of the concept-driven framework, such as scalability, scope of applicability, relevance to functional requirements, and capability to deal with complex specifications. It is of critical importance to justify the level of effort involved in applying our approach, and to examine whether the effort expended (at such an early stage) will really affect the bottom line in the long run. We look forward to collaborating with researchers and practitioners in designing experiments and case studies to investigate these issues.

Our future work also includes developing efficient methods for producing a core set of common elements that a group of participants can all meaningfully construe. This is critical to all RGT-based approaches, and can lead discussion to exploring the ongoing debate about "whether elements exist independently of constructs, or whether in fact elements are also constructs". Also of interest would be addressing the need for improvement in some areas of FCA tool support, such as focused projections of concept lattice, query languages, line diagram slicing algorithms, etc. Finally, we plan to develop concept-driven conflicts resolution and requirements prioritization methods to explore aspects weaving.

All in all, the repertory grid and the concept analysis are truly techniques: a grid or a formal context of itself is nothing more than a matrix of blank cells. They are only limited by the user's imagination. We hope that our work has shed some light on their applications to new situations, especially, to aspect-oriented software development.

Acknowledgement. We would like to thank Paul Clements, Awais Rashid, João Araújo, Ana Moreira, Yijun Yu, Ruzanna Chitchyan, Haifeng Liu, Harvey Siy, and Erik Simmons for helpful discussions, and for insightful comments on the media shop example. We also thank the anonymous reviewers for their constructive suggestions. Financial support was provided by NSERC and BUL.

References

[1] Baniassad, E., Clements, P.C., Araújo, J., Moreira, A., Rashid, A., Tekinerdoğan, B.: Discovering early aspects. IEEE Software 23(1), 61–70 (2006)
[2] Becker, P., Correia, J.H.: The TosCanaJ suite for implementing conceptual information systems. In: Ganter, B., Stumme, G., Wille, R. (eds.) Formal Concept Analysis. LNCS (LNAI), vol. 3626, pp. 324–348. Springer, Heidelberg (2005)
[3] Birkhoff, G.: Lattice Theory. Providence, RI.: Am. Math. Soc., 25 (1940)
[4] Castro, J., Kolp, M., Mylopoulos, J.: Towards requirements-driven information systems engineering: the Tropos project. Information Systems 27(6), 365–389 (2002)
[5] Chung, L., Nixon, B.A., Yu, E., Mylopoulos, J.: Non-Functional Requirements in Software Engineering. Kluwer Academic, Dordrecht (2000)
[6] Clarke, S., Baniassad, E.: Aspect-Oriented Analysis and Design: The Theme Approach. Addison-Wesley, Reading (2005)
[7] Delugach, H.S., Lampkin, B.E.: Troika: using grids, lattices and graphs in knowledge acquisition. In: Intl. Conf. on Conceptual Structures, pp. 201–214 (2000)
[8] Early aspects portal: (Cited on March 7, 2007), http://www.early-aspects.net/
[9] Eisenbarth, T., Koschke, R., Simon, D.: Locating features in source code. IEEE Transactions Software Engineering 29(3), 195–209 (2003)
[10] Fransella, F., Bell, R., Bannister, D.: A Manual for Repertory Grid Technique, 2nd edn. Wiley, New York (2004)
[11] Gaines, B.: An overview of knowledge acquisition and transfer. International Journal of Human-Computer Interaction 12(3-4), 441–459 (2000)
[12] Ganter, B., Wille, R.: Formal Concept Analysis. Springer, Heidelberg (1996)

[13] Hickey, A.M., Davis, A.M.: Elicitation technique selection: how do experts do it? In: International RE Conference, pp. 169–178 (2003)

[14] IDEF0 portal: http://www.idef.com/idef0.html (Cited on March 7, 2007)

[15] Jackson, M.: Problems, subproblems and concerns. In: Early Aspects Workshop, International Conference on AOSD (2004)

[16] Jutras, J.: An automatic reviser: the transcheck system. In: Christodoulakis, D.N. (ed.) NLP 2000. LNCS (LNAI), vol. 1835, pp. 127–134. Springer, Heidelberg (2000)

[17] Kaindl, H., Brinkkemper, S., Bubenko Jr., J.A., Farbey, B., Greenspan, S.J., Heitmeyer, C.L., do Prado Leite, J.C.S., Mead, N.R., Mylopoulos, J., Siddiqi, J.I.A.: Requirements engineering and technology transfer: obstacles, incentives and improvement agenda. RE Journal 7(3), 113–123 (2002)

[18] Kelly, G.: The Psychology of Personal Constructs, Norton, New York (1955)

[19] Kiczales, G., Lamping, J., Menhdhekar, A., Maeda, C., Lopes, C., Loingtier, J.-M., Irwin, J.: Aspect-oriented programming. In: Aksit, M., Matsuoka, S. (eds.) ECOOP 1997. LNCS, vol. 1241, pp. 220–242. Springer, Heidelberg (1997)

[20] Krone, M., Snelting, G.: On the interference of configuration structures from source code. In: ICSE, pp. 49–57 (1994)

[21] Lethbridge, T.C., Sim, S.E., Singer, J.: Studying software engineers: data collection techniques for software field studies. Empirical SE 10(3), 311–341 (2005)

[22] McKnight, C.: The personal construction of information space. Journal of the American Society for Information Science 51(8), 730–733 (2000)

[23] Murphy, G., Schwanninger, C.: Aspect-oriented programming. IEEE Software 23(1), 20–23 (2006)

[24] Niu, N., Easterbrook, S., Yu, Y.: A taxonomy of asymmetric requirements aspects. In: Early Aspects Workshop at AOSD (2007) (in press)

[25] Niu, N., Easterbrook, S.: Discovering aspects in requirements with repertory grid. In: Early Aspects Workshop at ICSE, pp. 35–41 (2006)

[26] Niu, N., Easterbrook, S.: Managing terminological interference in goal models with repertory grid. In: International RE Conference, pp. 303–306 (2006)

[27] Niu, N., Easterbrook, S.: So, you think you know others' goals? A repertory grid study. IEEE Software 24(2), 53–61 (2007)

[28] Novak, J.D.: Learning, Creating, and Using Knowledge. Lawrence Erlbaum, Hillsdale (1998)

[29] Nuseibeh, B., Easterbrook, S.M.: Requirements Engineering: A Roadmap. In: The Future of Software Engineering (2000)

[30] Nuseibeh, B.: Weaving together requirements and architectures. IEEE Computer 34(3), 115–117 (2001)

[31] Nuseibeh, B.: Crosscutting requirements. In: International Conference on AOSD, pp. 3–4 (2004)

[32] Parnas, D.: On the criteria to be used in decomposing systems into modules. Communications of the ACM 15(12), 1053–1058 (1972)

[33] Pisan, Y.: Extending requirement specifications using analogy. In: ICSE, pp. 70–76 (2000)

[34] Popper, K.: Epistemology without a knowing subject. In: International Congress for Logic, Methodology and Philosophy of Science, pp. 333–372 (1968)

[35] Potts, C., Takahashi, K., Anton, A.: Inquiry-based requirements analysis. IEEE Software 11(2), 21–32 (1993)

[36] Richards, D.: Merging individual conceptual models of requirements. RE Journal 8(4), 195–205 (2003)

[37] Richards, L.: Handling Qualitative Data: A Practical Guide. Sage, Beverely Hills (2005)

[38] Rogers, E.M.: Diffusion of Innovations, 4th edn. Free Press, NewYork (1995)

[39] Ryle, A.: Frames and Cages: The Repertory Grid Approach to Human Understanding. Sussex University Press, Sussex (1975)

[40] Sabetzadeh, M., Easterbrook, S.: Traceability in viewpoint merging: a model management perspective. In: International Workshop on Traceability in SE (2005)

[41] Sampaio, A., Chitchyan, R., Rashid, A., Rayson, P.: EA-Miner: a tool for automating aspect-oriented requirements identification. In: International Conference on ASE, pp. 352–355 (2005)

[42] Shaw, M.: On Becoming A Personal Scientist: Interactive Computer Elicitation of Personal Models of the World. Academic Press, Dublin (1980)

[43] Shaw, M., Gaines, B.: Comparing conceptual structures: consensus, conflict, correspondence and contrast. Knowledge Acquisition 1(4), 341–363 (1989)

[44] Snelting, G., Tip, F.: Reengineering class hierarchies using concept analysis. ACM Transactions on Programming Languages System 22(3), 540–582 (2000)

[45] Sowa, J.F.: Conceptual Structures: Information Processing in Mind and Machine. Addison-Wesley, Reading (1984)

[46] Suen, R., Baniassad, E.: Isolating concerns in requirements using latent semantic analysis. In: Early Aspects Workshop, OOPSLA (2005)

[47] Sutton, D.C.: Linguistic problems with requirements and knowledge elicitation. RE Journal 5(2), 114–124 (2000)

[48] Tilley, T.: Tool support for FCA. In: Eklund, P.W. (ed.) ICFCA 2004. LNCS (LNAI), vol. 2961, pp. 104–111. Springer, Heidelberg (2004)

[49] Tilley, T., Cole, R., Becker, P., Eklund, P.: A survey of formal concept analysis support for software engineering activities. In: Ganter, B., Stumme, G., Wille, R. (eds.) Formal Concept Analysis. LNCS (LNAI), vol. 3626, pp. 250–271. Springer, Heidelberg (2005)

[50] Tonella, P.: Concept analysis for module restructuring. IEEE Transactions Software Engineering 27(4), 351–363 (2004)

[51] Tonella, P.: Formal concept analysis in software engineering. In: ICSE, pp. 743–744 (2004)

[52] Tonella, P.: Using a concept lattice of decomposition slices for program understanding and impact analysis. IEEE Transactions Software Engineering 29(6), 495–509 (2003)

[53] Yu, E.: Modeling strategic actor relationships for process reengineering. PhD Thesis, University of Toronto (1994)

[54] Yu, Y., do Prado, J.C.S., Mylopoulos, J.: From goals to aspects: discovering aspects from requirements goal models. In: International RE Conference, pp. 38–47 (2004)

[55] Zave, P., Jackson, M.: Four dark corners of requirements engineering. ACM TOSEM 6(1), 1–30 (1997)

Analysis of Crosscutting in Early Software Development Phases Based on Traceability

Klaas van den Berg[1], José María Conejero[2], and Juan Hernández[2]

[1] Software Engineering Group University of Twente
P.O. Box 217, 7500 AE Enschede, The Netherlands
`k.g.vandenberg@ewi.utwente.nl`
[2] Quercus Software Engineering Group, University of Extremadura
Avda. de la Universidad s/n, 10071, Cáceres, Spain
`{chemacm,juanher}@unex.es`

Abstract. Crosscutting is usually described in terms of scattering and tangling. However, the distinction between these three concepts is vague. Precise definitions are mandatory for certain research areas such as the identification of crosscutting concerns at phases of the software life cycle. We propose a conceptual framework for crosscutting where crosscutting is defined in terms of trace relations. The definition of crosscutting is formalized using linear algebra, and represented with matrices and matrix operations. In this way, crosscutting can be clearly distinguished from scattering and tangling. With this definition and transitivity of trace relations, crosscutting can be identified and traced through software development, also in early phases. We describe some illustrative case studies to demonstrate the applicability of the analysis.

Keywords: aspect-oriented software development, traceability, scattering, tangling, crosscutting, crosscutting concerns.

1 Introduction

In Aspect-Oriented Software Development (AOSD), crosscutting is usually described in terms of scattering and tangling. However, the distinction between these concepts is vague, sometimes leading to ambiguous statements and confusion, as stated in [20]:

.. the term "crosscutting concerns" is often misused in two ways: To talk about a single concern, and to talk about concerns rather than representations of concerns. Consider "synchronization is a crosscutting concern": we don't know that synchronization is crosscutting unless we know what it crosscuts. And there may be representations of the concerns involved that are not crosscutting.

A precise definition of crosscutting is mandatory for the identification of crosscutting concerns at any phase of the software life cycle. The earlier we identify crosscutting concerns in software development, the easier we can cope with these concerns and increase quality of software. In addition, the identification of crosscutting concerns in different stages of software development makes it possible to trace such concerns throughout the whole software development process.

A. Rashid and M. Aksit (Eds.): Transactions on AOSD III, LNCS 4620, pp. 73–104, 2007.
© Springer-Verlag Berlin Heidelberg 2007

Traceability is the degree to which dependencies are made explicit between different artifacts such as stakeholder needs, requirements, design, system components, source code, etc. [27]. This issue has been investigated especially in early phases of software development such as requirements engineering. Trace dependencies can have different types, such as usage and abstraction dependencies (e.g. refinement and tracing [31]), and traceability matrices [15] have been widely used to record such dependencies. Since a change in an early phase can be traced through the development process, traceability matrices allow developers to improve software understanding and maintainability. They may ensure, for example, whether there are test cases for all requirements or whether stakeholders' requirements are fulfilled in the final system, both forward and backward. We claim that these matrices may be further exploited beyond their current use. In particular, the evaluation of the information captured by traceability matrices provides a means both to detect crosscutting and to assess the degree of crosscutting in software systems.

In this paper, we propose a definition of crosscutting based on the study of trace dependencies through an extension to traceability matrices. This definition allows developers both to identify crosscutting concerns in early phases [6] and to trace crosscutting concerns from early stages to subsequent phases of the software life cycle. We describe a conceptual framework with precise definitions of scattering, tangling and crosscutting. Although there are other definitions of crosscutting in the literature, these definitions are usually very tied to the implementation level, such as [23]. A study of similarities and differences of such definitions and ours is out of the scope of this paper. An extended description of our definition can be found in [8–9].

The rest of the paper is structured as follows. In Sect. 2, we introduce our definition of crosscutting based on trace dependencies. In Sect. 3, we describe how to represent and visualize crosscutting in a matrix and how to derive this matrix from the dependency matrix using a scattering and tangling matrix. Transitivity of trace relations is shown in Sect. 4. Then in Sect. 5, we show some case studies where we apply the concepts introduced in the previous sections. We discuss the relationship between crosscutting and related concepts such as coupling and decomposition in Sect. 6, also making some observations about our framework. Finally, in Sect. 7 and 8 we present related work and conclusions of the paper.

2 Crosscutting Pattern

In this section, we first introduce an intuitive notion of crosscutting, which will be generalized in a crosscutting pattern. Based on this pattern we provide precise definitions of scattering, tangling and crosscutting, and their relations.

For example, assume we have three concerns shown as elements of a source in Fig. 1, and four requirements (e.g., use cases) shown as elements of a target.

This picture is consistent with the citation at the beginning of the Introduction. Intuitively, we could say that s1 crosscuts s3 for the given relation between source and target elements. In this figure we only show two abstraction levels, but multiple intermediate levels between source and target may exist. This picture also fits other

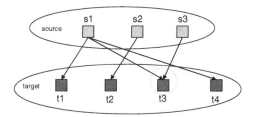

Fig. 1. Trace relations between source and target elements

intuitive notions of crosscutting, scattering and tangling which we can find in the literature such as *"an aspect in requirements is a concern that crosscuts requirements artifacts; an aspect in architecture is a concern that crosscuts architectural artifacts"* [6] or *"scattering occurs when the design of a single requirement is necessarily scattered across multiple classes and operations in the object-oriented design"*, *"tangling occurs when a single class or operation in the object-oriented design contains design details of multiple requirements"* both in [5]. As we can see in these citations, the notion of crosscutting, scattering and tangling is based on the relationship of elements at two levels or domains, depicted here as source and target. We discuss this in Sect. 6.

In the following section we generalize this intuition by means of a crosscutting pattern. Furthermore, we focus on definitions of crosscutting, tangling and scattering.

2.1 Generalization

Our proposition is that crosscutting can only be defined in terms of *"one thing"* with respect to *"another thing"*. Accordingly and from a mathematical point of view, what this means is that we have two domains related to each other through a mapping. We use here the general terms *source* and *target* (as in [24]) to denote these two domains, and the trace relationship is the mapping relating elements in these domains (see Fig. 2).

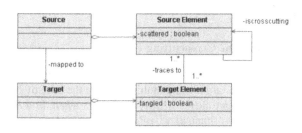

Fig. 2. Crosscutting pattern

We use the term *Crosscutting Pattern* to denote the situation where source and target are related to each other through trace dependencies. We use the term *pattern* as in design patterns [18], in the sense of being a general description of frequently encountered situations [23,25].

Although the terms source and target could represent two different domains, levels or phases of a software development process, we abstract from specific phases such as concern modeling, requirements elicitation, architectural design and so on. The only proposition is that we define crosscutting for two levels, which we called source and target. This approach can be applied to early phases in software development, e.g. concerns and requirements, but also to other phases near implementation, e.g., a UML design and Java code. In each case we have to define the trace relations between the respective source elements and target elements. We show a traceability model in Sect. 6.1 where we discuss the mapping between source and target in more detail.

In Table 1 we show some situations where the crosscutting pattern can be applied, with examples of source and target elements.

Table 1. Some examples of source and target domains

Examples	Source	Target	We may identify
Ex. 1	Concerns	Requirements Statements	Crosscutting Concerns with respect to mapping to Requirements Statements
Ex. 2	Concerns	Use Cases	Crosscutting Concerns with respect to mapping to Use Cases
Ex. 3	Concerns	Design Modules	Crosscutting Concerns with respect to mapping to Design Modules
Ex. 4	Use Cases	Architectural Components	Crosscutting Use Cases with respect to mapping to Architectural Components
Ex. 5	Use Cases	Design Modules	Crosscutting Use Cases with respect to mapping to Design Modules
Ex. 6	Design Modules	Programming Artifacts	Crosscutting Design Modules with respect to mapping to Programming Artifacts
Ex. 7	PIM artifacts (MDA)	PSM artifacts (MDA)	Crosscutting in PIM artifacts with respect to mapping to PSM artifacts

The definitions of tangling, scattering and crosscutting are relative to the source and target in the crosscutting pattern. Therefore, scattering, tangling and crosscutting are defined as specific cases of the mapping between source and target. We denote this mapping between source and target as (Source x Target). This is explained in the following section.

2.2 Definitions Based on the Crosscutting Pattern

As we can see in Fig. 2, there is a mapping from source elements to target elements. This mapping from source to target has a multiplicity. In the case of 1:many mappings we have scattering, defined as follows: *Scattering occurs when, in a mapping between source and target, a source element is related to multiple target elements.* The correspondence between two given domains, source and target, is defined as follows. For $s \in Source$, $f(s) = \{t \in Target \ / \ t$ is related to s in the target domain$\}$. We can define scattering as: An element $s \in Source$ is scattered if and only if $card(f(s)) > 1$, where card is the cardinality. In Fig. 1 we can see how the source element $s1$ is scattered over the target elements $t1$, $t3$ and $t4$.

Similarly, we can focus on the relation between target elements and source elements. This relation (here also called mapping) is the reverse of the mapping above. In the case of 1:many mappings from target to source we have tangling, defined as follows: *Tangling occurs when, in a mapping between source and target, a target element is related to multiple source elements.* In other words, an element t $\in$ Target is tangled if and only if card($f^{-1}(t)$)> 1, where f^{-1} is the inverse application. In Fig. 1 target element t3 is tangled with respect to the source elements s1 and s3.

There is a specific combination of scattering and tangling which we call crosscutting, defined as follows: *Crosscutting occurs when, in a mapping between source and target, a source element is scattered over target elements and where in at least one of these target elements, some other source element is tangled.* In other words, crosscutting can be defined as follows. For element s1, s2 $\in$ Source / (s1 $\neq$ s2), s1 crosscuts s2 if and only if card ($f(s1)$) > 1 and t $\in$ f(s1) : card ($f^{-1}(t)$) > 1 and s2 $\in$ f^{-1} (t). We do not require that the second source element is scattered. In that sense, our definition is not symmetric, in contrast to the definition in [23] (see Sect. 7). In Fig. 1, source element s1 is crosscutting source element s3 with respect to the given mapping between source and target but not the opposite. Following on with this example, and according to our definition, this means that we should redesign s1 but not s3 in order to remove crosscutting (i.e., through the use of aspect-oriented techniques). On the other hand, assuming crosscutting as a symmetric property implies that redesign of either s1 or s3 is feasible.

2.3 Case Analysis of Crosscutting

In the previous section we defined scattering, tangling and crosscutting for a mapping between source and target. Now, we discuss a case analysis of possible combinations. Assuming that the properties tangling, scattering, and crosscutting may be true or false, there are eight combinations (see Table 2). Each case addresses a certain mapping from source to target. However, crosscutting requires tangling and scattering, which eliminates 3 of these combinations (Cases 6, 7 and 8: not feasible).

Table 2. Feasibility of combinations of tangling, scattering and crosscutting

	tangling	scattering	crosscutting	feasibility
Case 1	no	no	no	feasible
Case 2	yes	no	no	feasible
Case 3	no	yes	no	feasible
Case 4	yes	yes	no	feasible
Case 5	yes	yes	yes	feasible
Case 6	no	no	yes	not feasible
Case 7	no	yes	yes	not feasible
Case 8	yes	no	yes	not feasible

There are five feasible cases listed in Table 4. In Case 4, we have scattering and tangling in which no common elements are involved. With our definition of crosscutting we clearly separate the cases with just tangling, just scattering and on the other hand crosscutting. Our proposition is that tangling and scattering are necessary but not sufficient conditions for crosscutting. An example of this situation is explained in one of the case studies (Sect. 5.1). We will now describe the representation of trace dependencies in traceability matrices.

3 Matrix Representation of Trace Relations

In this section we show how crosscutting can be represented and identified by means of an extension to traceability matrices. Trace relations are captured in a dependency matrix, representing the mapping between source and target. As an extension, we derive the crosscutting matrix from the dependency matrix. We describe how the crosscutting matrix can be constructed from the dependency matrix with some auxiliary matrices. This is illustrated with some examples.

3.1 Tracing from Source to Target

Traceability matrices have usually been used to show the relationships between requirements elicitation and the representation of these requirements in a particular engineering approach (such as use cases [31] or viewpoints [16]).

In terms of linear algebra, traceability matrices show the mappings between source and target. We show these mappings in a special kind of traceability matrix that we called a dependency matrix. *A dependency matrix (source x target) represents the dependency relation between source elements and target elements (inter-level relationship).* In the rows we have the source elements, and in the columns we have the target elements. In this matrix a cell with 1 denotes that the source element (in the row) is *mapped* to the target element (in the column). Reciprocally this means that the target element *depends on* the source element. Scattering and tangling can easily be visualized in this matrix (see the examples below).

We define a new auxiliary concept *crosscutpoint* used in the context of dependency matrices to denote *a matrix cell involved in both tangling and scattering* (see dark grey cell in Table 3). If there are one or more crosscutpoints then we say we have crosscutting.

Crosscutting between source elements for a given mapping to target elements, as shown in a dependency matrix, can be represented in a crosscutting matrix. *A crosscutting matrix (source x source) represents the crosscutting relation between source elements for a given source-to-target mapping (represented in a dependency matrix).* In the crosscutting matrix, a cell with 1 denotes that the source element in the row is crosscutting the source element in the column. In the next Sect. 3.2, we explain how this crosscutting matrix can be derived from the dependency matrix.

A crosscutting matrix should not be confused with a coupling matrix. A *coupling matrix* shows coupling relations between elements at the same level of abstraction (intra-level dependencies). In some sense, the coupling matrix is related to the design structure matrix [3]. On the other hand, a crosscutting matrix shows crosscutting relations between elements at one level with respect to a mapping onto elements at some other level (inter-level dependencies).

We now give an example and use the dependency matrix and crosscutting matrix to visualize the definitions (S denotes a scattered source element — a grey row; NS denotes a non-scattered source element; T denotes a tangled target element — a grey column; NT denotes a non-tangled target element). The example is shown in Table 3.

In this example, we have one scattered source element s[1] and one tangled target element t[3]. We apply our definition of crosscutting and arrive at the crosscutting matrix. Source element s[1] is crosscutting s[3] (because s[1] is scattered over {t[1], t[3], t[4]} and s[3] is tangled in one of these elements, namely t[3]). The reverse is not true: the crosscutting relation is not symmetric.

Table 3. Example dependency and crosscutting matrix with tangling, scattering and one crosscutpoint

dependency matrix

		target				
		t[1]	t[2]	t[3]	t[4]	
source	s[1]	1	0	1	1	S
	s[2]	0	1	0	0	NS
	s[3]	0	0	1	0	NS
		NT	NT	T	NT	

crosscutting matrix

		source		
		s[1]	s[2]	s[3]
source	s[1]	0	0	1
	s[2]	0	0	0
	s[3]	0	0	0

3.2 Constructing Crosscutting Matrices

In this section, we describe how to derive the crosscutting matrix from the dependency matrix. We now show an extended example with more than one crosscutpoint, in this example eight points (see Table 4; the dark grey cells).

Table 4. Example dependency matrix with tangling, scattering and several crosscutpoints

dependency matrix

		target						
		t[1]	t[2]	t[3]	t[4]	t[5]	t[6]	
source	s[1]	1	0	0	1	0	0	S
	s[2]	1	0	1	0	1	1	S
	s[3]	1	0	0	0	0	0	NS
	s[4]	0	1	1	0	0	0	S
	s[5]	0	0	0	1	1	0	S
		T	NT	T	T	T	NT	

crosscutting matrix

		source				
		s[1]	s[2]	s[3]	s[4]	s[5]
source	s[1]	0	1	1	0	1
	s[2]	1	0	1	1	1
	s[3]	0	0	0	0	0
	s[4]	0	1	0	0	0
	s[5]	1	1	0	0	0

Based on the dependency matrix, we define some auxiliary matrices: the *scattering matrix* (source x target) and the *tangling matrix* (target x source). For our example in Table 4 these matrices are shown in Table 5. These two matrices are defined as follows:

- In a scattering matrix, a row contains only dependency relations from source to target elements if the source element in this row is scattered (mapped onto multiple target elements); otherwise, the row contains just zeroes (no scattering).
- In a tangling matrix, a row contains only dependency relations from target to source elements if the target element in this row is tangled (mapped onto multiple source elements); otherwise, the row contains just zeroes (no tangling).

Table 5. Scattering and tangling matrices for dependency matrix in Table 4

scattering matrix

		target					
		t[1]	t[2]	t[3]	t[4]	t[5]	t[6]
source	s[1]	1	0	0	1	0	0
	s[2]	1	0	1	0	1	1
	s[3]	0	0	0	0	0	0
	s[4]	0	1	1	0	0	0
	s[5]	0	0	0	1	1	0

tangling matrix

		source				
		s[1]	S[2]	s[3]	s[4]	s[5]
target	t[1]	1	1	1	0	0
	t[2]	0	0	0	0	0
	t[3]	0	1	0	1	0
	t[4]	1	0	0	0	1
	t[5]	0	1	0	0	1
	t[6]	0	0	0	0	0

We now define the crosscutting product matrix, showing the number of crosscutting relations. The *crosscutting product matrix* ccpm can be obtained through the matrix multiplication of the scattering matrix sm and the tangling matrix tm: ccpm = sm x tm where ccpm [i][k] = sm[i][j] x tm[j][k]. We use this matrix to derive the final crosscutting matrix. In the crosscutting matrix, a matrix cell denotes the occurrence of crosscutting; it abstracts from the quantity of crosscutting. The *crosscutting matrix* ccm can be derived from the crosscutting product matrix ccpm using a simple conversion: ccm[i][k] = if (ccpm[i][k] > 0) $\wedge$ (i $\neq$ j) then 1 else 0.

The crosscutting product matrix for the example is given in Table 6. From this crosscutting product matrix we derive the crosscutting matrix shown in Table 4.

In this example there are no cells in the crosscutting product matrix larger than one, except on the diagonal where it denotes a crosscutting relation with itself and which we disregard here. In the crosscutting matrix, we set the diagonal cells to zero because, we assume that an element cannot crosscut itself.

In the crosscutting matrix in Table 4 there are now ten crosscutting relations between the source elements. The crosscutting matrix shows again that our definition

Table 6. Crosscutting product matrix for dependency matrix in Table 4

crosscutting product matrix

		source				
		s[1]	s[2]	s[3]	s[4]	s[5]
source	s[1]	2	1	1	0	1
	s[2]	1	3	1	1	1
	s[3]	0	0	0	0	0
	s[4]	0	1	0	1	0
	s[5]	1	1	0	0	2

of the crosscutting relation is not symmetric. For example, s[1] is crosscutting s[3], but s[3] is not crosscutting s[1] because s[3] is not scattered (scattering and tangling are necessary but not sufficient conditions for crosscutting).

In Fig. 3, we show the four steps we should perform in order to complete the process. The matrix operations described above drive the process until obtaining the final crosscutting matrix. For convenience, these formulas can be calculated by means of simple mathematic tools (such as Mathematica or Maple). By filling in the cells of the dependency matrix, the other matrices are calculated automatically.

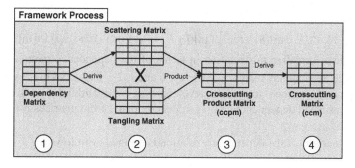

Fig. 3. Overview of steps in the framework

In the next section we show traceability of crosscutting, which implies the application of the framework to several consecutive levels.

4 Transitivity of Trace Relations

Usually, we encounter a number of consecutive levels or phases in software development. From the perspective of software life cycle phases we may distinguish Domain Analysis, Concern Modeling, Requirement Analysis, Architectural Design, Detailed Design and Implementation.

We consider here the cascading of two consecutive mappings: the target of the first mapping serves as source for the second one. For convenience, we call the first target our intermediate level (see Fig. 4).

Each of these mappings can be described with a dependency matrix. We describe how to combine two consecutive dependency matrices in an operation we call cascading. Cascading is an operation on two dependency matrices resulting in a new dependency matrix, which represents the dependency relation between source elements of the first matrix and target elements of the second matrix.

Fig. 4. Cascading of consecutive levels

For cascading, it is essential to define the transitivity of dependency relations. Transitivity is defined as follows. Assume we have a source, an intermediate level and a target, as shown in Fig. 4. There is a dependency relation between an element in the source and an element in the target if there is some element at the intermediate level that has a dependency relation with this source element and a dependency relation with this target element. In other words, the transitivity dependency relation f for source s, intermediate level u and target t, where card(u) is the number of elements in u, is defined as:

$$\exists\, k \in (1..\text{card(u)}): (\, s[i]\, f\, u[k]\,) \wedge (\, u[k]\, f\, t[m]\,) \Rightarrow (\, s[i]\, f\, t[m]\,).$$

We can also formalize this relation in terms of the dependency matrices. Assume we have three dependency matrices m1 :: s $\times$ u and m2 :: u $\times$ t and m3 :: s $\times$ t, where s is the source, u is some intermediate level, card(u) is the cardinality of u, and t is the target. The cascaded dependency matrix m3 is computed from matrices m1 and m2 as follows: m3 = m1 $\times$ m2

Then, *transitivity* of the dependency relation is defined as follows:

$$\exists\, k \in (1..\text{card(u)}): \text{m1}[i,k] \wedge \text{m2}[k,m] \Rightarrow \text{m3}[i,m].$$

In terms of linear algebra, the dependency matrix is a relationship between two given domains, source and target (see Section 0). Accordingly, the cascading operation can be generalized as a composition of relationships as follows. Let Dom_K, $k = 1..n$, be n domains, and let f_i be the relationship between domains Dom_i and Dom_{i+1}, $1 \leq i < n$, denoted as $Dom_i \xrightarrow{f_i} Dom_{i+1}$. Let Source and Target be the domains Dom_1 and Dom_n, respectively. Consequently, we have the following relationship between the domains: $Source \xrightarrow{f_1} Dom_2 \xrightarrow{f_2} Dom_3 \xrightarrow{f_3} ...Dom_{n-1} \xrightarrow{f_{n-1}} Target$. As a result, the dependency relationship between the Source and the Target is defined as $DM \equiv f_{n-1} \circ f_{n-2} \circ ... \circ f_1$. In this way, the dependency matrix between a source and target is obtained through matrix multiplication of the dependency matrices representing each f_i, $1 \leq i < n$.

As an example, we explain the cascading of two dependency matrices: one for concerns x requirements and one for requirements x modules. The two dependency

Table 7. Two dependency matrices to be cascaded

dependency matrix 1

		requirements			
		r[1]	r[2]	r[3]	r[4]
concerns	c[1]	1	0	0	1
	c[2]	0	1	0	0
	c[3]	0	0	1	1

dependency matrix 2

		modules				
		m[1]	m[2]	m[3]	m[4]	m[5]
requirements	r[1]	1	0	0	0	1
	r[2]	0	1	0	0	0
	r[3]	0	1	1	0	0
	r[4]	0	0	0	1	1

matrices are shown in Table 7. The first dependency matrix relates concerns with requirements. The second dependency matrix relates requirements with modules. The resulting dependency matrix relates concerns with modules (see Table 8). This matrix can be used to derive the crosscutting matrix for concern x concern with respect to modules.

The crosscutting matrix in Table 8 is not symmetric. Based on this matrix we conclude, for the given dependency relations between concerns and modules, that: concern c[1] is crosscutting concern c[3]; concern c[2] does not crosscut any other concern; concern c[3] is crosscutting concerns c[1] and c[2].

Table 8. The resulting dependency matrix and crosscutting matrix based on cascading of the matrices in Table 7

resulting dependency matrix

		modules				
		m[1]	m[2]	m[3]	m[4]	m[5]
concerns	c[1]	1	0	0	1	2
	c[2]	0	1	0	0	0
	c[3]	0	1	1	1	1

crosscutting matrix

		concerns		
		c[1]	c[2]	c[3]
concerns	c[1]	0	0	1
	c[2]	0	0	0
	c[3]	1	1	0

We summarize the cascading operation in Fig. 5. From this description it is clear that cascading can be used for traceability analysis across multiple levels, e.g., from concerns to implementation elements, via requirements, architecture and design (c.f. [30]).

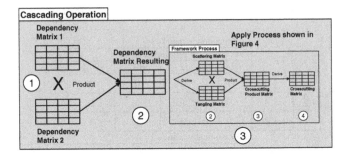

Fig. 5. Overview of cascading operation

We can trace concerns throughout the development process by applying the crosscutting analysis at each level. Once the crosscutting concerns have been identified at a particular level, we can compare the results with the results obtained in previous or subsequent levels.

5   Case Studies

In this section we show the application of our approach to some case studies. Firstly we apply the framework to a Remote Calculator, a simple software program which follows the Model-View-Controller (MVC) pattern. This is a case with scattering and tangling but no crosscutting. Secondly in Sect. 5.2, we show the application to a Portuguese Highways Toll System, a well known example shown in other publications [2, 28]. We obtain the same results as the ones described in the aforementioned publications. We only consider concerns which are related to non-functional properties of the system. In Sect. 5.3, we show how our approach may complement other approaches such us Theme/Doc [4] for the identification of crosscutting themes. In Section 0, we apply the framework to a Conference Review System (CRS), a case study which has been used in some workshops [17] where concerns are related to functional and non-functional properties. We show how to analyze crosscutting across several phases in the software life cycle. In the last Sect. 5.5, we extend the CRS system with aspects and analyze the impact of the selected decomposition.

5.1   Remote Calculator

In this section, we show the application of the framework to a simple example, a calculator with remote access. We apply the framework at concern level with respect to the design level (represented in a UML class diagram). Thus, this case study shows how the framework can be applied to other abstraction levels such as the implementation phase. The application of the framework in this example will show how crosscutting can be distinguished from scattering and tangling.

The case study consists of a distributed Java application which allows a user to calculate the sum of integer numbers. The distribution is accomplished by means of sockets. The MVC pattern [12] is applied in order to perform a separation of representation and control concerns from the functional concerns of an application.

In order to study the crosscutting in this case, we consider three main concerns in the system: Distribution to Client, Distribution to Server and Calculation. We take these concerns as source elements in our dependency matrix (see Sect. 3.1) and the UML design classes are considered to be the target elements.

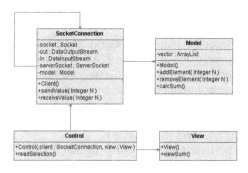

Fig. 6. UML class diagram of Remote Calculator

In Fig. 6 we show a UML class diagram representing the design. We have developed the main functionality regarding the socket concerns in a class called SocketConnection. This class just performs the remote connection and sends and receives integer values. We may say that this class has a low cohesion. Depending on the operation (sending or receiving), this class will invoke methods of the other classes. The Model, View and Control classes perform the actions to sum the integer, read user's selections and shows the results on screen respectively. Therefore, the application has a good separation between model (a class with a vector of numbers and which performs the sum), view (a class which shows the result on the screen) and control (a class which reads the user's inputs). Although such classes are coupled by means of method calls, their level of cohesion is high because each class is only addressing its main functionality (concern).

Table 9. Dependency and crosscutting matrix for the Remote Calculator

	dependency matrix				
	classes				
concerns	SocketConnection	Model	View	Control	
Distribution-to-Client	1	0	0	0	NS
Distribution-to-Server	1	0	0	0	NS
Calculation	0	1	1	1	S
	T	NT	NT	NT	

Table 9. (*continued*)

crosscutting matrix WRT[1] classes

concerns	concerns		
	Distribution-to-Client	Distribution-to-Server	Calculation
Distribution-to-Client	0	0	0
Distribution-to-Server	0	0	0
Calculation	0	0	0

[1] WRT are the abbreviation of "with respect to".

So, taking such a decomposition (in classes) and applying the framework, we obtain the dependency matrix shown in Table 9. As we can see in the matrix, concerns Distribution-to-Client and Distribution-to-Server are tangled in the same class SocketConnection, whereas Calculation concern is scattered over the other classes. However, as can be seen in the table, the matrix has no crosscutpoint. By means of the operations described in Sect. 3.2 we obtain the crosscutting matrix shown in Table 9: there are no crosscutting concerns in the system.

In many situations, we have tangling, scattering and at the same time crosscutting. With our definitions, we clearly distinguished scattering and tangling from crosscutting and, as we stated in Sect. 2.3, scattering and tangling are necessary but not sufficient conditions for crosscutting. The analysis depends on the chosen decomposition of source and target, other decompositions being feasible.

5.2 Portuguese Highways Toll System

In order to validate our framework, in this section we apply it to a well-known case study — the Portuguese Highways Toll System — which has been widely explained in some publications on the early aspects topic [2, 28]. As we will see at the end of the section, the results obtained are similar. As a starting point we take the same decompositions made by the authors of the original case. It can be seen that the concern decomposition is related to non-functional properties of the system.

The system is based on a road traffic price system where drivers of authorized vehicles are charged automatically at toll gates. The gates have sensors able to read information provided by a device installed in the vehicle when it passes through. This device is called a "gizmo" [28]. When an authorized vehicle passes through the toll gate, a green light turns on and a display shows the amount to be paid by the driver. If the car is not authorized, a yellow light turns on and a camera takes a photo of the license plate.

In [28] the authors identified the following stakeholders' requirements (which are represented by means of viewpoints [16]): ATM (allows the drivers to enter their information for registration in the system), Vehicle, Gizmo, Police (receives information about unauthorised vehicles), Debiting System (interacts with the bank to allow the payment), Toll Gate, Vehicle Owner and System Administrator (modifies information in the system). Some of these viewpoints have sub-viewpoints. On the other hand, after analyzing the initial requirements the authors specified the following concerns: Security, Response Time, Multi-Access System, Compatibility, Legal Issues, Correctness and Availability.

Table 10. Dependency matrix for Portuguese Highways Toll System

concerns	P	Gz	DS	ATM	TG	PT	ST	ExT	ET	Vh	UV	VO	Reg	Act	Bill	Adm
viewpoints (P:Police, Gz:Gizmo, DS:Debiting system, TG:Toll Gate, PT: Paying Toll, ST:Single Toll, ExT:Exit Toll, ET:Entry Toll, Vh:Vehicle, UV: Unauthorised Vehicle, VO:Vehicle Owner, Act:Activation, Reg:Registration, Bill:Billing, Adm:Administration)																
Response Time	0	1	0	1	1	1	1	1	1	1	1	0	0	0	0	0
Availability	0	1	0	1	1	1	1	1	1	0	0	0	1	1	0	1
Security	1	0	1	1	0	0	0	0	0	0	0	1	1	1	1	1
Legal Issues	1	0	0	0	0	0	0	1	0	0	0	0	1	0	1	0
Compatibility	1	0	1	1	0	0	0	0	0	0	0	0	0	1	0	0
Correctness	1	1	1	0	1	1	1	1	1	0	0	1	1	1	1	0
Multi-Access	0	1	0	1	1	1	1	1	1	1	1	0	1	1	0	0

Having these requirements and concerns, we apply our framework to identify crosscutting in the requirements analysis phase. We take the concerns and requirements (represented as viewpoints) as source and target of the mappings respectively. The dependency matrix for this case is shown in Table 10. The mappings between source and target are extracted from [28] where the authors specify in a similar table which concerns are being addressed by the requirements.

Once we have defined the dependency matrix, we obtain scattering and tangling matrices (see Sect. 3.2). Performing the multiplication of such matrices we obtain the crosscutting matrix shown in Table 11.

Table 11. Crosscutting matrix in Portuguese Highways Toll System

Concerns	Response-Time	Availability	Security	Legal Issues	Compatibility	Correctness	MultiAccess
	concerns						
Response Time	0	1	1	1	1	1	1
Availability	1	0	1	1	1	1	1
Security	1	1	0	1	1	1	1
Legal Issues	1	1	1	0	1	1	1
Compatibility	1	1	1	1	0	1	1
Correctness	1	1	1	1	1	0	1
Multi-Access	1	1	1	1	1	1	0

As we can see in the matrix in Table 11, every concern is crosscutting the other concerns. We obtain the same results that are explained in [28]. Since all concerns are related to non-functional properties of the system, the results are rather predictable. In order to make a more realistic study of crosscutting in systems, both concerns related to functional and non-functional properties must be analyzed. Otherwise, we obtain results where every concern is crosscutting the other concerns as shown in this case.

5.3 Course Management System

We show in this section the application of the framework to another previously published case study, a Course Management System (CMS). The case study consists of a system for managing the students who register for several courses. This example was introduced in [4] where the authors present an approach for identifying and modeling crosscutting concerns at requirement and design stages. This approach is based on the concept of theme. A theme is an element of design (collection of structures and behaviors that represent one feature) and can be one of two different kinds in the approach: base and crosscutting themes. In order to identify the crosscutting themes at requirement level in the system, the authors introduce the concept of action view. The action view is a representation of the requirements, grouping them in the form of actions and relating them with the original requirements. The actions are key words which the developer must identify by looking at the requirements document and picking out sensible words.

In [4], the authors present the following requirements for the CMS:

- R1: Students can register for courses
- R2: Students can unregister for courses
- R3: When a student registers then it must be logged in his record
- R4: When a student unregisters it must also be logged
- R5: Professors can unregister students
- R6: When a professor unregisters a student it must be logged
- R7: When a professor unregisters a student it must be flagged as special
- R8: Professors can give marks for courses
- R9: When a professor gives a mark this must be logged in the student's record.

For these requirements, the authors [4] presented the following actions: register, unregister, logged, give and flagged. Taking these actions and requirements, the authors present an *action view* where such requirements are related with the corresponding actions. We apply the framework to identify crosscutting by filling in the dependency matrix in the same way as it is done in the action view [4]. As we can see in Table 12, the results offered by the crosscutting matrix are the same as those shown in the action view in [4].

In the crosscutting matrix we can observe how there are several actions which are considered to be crosscutting themes. Obviously, in real systems, requirements often refer to more than one action so that we usually obtain many crosscutting themes. In [4], the authors assume the same. In order to avoid this problem, they remove some relationships between actions and requirements by analyzing the requirements and deciding the main action addressed by each requirement. The result of this process is a new action view which is called *clipped action view*. However, this is an ad-hoc approach that could lead to (un)predictable results. Our framework may complement Theme/Doc in order to properly take such decisions by means of the number of

Table 12. Dependency matrix and crosscutting matrix for *action view* presented in [4]

dependency matrix (actions x requirements)

		requirements									
		R1	R2	R3	R4	R5	R6	R7	R8	R9	
actions	register	1	0	1	0	0	0	0	0	0	S
	unregister	0	1	0	1	1	1	1	0	0	S
	logged	0	0	1	1	0	1	0	0	1	S
	give	0	0	0	0	0	0	0	1	1	S
	flagged	0	0	0	0	0	0	1	0	0	NS
		NT	NT	T	T	NT	T	T	NT	T	

crosscutting matrix (actions x actions) WRT requirements

		actions				
		register	unregister	logged	give	flagged
actions	register	0	0	1	0	0
	unregister	0	0	1	0	1
	logged	1	1	0	1	0
	give	0	0	1	0	0
	flagged	0	0	0	0	0

crosscutting relations obtained firstly in the crosscutting product matrix and finally in the crosscutting matrix. As we can see in the crosscutting matrix, the logged action has more crosscutting cells than the other ones. Such results encourage the developer to classify Login as a main crosscutting theme.

5.4 Conference Review System

In this section we show the case study of a Conference Review System (CRS). In contrast to the previous case studies, here we show the application of the framework to an example where concerns are related to both functional and non-functional properties, and the results obtained in this case are more significant than those obtained in the previous one. This case study has been presented in some workshops, e.g. [17]. The general purpose of the original system is to assist a conference's program committee to perform the review of papers and registration of conference participants [13]. For space reasons, we have used a simplification of this system.

There are four different user types in the system: PcChair, PcMembers, Authors and Participants. A PcChair is the main person responsible for the review process, and has access to every paper and every review in the system. A PcMember takes over the reviews of the papers and can see paper information but not reviews by other PcMembers. An Author can submit papers to the system, being permitted to see only information about his own submission. A Participant must register in order to attend the conference. The registration process is completely separated from the login process. However, once a user has registered he needs to login whenever he accesses the system. This login process checks the role of the user in the system.

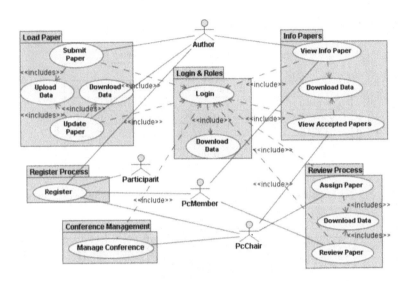

Fig. 7. Use case model of the Conference Review System

The use case model of the conference review system is shown in Fig. 7. The complete requirements analysis can be seen in [13].

We identify the following eight concerns: Papers Submission, Papers Queries, Registration, Conference, Review, Information Retrieval/Supply, Login and User Types. Furthermore, we take the elements in the use case model (each package) shown in Fig. 7 and the set of actors which take part in system as decomposition of requirements. We apply our approach to identify crosscutting in these domains. In Table 13 we show the dependency matrix with trace dependencies between concerns and requirements and in Table 14 the crosscutting matrix obtained from the former. Other decompositions of both concerns and requirements would be possible and the results obtained would be different.

Table 13. Dependency matrix for the Conference Review System

dependency matrix (concerns x requirements)

		requirements							
		Register Process	Info Papers	Load Papers	Review Process	Conf. Manag.	Login &Roles	Actors	
concerns	Papers Submission	0	0	1	0	0	0	0	NS
	Papers Queries	0	1	0	0	0	0	0	NS
	Registration	1	0	0	0	0	0	0	NS
	Conference	0	0	0	0	1	0	0	NS
	Review	0	0	0	1	0	0	0	NS
	Information Ret/Sup	1	1	1	1	1	1	0	S
	Login	0	1	1	1	1	1	0	S
	User Types	0	0	0	0	0	0	1	NS
		T	T	T	T	T	T	NT	

Table 14. Crosscutting matrix for the Conference Review System

crosscutting matrix (concerns x concerns) WRT requirements

		concerns							
		Papers Submis-sion	Papers Queries	Registra_tion	Confe-rence	Review	Information Ret/Sup	Login	User Types
concerns	Papers Submission	0	0	0	0	0	0	0	0
	Papers Queries	0	0	0	0	0	0	0	0
	Registration	0	0	0	0	0	0	0	0
	Conference	0	0	0	0	0	0	0	0
	Review	0	0	0	0	0	0	0	0
	Information Ret/Sup	1	1	1	1	1	0	1	0
	Login	1	1	0	1	1	1	0	0
	User Types	0	0	0	0	0	0	0	0

As we can see in Table 14, the Login concern crosscuts every concern where the user must authenticate himself and the system must check the role of such user. Similarly, the Information Retrieval/Supply concern crosscuts the concerns which need an access to the correspondence information to perform their actions.

Once we have identified the crosscutting concerns with respect to the requirements domain, we can observe how the concerns are related to the design of the system. We show in Fig. 8 a simple UML class diagram representing the static structure of the design.

Now, we take the requirements as represented in the use case model as source elements, and the classes in the class diagram of the design as target elements. We can

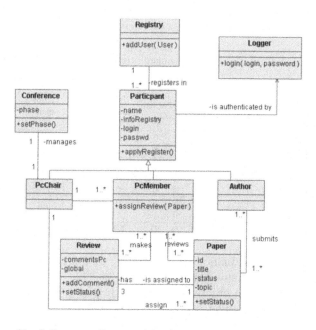

Fig. 8. Structure diagram of the Conference Review System

Table 15. Dependency matrix (requirements x classes) for CRS

		classes									
		Paper	Review	Confe-rence	Pc Chair	Pc Member	Author	Partici-pant	Logger	Registry	
requirements	Register Process	0	0	0	0	0	0	1	0	1	S
	Info Papers	1	0	0	0	0	0	0	0	0	NS
	Load Papers	1	0	0	0	0	0	0	0	0	NS
	Review Process	0	1	0	0	0	0	0	0	0	NS
	Conf. Manag	0	0	1	0	0	0	0	0	0	NS
	Login&Roles	0	0	0	0	0	0	1	1	0	S
	Actors	0	0	0	1	1	1	1	0	0	S
		T	NT	NT	NT	NT	NT	T	NT	NT	

build the dependency matrix shown in Table 15 to show the trace dependencies between requirements and design elements.

As we can see in Table 15, the trace dependencies between requirements and classes are direct mappings except for *Register Process* and *Login&Roles* because of information added in the *Participant* class for such register and login purposes respectively (*infoRegistry* and *login, passwd* attributes of Participant class). These requirements are tangled in this class with the own functionality of the Participant class (User Type).

We apply the cascading operation (as defined in Sect. 4) between the dependency matrix concerns x requirements (Table 13) and the dependency matrix requirements x design (Table 15) to obtain trace dependencies between concerns and design elements. This derived dependency matrix concerns x design is shown in Table 16.

Table 16. Cascaded dependency matrix (concerns x classes) for CRS

		classes									
		Paper	Review	Confe-rence	PcChair	Pc-Member	Author	Partici-pant	Logger	Registry	
concerns	Papers Submission	1	0	0	0	0	0	0	0	0	NS
	Papers Queries	1	0	0	0	0	0	0	0	0	NS
	Registration	0	0	0	0	0	0	1	0	1	S
	Conference	0	0	1	0	0	0	0	0	0	NS
	Review	0	1	0	0	0	0	0	0	0	NS
	Information Ret/Sup	2	1	1	0	0	0	1	0	1	S
	Login	2	1	1	0	0	0	1	1	0	S
	User Types	0	0	0	1	1	1	1	0	0	S
		T	T	T	NT	NT	NT	T	NT	T	

Finally, applying our definition of crosscutting to the last derived dependency matrix, we obtain the crosscutting matrix shown in Table 17.

From this matrix we can observe that — with respect to the design — we have obtained some new crosscutting concerns. The Registration concern crosscuts the

Table 17. Crosscutting matrix for CRS based on cascaded matrix in Table 16

		concerns							
		Papers Submis-sion	Papers Queries	Registra-tion	Confe-rence	Review	Information Ret/Sup	Login	User Types
concerns	Papers Submission	0	0	0	0	0	0	0	0
	Papers Queries	0	0	0	0	0	0	0	0
	Registration	0	0	0	0	0	1	1	1
	Conference	0	0	0	0	0	0	0	0
	Review	0	0	0	0	0	0	0	0
	Information Ret/Sup	1	1	1	1	1	0	1	1
	Login	1	1	1	1	1	1	0	1
	User Types	0	0	1	0	0	1	1	0

Information Ret/Sup, Login and User Types concerns. Similarly, the User Types concern crosscuts the Registration, Information Ret/Sup and Login concerns. As we showed in the dependency matrix obtained by means of the cascading operation (see Table 16), all these concerns are scattered in several design modules and in at least one of these modules some other concern is tangled.

Obviously, this conclusion about crosscutting depends very much on the decomposition at each level and the dependencies between elements at these levels. There are many alternatives, which could aim at avoiding crosscutting by using another modularization (e.g., aspect-oriented techniques such as [5]). Here, we showed how to analyse crosscutting across several phases in the software life cycle. The impact of the selected decomposition in the framework is explained in the next section.

5.5   CRS with Aspects

Following the CRS case study, we detected that the Login concern crosscuts other concerns at the requirements phase. In this section we add aspect-oriented support at requirement level to properly model such a concern. Note that we can decide to postpone this refactoring and face up to the problem at later stages of the development. This means, for example, dealing with the crosscutting concerns at design level using techniques such as Theme/UML [5] or at implementation level by means of an AOP language.

In [26], the authors present an approach to model volatile concerns — represent business rules that the stakeholders would like to be able to change quickly — as crosscutting concerns. They apply aspect-oriented techniques to model concerns which require a high degree of evolution. Their approach presents a methodology based on several steps: concern identification, concern classification and finally concern representation based on the previous classification. The concerns which are classified as volatile or crosscutting are marked as roles (using the special symbol "|") and they are modeled using a pattern specification model. In particular the authors utilize a Use Case Pattern Specification and an Activity Pattern Specification. By

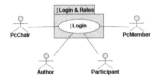

Fig. 9. Login&Roles marked as a crosscutting concern

means of the Pattern Specification we can formalize the reuse of models. See [26] to obtain more details about Pattern Specifications. The purpose of this section is to show the application of such Pattern Specification to model the Login concern of our CRS. Accordingly, we add the "l" mark before the name of the use case which addresses the Login concern (*Login&Roles package*), see Fig. 9.

In [26], the authors present a template to represent each concern. In this template, relationships with other concerns are shown. Since the Login concern is related to other ones, we show in its template the relationships with such concerns (see Table 18). These relationships are extracted from Table 13, where we show concerns which are crosscut by Login one.

Table 18. Template for Login concern

Concern Name	Login
Classification	Constraint
Stakeholders	Participant, PcMember, PcChair and Authors
Interrelationships	PaperSubmission, PaperQueries, Conference, Review, Information Ret/Sup
List of Preconditions	
(1) User must have a user name and password.	
List of Responsibilities	
(1) Check user name	
(2) Check password	
(3) Check user role	

In order to compose the crosscutting concern with the base concerns, in [26] the authors use Activity Patterns Specifications. In these Activity Patterns, Activities describe use cases and activity roles (marked as "l") describe use case roles or crosscutting use cases. Each responsibility listed in the concern's template corresponds to an activity in an activity diagram or an activity role in an APS. The nature of the concern (crosscutting, enduring or volatile) decides whether activities or activity roles are used [26].

We show in Fig. 10a the activity diagram for the Review Paper use case. As we can see in the figure, we have externalized from this activity the Login process which is shown in Fig. 10b.

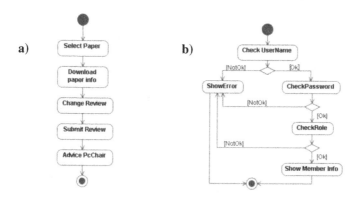

Fig. 10. Activity diagrams for (a) ReviewPaper and (b) Login&Roles

Secondly, a composition rule is defined to merge both activity diagrams. This composition rule allows us to define the places where we apply the Login concern. In Fig. 11 we show the composition rule to compose the Login process with the Review use case. We assign the name of *ReviewPaper* to the activity diagram for the reviewing process. Similar rules could be defined to compose the Login crosscutting concern with the rest of related concerns (concerns which it crosscuts).

Compose ReviewPaper **with** Login&Roles
   1. **Insert** CheckUserName **before** SelectPaper

Fig. 11. Rule to compose the crosscutting concern with the base system

Since we have applied an early aspects technique to model the previously identified crosscutting concern, the application of our framework to such an example shows the difference results after changing the selected decomposition. In this case, the dependencies of several use cases to the Login concerns have been removed, so the correspondent cells in the dependency matrix have been changed to zero. In Table 19 and

Table 19. Dependency matrix concerns x requirements

dependency matrix (concerns x requirements)

		requirements							
		Register Process	Info Papers	Load Papers	Review Process	Conf. Manag.	Login &Roles	Actors	
concerns	Papers Submission	0	0	1	0	0	0	0	NS
	Papers Queries	0	1	0	0	0	0	0	NS
	Registration	1	0	0	0	0	0	0	NS
	Conference	0	0	0	0	1	0	0	NS
	Review	0	0	0	1	0	0	0	NS
	Information Ret/Sup	1	1	1	1	1	0	0	S
	Login	0	0	0	0	0	1	0	S
	User Types	0	0	0	0	0	0	1	NS
		T	T	T	T	T	NT	NT	

Table 20. Crosscutting matrix for CRS with aspects

crosscutting matrix (concerns x concerns) WRT requirements

	concerns							
	Papers Submission	Papers Queries	Registra-tion	Confe-rence	Review	Informa-tion Ret/Sup	Login	User Types
Papers Submission	0	0	0	0	0	0	0	0
Papers Queries	0	0	0	0	0	0	0	0
Registration	0	0	0	0	0	0	0	0
Conference	0	0	0	0	0	0	0	0
Review	0	0	0	0	0	0	0	0
Information Ret/Sup	1	1	1	1	1	0	0	0
Login	0	0	0	0	0	0	0	0
User Types	0	0	0	0	0	0	0	0

Table 20 we can observe the dependency and crosscutting matrix for concerns with respect to requirements for the aspect-oriented decomposition respectively. As we can see in these tables, the Login concern does not crosscut the other concerns anymore.

6 Discussion

In this section, we consider how to address some open issues according to our framework. In some cases, there could be better solutions to be considered; however, the main purpose of this section is to enhance the discussion about the following topics. We first analyze some trace dependency types which can be used in the crosscutting pattern. Then, we discuss how crosscutting is related to decompositions expressed in modeling or implementation languages. We conclude our discussion with the role of intra-level dependencies (coupling) for the transitivity of trace relations.

6.1 Trace Relationships

We introduced the crosscutting pattern in Sect. 2.1. We assumed that elements in the source are related to elements in the target through a mapping captured in trace dependency relationships. In order to determine when two elements from source and target are related to each other, we introduced a trace dependency model which

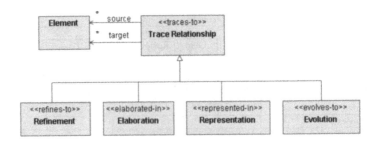

Fig. 12. Trace relationships

enhances the identification of such relations (see Fig. 12). Ramesh and Jarke [27] show a more detailed model about traceability where these and other more specific relations are explained. The UML 2.0 specification [31] also covers such relationships. In [19] the authors show another taxonomy of trace relationships. The model shown in Fig. 12 is based on the previous models covering some important trace relationships of interest for crosscutting identification.

As shown in Fig. 12, we focus just on the following types of trace relationships: refinement, elaboration, evolution and representation. These relationships may be applied to different domains where we can find them. For example:

- **Refinement:** In software development we usually find refinements between different abstraction levels. For instance, the first abstraction could refer to the concerns a system must deal with and the second one to the software artifacts which address such concerns (this could be extended to any phase in software development). As another example, the Model Driven Architecture (MDA) [24] provides a way to build software based on different refinements or transformations between models or artifacts belonging to different abstraction levels [e.g. Computational Independent Model (CIM), Platform Independent Model (PIM) and Platform Specific Model (PSM)]. In most of the case studies we showed in Sect. 5, we identified some examples of refinement relations. For instance, we related concerns to requirements artifacts or design classes.

- **Elaboration:** We can find relationships between models of the same abstraction level. In such situations, we elaborate or add some extra information to a model in order to get a new model. For instance at requirement level we can elaborate a use case based on a previous one. In MDA, model-to-model transformations at the same abstraction level (e.g., PIM-to-PIM) are also examples of this kind of trace relationship.

- **Representation:** In requirements engineering it is very common to have different representations of the same user needs. For instance, we can represent the requirements as statements extracted from a requirement elicitation document and we can also represent such requirements as viewpoints or use cases. We can link both kinds of representation by means of trace relationships. In the Course Management System shown in Sect. 5.3 we can identify this kind of relationships. In this case study we related requirements to actions. Actions are integrated into an *Action View* which is a different representation of the same requirements.

- **Evolution:** With this type of dependencies we can relate gradual changes of software artifacts over time (as in adaptive maintenance). The "evolves-to" relationship exists between modified (structural and/or behavioral) elements in artifacts.

Other types can be defined depending on the goal of traceability to be achieved.

6.2 Languages and Decomposition

Our definition of crosscutting is based on a mapping from source to target (represented in the dependency matrix with source and target elements). In some cases it is possible to avoid tangling, scattering and crosscutting by choosing another decomposition of source and target, a possibility determined by the expressive power of the languages in which the source and target are represented. The expressivity of languages is the leading theme in the seminal paper on aspect-oriented programming by Kiczales et al. [21]. This is also stated in [25]:

Crosscutting models are themselves not the problem. The problem is that our languages and decomposition techniques do not properly support crosscutting modularity.

The role of the source and target languages can be made clear in an extension to the crosscutting pattern (see Fig. 13) (cf. metamodel transformation pattern [24]). A source can be described using several languages at the same time, a fact which also applies to the target. In cases where limitations in the expressive power of the languages are the cause of tangling, scattering, and/or crosscutting, we can use the terms *intrinsic tangling, intrinsic scattering* and *intrinsic crosscutting* [9]. Usually, aspect-oriented languages solve the problem of such a kind of crosscutting.

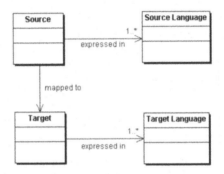

Fig. 13. Languages in the crosscutting pattern

In specific cases there must be debate and arguments to decide whether or not there are essential limitations in the languages. The extension of a language with new constructs and new composition operators — such as aspects or composition filters — may change the (de)composition of source and target. Hence, it will affect the dependency matrix and the related analysis of scattering, tangling and crosscutting.

Related to the problem of expressivity of languages, the creation of the actual decomposition and modularization is a very important research issue that is not addressed here. There are problems: the problem of decomposition (e.g. modularization) of source and target, dominant decompositions, composition operators, granularity of decomposition, the type of dependency relations between source elements and target elements, but also the intra-level dependency relations of source elements and of target elements.

Elements at a certain level can be decomposed into more basic elements at the same level (e.g., in the composite pattern in [18]). This may affect the set up of the dependency matrix: one has to choose at what granularity the relation between source and target will be analyzed. Composite elements occur at any level, for example in implementation components, but also in concern modeling. Depending on the goal of the analysis, one has to decide on the granularity of source and target elements. For example, one could consider a class with its attributes and operations as a single element (course granularity), or one could consider each operation and each attribute as separate elements (fine granularity). There is a clear compositional relation between a class and its attributes and operations. At course granularity, there could be tangling in mapping two concerns to a single class. At fine granularity, one concern could be mapped to an attribute and another concern to an operation, with no tangling in that decomposition. However, in the latter case, one has to consider the intra-level relationships as well (see Sect. 6.3).

There are usually alternative decompositions both in source and target, and alternative mappings between source and target. One has to compare combinations of alternative compositions on quality attributes such as adaptability, reusability and maintainability. In the last two case studies shown in Sect. 5.5, we presented two different decompositions of the same problem. On the one hand we decomposed the system using a traditional object-oriented model. On the other hand we used an aspect-oriented approach recently presented (see [26]) in order to model crosscutting concerns. As we showed in that example, depending on the selected decomposition, the results obtained applying the framework may be different, in some cases removing crosscutting concerns from the system. However, in order to detect the cases where aspect-oriented techniques should be used, we need the identification of crosscutting concerns in the system. The framework presented here is focused on such identification. Moreover the study of the values obtained in the crosscutting product matrix may help to assess the degree in which crosscutting is removed from the system.

6.3 Indirect Trace Dependencies

Elements at a certain level usually have some relationship with other elements at the same level (intra-level relationships): they are coupled. There are many coupling types: generalization/specialization, aggregation, data coupling, control coupling, message coupling, and so on. In the case of a dependency relation of a source element and a target element, which itself is coupled to a second target element, one could also conceive a dependency relation between the source element and the second target element.

Intra-level trace dependencies combined with inter-level trace dependencies may cause dependencies, which we call an *indirect trace dependency* based on a pseudo-transitivity which can be described as follows. Assume source element s[i] has a coupling relation R' with source element s[j] (see Fig. 14). Moreover, source element s[j] has a dependency relation R with target element t[k]. Then the indirect dependency relation is (s[i] R' s[j]) $\wedge$ (s[j] R t[k]) $\Rightarrow$ (s[i] R' $\circ$ R t[k]). In the same way, assume source element s[i] has a dependency relation R with target element t[j] and target element t[j] is coupled with target element t[k] by means of R'. In that case the indirect dependency relation is (s[i] R t[j]) $\wedge$ (t[j] R' t[k]) $\Rightarrow$ (s[i] R $\circ$ R' t[k]).

One should clearly distinguish the direct (inter-level) dependency relation from this indirect dependency relation. Once we have identified all the direct dependencies, we must consider the possible indirect dependency relationships emerged from coupling relations. Intuitively, we are considering such relationships in the different case studies we showed in Sect. 5. For instance, in the CRS example in Sect. 5.4, we

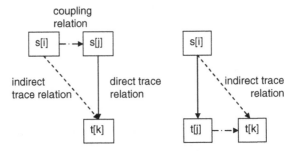

Fig. 14. Direct and indirect trace relations

added some mappings based on indirect trace relationships to the Login concern row in the dependency matrix shown in Table 13. Since some use cases are related with the Login use case by means of an "includes" relationship, such coupling relations imply that the Login concern is mapped to all these use cases. In Fig. 7 we can see that the Submit Paper use case is related with the Login use case by means of an "include" relationship. This relationship implies that the Login concern is mapped onto the Load Paper use case package. The same is applied to other use cases like Manage Conference, Assign Paper or View Info Paper. Although some relations are derived from obvious indirect relations, we mainly focus on this paper on inter-level relations. In a further study of transitivity between inter- and intra-level relations, we will consider the combination of transitive closure for both inter-level and intra-level dependencies.

7 Related Work

Several authors use matrices (design structure matrices, DSM) to analyze modularity in software design [3]. Lopes and Bajracharya [22] describe a method with clustering and partitioning of the design structure matrix for improving modularity of object-oriented designs. However, the design structure matrices represent intra-level dependencies (as coupling matrices in Sect. 3.1) and not the inter-level dependencies as in the dependency matrices used for our analysis of crosscutting. In [28], a relationship matrix (concerns x requirements) very similar to our dependency matrix is described and used to identify crosscutting concerns. However, there is no formalized definition of crosscutting.

In project management, an extension to design structure matrices is proposed by Danilovic and Sandkull [14]. In so-called domain mapping matrices (DMM) they capture the dynamics of product development. In their terminology the traditional DSMs support intra-domain analysis, whereas the DMMs support inter-domain analysis. The purpose of our dependency matrix is similar to these design mapping matrices.

The approach presented in [2] allows the requirements engineer to identify crosscutting concerns. However, the identification of crosscutting functional concerns is not yet clear. In [29] the authors have improved this approach by means of a mechanism based on a natural language processor to identify functional and non-functional crosscutting concerns from requirements documents. However, this approach is focused only on requirements phases, while our approach can be applied throughout the software life cycle.

The papers described above lack the application of their identification of crosscutting to consecutive levels. We used our formalization to trace crosscutting concerns across levels of a software development process, as shown by the cascading operation.

A definition of crosscutting similar to ours can be found in [23] and [25]. Our definition is less restrictive as explained in [8]. Moreover, our definition can be applied to consecutive levels of abstractions in software development, such as requirements, design and implementation. This can be achieved through the cascading of dependency matrices as shown in Sect. 4.

Knethen and Paech [19] present a survey about tracing approaches. In this survey, the authors sum up the main relationships which can be used in order to trace elements in software engineering. They also explain the different entities we should consider to be traced and the tools used to represent such trace relationships. The authors establish three kinds of relationships: between documentation entities on the same abstraction, between documentation entities at different abstractions and between documentation entities of different versions of a software product. According to this taxonomy of relationships, we can classify our mappings between source and target within the second kind of relationships (between different abstractions). For instance, the two different abstractions could refer to concerns and representation of concerns in a particular phase (as we stated in Sect. 2.1). However, these different abstractions could also refer to refinements within a same level. For instance, we can consider trace dependencies in requirements between textual requirements and use cases.

Finally, there are several tools to show or represent the mappings between entities. In [32] we find tools based on traceability matrices, graphical models and cross references. We have used traceability matrices to show the mappings. By means of an extension to such matrices we are able to represent both the mappings between source and target elements and scattering and tangling in the system.

8 Conclusions

We proposed a definition of crosscutting based on an extension to traceability matrices, formalized in a crosscutting pattern. In a dependency matrix, we show the mappings between source and target. As an extension, we used this matrix to derive a crosscutting matrix and to identify crosscutting. This can be applied to any phases or abstraction levels in a software development process, including early phases. In [10] we applied the framework to modeling phases. The approach can be applied to systems where well known crosscutting concerns exist, but also in systems where crosscutting concerns should be identified. Obviously, the earlier we identify crosscutting in system development, the easier it is to cope with crosscutting in order to improve the quality of the system. Important properties of software such as modularity, reusability, evolvability or adaptability can be enhanced by means of an early identification of crosscutting.

An interesting application of our framework is the analysis of crosscutting across several levels in software development, for example from concern modeling to requirements, or from architectural design to detailed design and implementation. This analysis is formalized by means of cascading the crosscutting pattern. As such, it provides an approach for traceability analysis. We showed the application of the approach to some case studies to identify crosscutting. The operationalization of crosscutting with matrices constitutes a helpful means to analyze crosscutting in different scenarios or domains.

Other applications of our framework have been studied. Since evolvability in systems can be influenced by crosscutting, change impact analysis of crosscutting has been carried out in [7]. The framework has been applied to analyze the impact of crosscutting on MDA model transformations [11]. On the other hand, the framework may help developers not only to identify crosscutting but also to assess the degree of crosscutting in a system. In that sense, the crosscutting product matrix described in Sect. 3.2 provides important information for this purpose. We are investigating the definition of crosscutting metrics based on the crosscutting product matrices. Further research should show the scalability of this approach and provide support for different types of trace relations.

Acknowledgment. This work has been carried out in conjunction with the AOSD-Europe Project IST-2-004349-NoE (see [1]) and also partially supported by MEC under contract TIN2005-09405-C02-02. We would like to thank Ana Moreira for her comments and suggestions. We would also like to thank the anonymous reviewers who provided constructive comments and suggestions to enhance this work.

References

1. AOSD-Europe. AOSD Ontology 1.0 – Public Ontology of Aspect-Orientation (Retrieved May, 2005) (2005), from http://www.aosd-europe.net/documents/d9Ont.pdf
2. Araujo, J., Moreira, A., Brito, I., Rashid, A.: Aspect-Oriented Requirements with UML. In: Workshop on Aspect-Oriented Modelling with UML at International Conference on Unified Modelling Language. Dresden, Germany (2002)
3. Baldwin, C.Y., Clark, K.B.: Design Rules, The Power of Modularity, vol. 1. MIT Press, Cambridge (2000)
4. Baniassad, E., Clarke, S.: Theme: An Approach for Aspect-Oriented Analysis and Design. In: 26th International Conference on Software Engineering, pp. 158–167. Edinburgh, Scotland (2004)
5. Baniassad, E., Clarke, S.: Aspect-Oriented Analysis and Design: The Theme Approach. Addison-Wesley, Reading (2005)
6. Baniassad, E., Clements, P., Araújo, P., Moreira, A., Rashid, A., Tekinerdogan, B.: Discovering early aspects. In IEEE Software 23(1), 61–70 (2006)
7. van den Berg, K.: Change Impact Analysis of Crosscutting in Software Architectural Design. In: Workshop on Architecture-Centric Evolution at 20th ECOOP, Nantes (2006)

8. van den Berg, K., Conejero, J.M.: A Conceptual Formalization of Crosscutting in AOSD. In: In Iberian Workshop on Aspect Oriented Software Development, TR-24/05 University of Extremadura, Granada, Spain, pp. 46–52 (2005)
9. van den Berg, K., Conejero, J.M.: Disentangling crosscutting in AOSD: A conceptual framework. Paper presented at the EIWAS2005, Brussels (2005b)
10. van den Berg, K., Conejero, J.M., Hernández, J.: Identification of crosscutting in software design. In: Aspect-Oriented Modeling Workshop at 5th AOSD, Bonn (2006b)
11. van den Berg, K., Tekinerdogan, B., Nguyen H.: Analysis of Crosscutting in Model Transformations. In: Aagedal, J., Neple, T., Oldevik, N.J. (eds) ECMDA-TW Traceability Workshop Proceedings 2006. SINTEF Report A219, pp. 51–64 (2006)
12. Bushmann, F., Meunier, R., Rohnert, H., Sommerlad, P., Stal, M.: Pattern-Oriented Software Architecture: A System of Patterns. Wiley, Chichester, UK (1996)
13. Cachero, C., Gómez, J., Párraga, A., Pastor, O.: Conference Review System: A Case of Study. In: [17] (2001)
14. Danilovic, M., Sandkull, B.: The use of dependence structure matrix and domain mapping matrix in managing uncertainty in multiple project situations. International Journal of Project Management 23(3), 193–203 (2005)
15. Davis, A.: Software Requirements: Objects, Functions and States, 2nd edn. Prentice-Hall, Englewood Cliffs (1993)
16. Finkelstein, A., Sommerville, I.: The Viewpoints FAQ. BCS/IEE Software Engineering Journal 11(1), 2–4 (1996)
17. In: First International Workshop on Web-Oriented Software Technology, Valencia, Spain (2001), http://www.dsic.upv.es/ west/iwwost01/
18. Gamma, E., Helm, R., Johnson, R., Vlissides, J.: Design patterns. Elements of reusable object-oriented software. Addison-Wesley, Reading (1995)
19. von Knethen, A., Paech, B.: A Survey on Tracing Approaches in Practice and Research. IESE-Report No. 095.01/E. v1.0. Fraunhofer Institut Experimentelles Software Engineering (2002)
20. Kiczales, G.: Crosscutting. AOSD.NET Glossary 2005 (2005), At http://aosd.net/wiki/index.php?title=Crosscutting
21. Kiczales, G., Irwin, J., Lamping, J., Loingtier, M., Lopes, C.V., Maeda, C.: Aspect-Oriented Programming. In: Aksit, M., Matsuoka, S. (eds.) ECOOP 1997. LNCS, vol. 1241, pp. 220–242. Springer, Heidelberg (1997)
22. Lopes, C.V., Bajracharya, S.K.: An analysis of modularity in aspect oriented design. In: 4th International Conference on Aspect-Oriented Software Development. Chicago, Illinois (2005)
23. Masuhara, H., Kiczales, G.: Modeling Crosscutting in Aspect-Oriented Mechanisms. In: Cardelli, L. (ed.) ECOOP 2003. LNCS, vol. 2743, pp. 2–28. Springer, Heidelberg (2003)
24. MDA. MDA Guide Version 1.0.1, document number omg/2003-06-01 (2003)
25. Mezini, M., Ostermann, K.: Modules for Crosscutting Models. In: Rosen, J.-P., Strohmeier, A. (eds.) Ada-Europe 2003. LNCS, vol. 2655, pp. 24–44. Springer, Heidelberg (2003)
26. Moreira, A., Araujo, J., Whittle, J.: Modeling Volatile Concerns as Aspects. In: Dubois, E., Pohl, K. (eds.) CAiSE 2006. LNCS, vol. 4001, pp. 973–978. Springer, Heidelberg (2006)
27. Ramesh, B., Jarke, M.: Toward reference models for requirements traceability. IEEE Transactions on Software Engineering 27(4), 58–93 (2001)
28. Rashid, A., Moreira, A., Araujo, J.: Modularisation and Composition of Aspectual Requirements. In: Second Aspect Oriented Software Conference. Boston, USA (2003)

29. Sampaio, A., Loughran, L., Rashid, A., Rayson, P.: Mining Aspects in Requirements. In: Early Aspects 2005 Workshop at Aspect Oriented Software Development Conference. Chicago, USA (2005)
30. Tekinerdogan, B.: ASAAM: Aspectual Software Architecture Analysis Method. In: 4th Working IEEE/IFIP Conference on Software Architecture (2004)
31. UML. Unified Modeling Language 2.0 Superstructure Specification. (Retrieved October, 2004) from (2004), http://www.omg.org/cgi-bin/doc?ptc/2004-10-02
32. Wieringa, R.J.: An introduction to requirements traceability. Technical Report IR-389, Faculty of Mathematics and Computer Science, Vrije Universiteit, Amsterdam (1995)

Visualizing Early Aspects with Use Case Maps

Gunter Mussbacher[1], Daniel Amyot[1], and Michael Weiss[2]

[1] SITE, University of Ottawa, 800 King Edward, Ottawa, ON, K1N 6N5, Canada
{gunterm, damyot}@site.uottawa.ca
[2] School of Computer Science, Carleton University, 1125 Colonel By Drive, Ottawa, ON, K1S 5B6, Canada
weiss@scs.carleton.ca

Abstract. Once aspects have been identified during requirements engineering activities, the behavior, structure, and pointcut expressions of aspects need to be modeled unobtrusively at the requirements level, allowing the engineer to seamlessly focus either on the behavior and structure of the system without aspects or the combined behavior and structure. Furthermore, the modeling techniques for aspects should be the *same* as for the base system, ensuring that the engineer continues to work with familiar models. This paper describes how, with the help of Use Case Maps (UCMs), scenario-based aspects can be modeled at the requirements level unobtrusively and with the same techniques as for non-aspectual systems. Use Case Maps are a visual scenario notation under standardization by the International Telecommunication Union. With Use Case Maps, aspects as well as pointcut expressions are modeled in a visual way which is generally considered the preferred choice for models of a high level of abstraction.

Keywords: aspect-oriented requirements engineering, Use Case Maps, scenario notations, User Requirements Notation.

1 Introduction

Aspects [26] expand object-oriented software development by adding means for encapsulating requirements-level concerns (also called requirements units, e.g., features, use cases, etc). Generally, such encapsulation cannot be achieved with classes/objects alone as "the units of interest in the requirements domain are fundamentally different from the units of interest in object-oriented software" [21]. In object-oriented software, this manifests itself in scattering (parts of a concern are scattered over many classes) and tangling (one class contains parts of many different concerns). Aspects address these problems (see [25] for an example on how use cases can be encapsulated throughout the whole software development process). Note that although this paper focuses on object-oriented techniques, similar arguments in support of aspects can be made for other development paradigms. As Use Case Maps (UCMs) also have been used in the context of various software development paradigms (see Sect. 2.1 for examples), aspect-oriented UCMs (AoUCM) are applicable to a wide variety of development paradigms.

A. Rashid and M. Aksit (Eds.): Transactions on AOSD III, LNCS 4620, pp. 105–143, 2007.

UCMs [38] are part of the User Requirements Notation (URN) [39], a standardization effort of the International Telecommunication Union (ITU). The UCM notation is a visual scenario language that focuses on the causal flow of behavior superimposed on a structure of components. UCMs depict the interaction of architectural entities while abstracting from message and data details. UCMs have been used to drive performance analysis, scenario interaction detection, testing activities, and the evaluation of architectural alternatives at a very early stage in the software development process. In addition to UCMs, URN contains a second language for goal modeling and the description of non-functional requirements (GRL — the Goal-oriented Requirement Language [37]), making it the first standardization effort to address non-functional requirements explicitly in a graphical way.

This paper describes the first step in unifying URN concepts and aspects concepts, both on a notational level as well as on a process level, in order to take advantage of mutual benefits. Aspects can improve the modularity, compositionality, reusability, scalability, and maintainability of URN models. Considering the strong overlap between non-functional requirements and concerns encapsulated by aspects, aspects can help bridge the gap between goals (non-functional requirements described with GRL) and operational scenarios (the UCM scenarios which describe how a goal is achieved). On the other hand, aspects can benefit from a standardized way of modeling non-functional requirements (and therefore concerns) with URN.

The aforementioned first step endeavors to unify UCMs and aspects by using existing notational elements of UCMs to describe aspect-oriented concepts. Aligning UCM and aspect concepts makes it possible to visually describe aspect-oriented models with UCM models (as long as the aspect models are scenario-based). Furthermore, it allows aspect concepts to be used as first class modeling elements when building UCM models.

The remainder of the paper gives an overview of UCMs in Sect. 2.1 and an overview of modeling techniques for early aspects in Sect. 2.3. Section 3 describes how aspects can be modeled with UCMs at the requirements level and explains extensions to the URN metamodel in order to accommodate aspect-oriented UCMs. Section 4.1 discusses a matching algorithm for aspect-oriented UCMs and Sect. 4.2 a composition algorithm for aspect-oriented UCMs. Section 4.4 talks about additional features and tool support for them. Throughout the paper, a hotel reservation system is used as an example to illustrate standard UCMs in Sect. 2.2, aspect-oriented UCMs in Sect. 3.5, and the composed system in Sect. 4.3. The paper ends with a conclusion and a discussion of future work in Sect. 5.

2   Background

This section provides an overview of UCMs and modeling techniques for scenario/use case-based approaches to aspect-oriented requirements engineering.

2.1 Use Case Maps

UCMs [38] are an integral part of the ITU's effort to standardize the URN [39]. UCMs are a visual scenario notation for the description of functional requirements and, if desired, high-level design. Paths describe the causal flow of behavior of a system (e.g., one or many use cases). Optionally, paths are superimposed over components which represent the architectural structure of a system (e.g., classes or packages). UCMs abstract from the details of message exchange and communication infrastructures while still showing the interaction between architectural entities. As UCMs integrate many scenarios and use cases into one combined model of a system, it is possible to reason about undesired interactions between scenarios [4], analyze performance implications [34, 35], and drive testing efforts based on UCM specifications [6]. As UCMs show architectural structures, various architectural alternatives can be analyzed [7, 8, 40]. Over the last decade, UCMs have successfully been used for service-oriented, concurrent, distributed, and reactive systems such as telecommunications systems [3, 8], e-commerce systems [5], agent systems [23], operating systems [16], and health information systems [1]. UCMs have also been used for business process modeling [40].

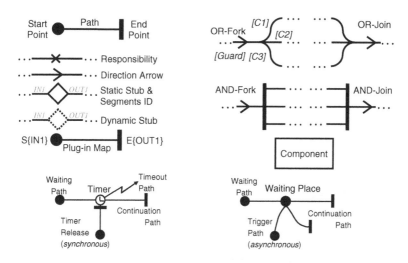

Fig. 1. Basic elements of UCM notation

The basic elements of the UCM notation are shown in Fig. 1. A *map* contains any number of *paths* and structural elements (*components*). Paths express causal sequences and may contain several types of path nodes. *Responsibilities* describe required actions or steps to fulfill a scenario. *OR-forks* (possibly including guarding *conditions*) and *OR-joins* are used to show alternatives, while *AND-forks* and *AND-joins* depict concurrency. Loops can be modeled implicitly with OR-joins and OR-forks. As the UCM notation does not impose any nesting constraints,

joins and forks can be freely combined and a fork does not need to be followed
by a join.

UCM models can be decomposed using *stubs* which contain sub-maps called
plug-ins. Plug-in maps are reusable units of behavior and structure. *Plug-in
bindings* connect in-paths and out-paths of stubs with start and end points of a
plug-in map, respectively (see Fig. 2a for an example; note that the arrows have
been added to this and following figures to clearly indicate plug-in bindings for
the UCM model — UCM editing tools do not display such arrows but manage
plug-in bindings much more concisely). Stubs without plug-in bindings for start
or end points can be shown visually without an in-path or out-path, respectively
(see Fig. 2b). A stub may be *static* which means that it can have at most one
plug-in, whereas a *dynamic* stub may have many plug-ins which may be selected
at runtime. A *selection policy* decides which plug-ins of a dynamic stub to choose
at runtime.

Map elements which reside inside a component are said to be *bound* to the
component. Components have various types and characteristics (not discussed
in this paper) and can contain sub-components.

Other notational elements of UCMs are *timers* and *waiting places*. A timer
may have a *timeout path* which is indicated by a zigzag line. A waiting place
denotes a location on the path where the scenario stops until a condition is
satisfied. If an endpoint is connected to a waiting place or a timer, the stopped
scenario continues when this end point is reached (synchronous interaction).
Asynchronous, in-passing triggering of waiting places and timers is also possible.
End points can also be connected to start points as shown in Fig. 2c to indicate
simple sequences of paths. A more complete coverage of the notation elements
is available in [17, 19, 38].

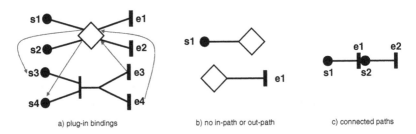

a) plug-in bindings   b) no in-path or out-path   c) connected paths

Fig. 2. Connecting stubs, plug-in maps, and paths

UCMs also support the definition of scenarios. For each choice point in the
UCM model (e.g., an OR-fork), Boolean expressions are defined for all alternatives. A scenario describes a specific path through the UCM model (only one
alternative at a choice point is taken) by initializing the variables used in the
Boolean expressions. For each scenario, its pre-conditions and post-conditions
are additionally specified as well as its start points and expected end points.

UCMs share many characteristics with UML activity diagrams but UCMs
offer more flexibility in how sub-diagrams can be connected, how sub-components

can be represented, and how dynamic responsibilities and dynamic components (not shown here) can be used to capture requirements for agent systems. UCMs also integrate a simple data model, performance annotations, and a simple action language used for analysis. However, activity diagrams have better support for object flows and a better integration with the rest of UML.

On the other hand, UCMs are integrated with goal-oriented models described with the *Goal-oriented Requirement Language* (GRL), the second modeling notation in the URN. With URN, the goals of stakeholders and the system are modeled on GRL graphs, showing the impact of often conflicting goals and various alternative solutions proposed to achieve the goals. Softgoals (which relate to non-functional requirements), hard goals (which relate to functional requirements), and solutions impact each other in either a negative or positive way. The solutions from the GRL graphs are refined by the UCM model which provides the structural and behavioral details of scenarios for the solution.

Two editing tools for UCMs have been developed at Carleton University and the University of Ottawa. The tools make it possible to create, maintain, analyze, and transform UCM models. The original UCM Navigator (UCMNAV) [27] is only a UCM tool whereas the new Eclipse-based jUCMNav [33] is a true URN tool that offers GRL modeling in addition to UCM modeling.

2.2   Use Case Maps Example

This section discusses a simplified example which further illustrates the UCM notation. Given the following requirements, the basic UCM model in Fig. 3 can be created consisting of two use cases:

R1. Users shall be able to make reservations.
R2. System shall authenticate users before any access to a reservation (such as making, canceling, ...).
R3. System shall add failed reservation attempts to a waiting list from which they will be taken when another reservation is canceled in the future.

In the make reservation use case, the system first checks for authorization and only if the user is authorized is the reservation made. If the reservation is not successful, the reservation is added to a waiting list. In the cancel reservation use case, the system again checks for authorization and only if the user is authorized is the cancellation performed. After the cancellation, the system tries to fulfill a reservation from the waiting list. Note that the components in this case correspond to objects, but this is just one of the possible interpretations of a UCM component. Considering that there exist other non-functional requirements (such as security) that need to be added to the use cases and considering that there exist other features that interact with making and canceling reservations (such as waiting lists) and that need to be added to the use cases, there is clearly a need for better modularization. A more advanced UCM model which extracts the common behavior into a plug-in map is shown in Fig. 4.

Even though stubs structure the UCM model considerably better, the cancel and make reservation use cases still include descriptions of non-related behavior

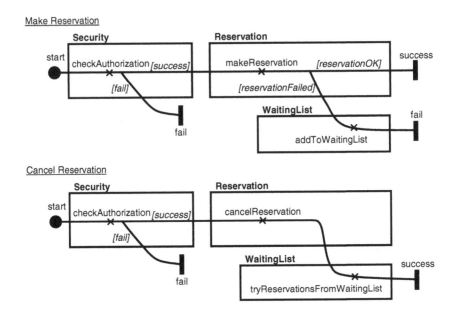

Fig. 3. Basic UCM reservation use cases

(the stubs related to authorization and the responsibilities related to waiting lists). A further improvement of the UCM model in Fig. 4 is shown in Fig. 5. Now, each individual plug-in map only deals with one concern. Top-level maps (often called root maps) describe how the different concerns are composed together. However, root maps often turn out to be rather complicated. Scalability is also an issue as, for example, the Authorization stub has to be added explicitly to each root map. Furthermore, the description of making a reservation is in one plug-in map only because no other use case exists that needs to be interleaved with making a reservation. Figure 5 only shows the situation where behavior has to be added before or after making and canceling reservations. Often however, use cases are interleaved, causing the behavior for making a reservation to be split up into several maps (see Fig. 6 — the disjoint plug-in maps in Make Reservation Part 1 and Part 2 only contain parts of the behavior for making a reservation). This makes it much harder to understand and maintain individual use cases. AoUCM address these problems.

2.3 Modeling Techniques for Aspect-Oriented Requirements

About a decade ago, *aspect-oriented programming* (AOP) [26] introduced a new way of structuring software systems. With this new modularization, it is possible to address problems of object-oriented software engineering that occur because the units of interest to the requirements engineer cannot readily be encapsulated with object-oriented units [21]. This results in *scattering* (parts of a requirements unit are scattered over many classes) and *tangling* (one class contains parts of

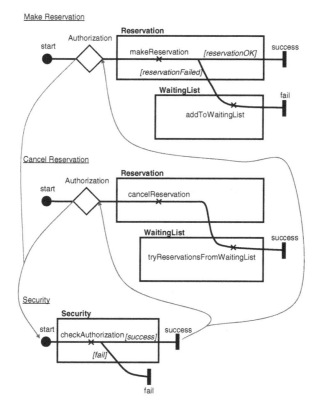

Fig. 4. Advanced UCM reservation use cases — first attempt

many different requirements units). This problem has also been referred to as the tyranny of the dominant decomposition [36], as a chosen modularization technique (e.g., objects) inevitably will cause unwanted side-effects in the software design (e.g., scattering and tangling). The UCM model in Fig. 5 exhibits signs of scattering and tangling. The Authorization stub is scattered over multiple root maps and various concerns are tangled in each of the root maps. Examples for requirements units (or *concerns*) for which aspects provide a better encapsulation than objects are authorization/authentication, caching, concurrency management, debugging, distribution, logging, testing, transaction management, or even a feature or use case [25].

Initially, aspect-orientation focused on the implementation level leading to an ever-growing number of tools that provide extensions for aspects to major programming languages [9, 10]. Essentially, aspects identify locations in a program (called *joinpoints*) through parameterized expressions (called *pointcuts*). Aspects also specify behavior (called *advice*) which will be inserted into the specified locations. As advices may change the behavior of already existing structural entities thus violating proper object-oriented modularization, entities external to an aspect are referenced in a structured way (with the help of *intertype declarations*).

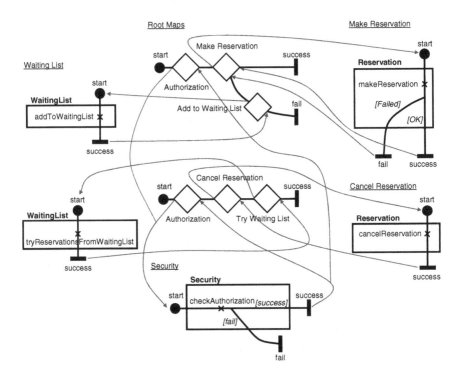

Fig. 5. Advanced UCM reservation use cases — second attempt

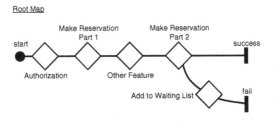

Fig. 6. Description of make reservation is spread out over multiple disjoint plug-in maps

Note that we are using AspectJ terms [14] but that the concepts also apply to other flavors of aspect-oriented programming.

Aspect-oriented modeling (AOM) or *early aspects* aims to apply aspect-oriented concepts earlier in the software development life cycle in order to manage more effectively concerns at the requirements and architecture stages. Many approaches to *aspect-oriented requirements engineering* (AORE) are described in a recent survey [20], grouped into viewpoint, goal, scenario/use case, concern, and component-based approaches. As our technique is more closely related to the group of scenario/use case-based approaches, we will briefly review this group in more detail.

In *Aspect-Oriented Software Development (AOSD) with Use Cases* [25], Jacobson and Ng view a well-written use case as a concern and add the notion of *pointcuts* to the traditional use case approach. Pointcuts in one use case reference extension points in other use cases in a textual way. The traditional usage of extension points is slightly altered as they do not directly reference a use case anymore but only identify a step in the use case where an extension may occur. Furthermore, a new kind of use case, the *infrastructure use case*, is used in addition to the traditional *application use cases*. It describes scenarios required to address non-functional requirements. Infrastructure use cases do not reference other use cases directly but pointcuts in a generic *perform transaction use case*. This particular use case models abstractly all types of interactions of an actor with the system, providing a generic description of the system. The perform transaction use case is eventually mapped to traditional use cases, effectively weaving aspect behavior described by infrastructure use cases into application use cases.

In *Scenario Modeling with Aspects* [41], Whittle and Araújo use UML sequence diagrams to describe non-aspectual scenarios and *interaction pattern specifications* (IPS) to describe aspectual scenarios. IPS are very similar to sequence diagrams but allow the definition of roles for classifiers, messages, and parameters. Binding the roles in IPS to elements of sequence diagrams produces a composed system, which is then translated into state machines for validation. Alternatively, the sequence diagrams and IPS are first both translated into state machine representations [finite state machines and *state machine pattern specifications* (SMPS), respectively] and then composed together at the state machine level [13] with the same binding technique. SMPS are very similar to state machines but also contain roles identified in IPS. In both cases, the binding is specified textually and identifies explicitly elements to be bound. On one hand, this allows for a very flexible composition. On the other hand however, the explicit binding may cause problems with scalability.

The *Aspectual Use Case Driven Approach* is the third major research direction discussed for scenario/use case-based approaches in [20]. Moreira et al. [12, 29] propose to add extensions to UML use case and sequence diagrams in order to visualize how crosscutting non-functional requirements are linked to functional requirements expressed by use case diagrams or sequence diagrams. Non-functional requirements are captured with the help of templates. Moreira and Araújo [28] builds on this work, extending the set of use case relationships to include "constrain", "collaborate", and "damage" relationships and making use of *activity pattern specifications* (APS). The new relationships describe how one use case impacts another (restricting it, contributing positively to it, or contributing negatively to it). APS extend UML activity diagrams by allowing the specification of roles similar to IPS [41] and SMPS [13]. APS are used to describe use cases in more detail. Various activity diagrams are composed by composition rules which are similar to the binding in [13, 41].

Rashid et al. [32] describe an approach for conflict identification and resolution for aspectual requirements. While the example presented in [32] uses a viewpoint-based approach to requirements engineering, it is argued that the technique can also be applied to other requirements engineering approaches including scenarios/use cases. The topic matter, however, is orthogonal to our proposed technique.

Araújo and Coutinho [11] discuss aspects in a viewpoint-based requirements engineering approach that also includes use cases. Non-functional requirements (defined with templates) and use cases are linked to viewpoints. Use cases that are included by or extend more than one use case or that crosscut several viewpoints are called *aspectual use cases*. This approach does not discuss composition of aspectual use cases with other use cases but focuses more on how to extend the work in [32] for conflict resolution.

Barros and Gomes [15] apply aspect-orientation to UML activity diagrams. The approach is based on an additional composition operation called *activity addition* which allows the fusing of stereotyped nodes in one activity diagram with nodes in another. Stereotyping is effectively used as a pointcut expression, identifying explicitly nodes in another activity diagram for behavior merging. Zdun and Strembeck [42] extend UML activity diagrams with nodes for start and end points of aspects in order to visualize aspects in a composed system.

In the UCM community, the applicability of UCMs to model aspects was identified very early on by Buhr [18] but received little attention since then with the exception of de Bruin and van Vliet [22]. The approach by de Bruin and van Vliet adds *Pre stubs* and *Post stubs* for each location on a UCM that requires a change. The stubs allow behavior to be added before or after the location by plugging *refinement maps* into the stubs. Components on UCMs are identified by a *Name:Type pair*. A refinement map can be placed in a Pre or Post stub only if the component type on the refinement map matches the component type to which the Pre or Post stub is bound.

Defining and representing aspects must consider a number of factors. It should be easy to switch from traditional modeling to aspect-oriented modeling. Preferably, there should not be a difference and the same modeling language should be used for both in order to avoid having to learn yet another modeling language. It should be possible to define aspects without influencing the base model. This is a crucial point of aspect-orientation as the base model must not be polluted by aspect-specific information. Breaking the modeling paradigm is best avoided, and therefore aspects, including advice, pointcut expressions, and intertype declarations should be modeled using the same modeling paradigm (e.g., without the use of graphical and purely textual representations at the same time). Pointcut expressions should be parameterized to avoid scalability issues. For scenario/use case-based aspect techniques to be effective at the requirements phase, the employed technique should be at the right abstraction level where message or data details of interactions are irrelevant. The composition technique should be flexible and exhaustive in that it allows all frequently encountered compositions to be expressed.

None of the scenario/use case-based approaches to aspect-oriented requirements engineering mentioned in this section excels in all of these factors (see Sect. 5 for a discussion on this). AoUCM aim to address this shortcoming.

Furthermore, the group of goal-based approaches to aspect-oriented requirements engineering is also of interest in the context of an aspect-oriented URN, e.g., work on aspects and the i^* framework [2]. As GRL borrows many concepts from the i^* framework, we believe that aspects can also be added to the GRL part of URN and that there is a need to synchronize aspect-oriented GRL models with aspect-oriented scenario models expressed with UCM. Gross and Yu [24] present an initial attempt at adding aspects to GRL. They introduce the concept of an intentional aspect as an abstraction for the design of aspects, the composition of actors and aspects, and linking aspects to implementation artefacts. Actors and intentional aspects encapsulate goals and alternative solutions of system modules and aspects, respectively. When actors and aspects are composed, their contributions to common non-functional requirements are merged. The main objective of the approach is to provide traceability between aspects and goals, and aspects and implementation artefacts. However, composition of actors and aspects is not presently supported by tools. Alencar et al. [2] suggest three rules to identify crosscutting concerns in i^* models. Based on the findings, the i^* model is restructured in an aspect-oriented way using a new notational element for aspects (a star). Both proposals are limited to adding aspects to goal models, and do not consider linking goal models to scenario models such as UCM models.

3   Aspect-Oriented Use Case Maps (AoUCM)

In order to unify aspect concepts with UCM concepts, the first step is to define a joinpoint model for UCMs. Furthermore, advice, intertype declarations, and pointcuts have to be defined in UCM terms. We will approach these tasks initially in an informal way. At the end of this section, however, the concepts mentioned above will be defined precisely in the URN metamodel. While previous work [30] reported only on early results, the remaining sections of this paper give a much more in-depth introduction to AoUCM. In summary, the following questions need to be answered:

- What are good joinpoints in UCMs?
- How is advice specified for an aspect?
- How are intertype declarations specified for an aspect?
- How are pointcuts specified and how are pointcuts and advice linked?

3.1   Joinpoint Model

In aspect-oriented programming, a joinpoint is a point in the dynamic flow of the program such as a method call, the execution of a method, the initialization of an object, set methods, get methods, or exception handling. Hence, a joinpoint has a behavioral dimension as well as a structural dimension. For use cases, Jacobson and Ng define a joinpoint as a step in a flow of the use case. In UCM terms, this translates directly into responsibilities (behavioral dimension) optionally bound to components (structural dimension). Responsibilities are just one kind of path node. Therefore, any path node could be a joinpoint (i.e., a location on the path). Defining any path node as a joinpoint gives the most flexibility to the requirements engineer without significantly increasing the complexity of AoUCM or requiring additional modeling constructs. Figure 7 shows UCM path nodes such as start points, dynamic and static stubs, responsibilities, OR-forks and OR-joins, AND-forks and AND-joins, waiting places, timers, and end points. Each of these path nodes is a joinpoint. The small diamonds in Fig. 7 do not indicate joinpoints but insertion points. An aspect can insert behavior at an insertion point, i.e., either before or after joinpoints. An insertion point is associated with exactly one joinpoint. Some joinpoints such as start and end points can only have two insertion points, one before and one after the joinpoint. Other joinpoints such as stubs, forks, and joins can have more than two insertion points. The component in Fig. 7 indicates that the joinpoint model does not concern itself only with behavioral specification but optionally also with structural specifications.

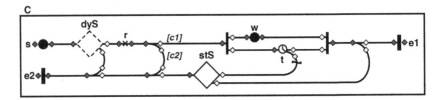

Fig. 7. Joinpoints and insertion points in UCMs

The small light-shaded diamonds indicate that more than one insertion point exist *before* or *after* the path node (i.e., joinpoint). Note that even though the figure only shows at the most three insertion points for one joinpoint, any joinpoint with three insertion points may also have more than three insertion points. The joinpoint model, however, does not need to concern itself with the number of insertion points. The joinpoint model simply identifies all path nodes as joinpoints. We will see in Sect. 3.4 how it is possible to reference each of these insertion points individually.

3.2   Advice Map

An advice describes the behavior of an aspect triggered in a certain situation. Intertype declarations identify the structural entities that either provide the advice or contribute to the advice. Describing behavior in UCMs is straightforward as UCMs are meant to do exactly that: describe behavior with paths on top of a structure of components. The semantic meaning of components in UCMs is cast very wide — anything that can provide a service is a component from classes to actors to roles. Therefore, structural entities identified by intertype declarations can certainly be described with UCM components. The resulting map is called *advice map*. An advice map does not differ syntactically from a non-aspectual map. Both describe behavior with a path, and both use components to indicate who is responsible for providing the behavior. The difference manifests itself in terms of how this map fits into the overall system. This is explained in Sect. 3.4.

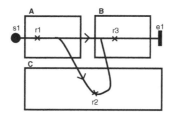

Fig. 8. Advice map with path and components

Figure 8 shows the description of an advice that requires r1 from component A, responsibility r2 from component C, and responsibility r3 from component B. All three components are contributing to the advice. There are three cases:

a. An advice may use an already existing responsibility.
b. An advice may add an aspect-specific responsibility to an already existing component.
c. An advice may define an aspect-specific responsibility for an aspect-specific component.

These three cases can of course be automatically identified by looking at the usage of the responsibilities and components in the whole UCM model, but there is no standard visual representation that indicates which case applies. Therefore, the differentiation between these three cases is a matter of naming conventions. For example, A could be called A (Shared) to indicate case (a), B could be called B (Extended) to indicate case (b), and C could be called C (Owned) to indicate case (c).

3.3   Pointcut Map

A pointcut defines a set of joinpoints either explicitly or in a parameterized way, thereby defining the structural context and behavioral context for the execution of an advice. In aspect-oriented programming, pointcuts can be rather lengthy and complex multi-line expressions. In aspect-oriented use case modeling, point-cuts reference extension points in a different use case. Both use text as the means to describe pointcuts. Considering the visual character of UCMs, a visual representation for pointcuts is a natural choice. More importantly, using a visual representation instead of defining separate textual representations of pointcuts avoids a modeling paradigm break. Therefore, pointcuts are defined on a UCM called *pointcut map* (see Figs. 10 and 11 for examples).

On first look, there is no difference between a pointcut map and other UCMs. Looking more closely, however, the pointcut map represents a partial map which identifies joinpoints when matched against all other maps in the UCM model. The parameterization of pointcuts is achieved by *wildcards* in the names of UCM elements on the pointcut map. Any of the named elements on a pointcut map may contain the wildcard * or logical expressions. The pointcut expressions in Fig. 9 match against (a) all start points starting with s, (b) all responsibilities, (c) all waiting places named ready or starting with w, and (d) all components starting with A. These examples are not complete pointcut maps — in fact, the first three examples are not even valid UCMs. They only illustrate expressions which may be used on a pointcut map. Figure 10 and Fig. 11 show complete pointcut maps.

Fig. 9. Four examples of visual pointcut expressions

As mentioned previously, pointcut maps are partial maps. This is evident in the usage of start and end points on the pointcut map. Start or end points without a name denote only the start or end of the partial map and are therefore not matched against start or end points on other maps in the UCM model (see gray path nodes in Fig. 10). For example, Fig. 10a matches against all maps with a responsibility r. Figure 10b matches against all maps with a start point s, followed by responsibility r, and followed by an end point e. Figure 10c, on the other hand, matches against all maps with a start point s followed by responsibility r.

Note that it is possible to use unnamed start and end points as markers for the start and end of the pointcut expression because the usage of unnamed start and end points in standard UCMs is strongly discouraged. Scenario definitions and plug-in bindings also prefer named start and end points.

Finally, the location of start and end points is also important for the meaning of the pointcut map. Figure 11a matches all maps with a responsibility starting with Get and bound to the component Reservation. Figure 11b matches all maps with a responsibility starting with Confirm. The responsibility must be immediately followed by an end point called confirmed. The responsibility and the

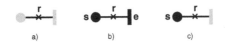

Fig. 10. Three pointcut maps

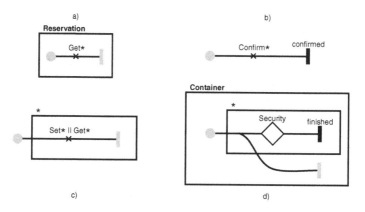

Fig. 11. More examples of pointcut maps

end point may or may not be bound to a component. Figure 11c matches all maps with a responsibility starting with Set or Get and bound to any component as the first path node of the component (because the start point is outside the component). Finally, Fig. 11d matches all maps with an OR-fork bound to any component inside component Container as the first path node. The OR-fork must be immediately followed on one branch by a static stub called Security and an end point called finished, and followed by nothing on the other branch before exiting the component (because the end point is outside the inner component).

In other words, if a path on the pointcut map crosses the boundary of a component because of the location of a start or end point, then the path in the matching UCM will also have to cross the boundary of the matching component. Note that the start and end points that are not matched are shown in gray in Fig. 11 and in Fig. 12. See Table 1 and Fig. 12 for a summary of all cases. The base maps and pointcut maps in Fig. 12 assume that after the start points all maps are identical. Therefore, whether a base map matches a pointcut map is solely dependent on the locations and the names of the start points. Note that the same matching rules apply to end points.

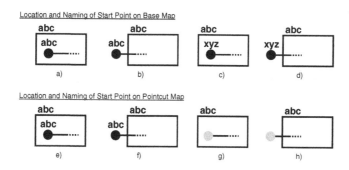

Fig. 12. Location and naming of start points on pointcut maps and base maps

Table 1. Matching rules for start points on pointcut maps and base maps

Do the base map and the pointcut map match?	Base map's start point [1] is *named* and *inside* component (Fig. 12 (a))	Base map's start point is *named* and *outside* component (Fig. 12 (b))	Base map's start point is *named differently* and *inside* component (Fig. 12 (c))	Base map's start point is *named differently* and *outside* component (Fig. 12 (d))
Pointcut map's start point [1] is *named* and *inside* component (Fig. 12 (e))	yes	no [2]	no [3]	no [3]
Pointcut map's start point is *named* and *outside* component (Fig. 12 (f))	no [2]	yes	no [3]	no [3]
Pointcut map's start point is *unnamed* and *inside* component (Fig. 12 (g))	yes	yes [4]	yes	yes [4]
Pointcut map's start point is *unnamed* and *outside* component (Fig. 12 (h))	no [5]	yes	no [5]	yes

1)   The same reasoning applies to end points.

2)   The pointcut expression stipulates that there has to be a start point with name abc inside or outside component abc. Therefore, there is no match if the start point in the base map is **not** inside or outside component abc, respectively.

3)   There is no match in this case because the names do not match.

4)   This pointcut expression does not require the path to cross component abc, but it also does not exclude it. Therefore, the base map is matched although the start point is outside of component abc.

5)   This pointcut expression requires the path to cross the component because the start point is outside of component abc. Therefore, the start point in the base map cannot be inside component abc.

3.4   Advice Map Revisited

At this point, the advice defined on advice maps still needs to be woven into the base system with the help of the pointcuts defined on pointcut maps. Somehow, advice and pointcuts need to be linked. Advice may be executed before, after, or around joinpoints identified by many pointcuts. To achieve this, a dynamic stub called the *pointcut stub* is added to the advice map introduced in Sect. 3.2. The plug-ins of the pointcut stub are the pointcut maps discussed in Sect. 3.3. For example, the pointcut map in Fig. 11d could be plugged into the pointcut stubs below by binding the one in-path to the one start point, one of the out-paths to one of the end points, and the other out-path to the other end point.

By keeping advice and pointcut expressions on separate UCMs (advice maps and pointcut maps, respectively), it is possible to reuse advice and pointcut expressions separately. For example, the same advice can be reused in a different UCM model with different pointcut maps plugged into the pointcut stub. Similarly, the same pointcut map can be used for different aspects.

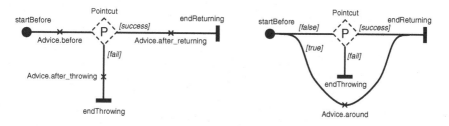

Fig. 13. Pointcut stub

The two advice maps in Fig. 13 show how advice and pointcuts are linked to each other. The requirements engineer can understand in one glance the relationship of the advice to the base system due to the visual representation. For example, the left map shows advice being executed before and after the pointcuts specified on the pointcut maps bound to the pointcut stub. The right map shows very clearly that advice is being executed *around* the specified pointcuts, allowing a situation to be modeled which occurs frequently in aspect-oriented modeling. The aspect in the right map overrides the behavior of the base. In more detail, the left map shows that before the specified pointcuts the responsibility Advice.before is executed and after the specified pointcuts the responsibility Advice.after_returning is executed in the success case and the responsibility Advice.after_throwing is executed in the fail case. The right map shows that the path elements defined by the specified pointcuts are never executed in the composed system because the [false] branch is never taken. The [true] branch is always taken and therefore the responsibility Advice.around is executed instead of the path elements matched by the pointcuts.

Note that many more composition rules (such as concurrency, loops, and interleaving) than the ones mentioned here (before/after/around) can easily be modeled with AoUCM (see [31] for details).

There are a number of observations to be pointed out regarding the use of the pointcut stub. First, the number of in-paths and out-paths for the pointcut stub is flexible. This makes it possible to take into account path nodes with more than one before or after location (e.g., stubs, forks, and joins — see Sect. 3.1). Advice can be specified individually for such locations. Second, the pointcut stub is a dynamic stub which may contain multiple plug-in maps, each of which may describe a different pointcut expression. Therefore, as many different pointcut expressions as necessary can be described for the aspect. Finally, each advice shown on the maps in Fig. 13 is very simple as it consists only of one responsibility. In reality, the responsibility may be replaced by much more complicated advice maps (e.g., see Fig. 8 and imagine a pointcut stub added somewhere on the path).

3.5   Aspect-Oriented Use Case Maps Example

This section revisits the reservation example from Sect. 2.2 and models it with AoUCMs. In Fig. 14, the base maps show the use cases for making and canceling a reservation. Two aspects are defined that describe authorization and waiting

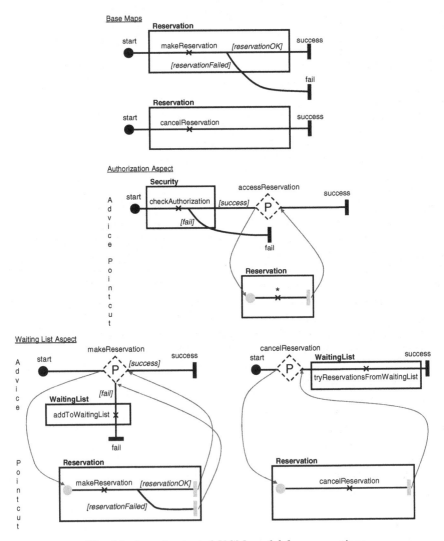

Fig. 14. Aspect-oriented UCM model for reservations

list behavior, respectively. The authorization aspect contains one advice map and one pointcut map. For the waiting list aspect, two advice maps and two pointcut maps are defined. The plug-in bindings are indicated by arrows. The authorization aspect adds an authorization check (checkAuthorization) before any responsibility in the Reservation component, while the waiting list aspect adds failed reservations to a waiting list (addToWaitingList) or tries to fulfill a reservation from the waiting list if a cancellation occurs (tryReservationsFromWaitingList).

The pointcut map for authorization matches any access to the Reservation component. Therefore, the responsibility in the authorization pointcut map is matched against makeReservation and cancelReservation in the base maps. Note that it is irrelevant for the match that the make reservation map contains two end points and the cancel reservation map only one because the end points (as well as the start points and the OR-fork) are not matched. The pointcut map requires only the responsibilities to be matched.

The pointcut maps for the waiting list match the makeReservation responsibility with the makeReservation responsibility in the base maps, the OR-fork including conditions with the OR-fork and conditions in the base maps, and the cancelReservation responsibility with the cancelReservation responsibility in the base maps.

3.6   URN Metamodel and Aspects

For the purpose of this paper, we are focusing on a subset of the UCM portion of the URN metamodel (Fig. 15) [33, 38]. A UCMmap consists of component references (ComponentRef) and PathNodes, reflecting structure and behavior, respectively. Components may contain other components as well as path nodes. There are a great number of different kinds of path nodes but only the Stub is of greater interest with regard to aspects. Stubs may contain plug-in maps and PluginBinding specifies how a stub and a plug-in map are connected.

In order to accommodate the new concepts introduced by aspects, the URN metamodel needs to be extended. The new concepts are advice map, pointcut map, pointcut stub, and joinpoint. UCMadviceMap and UCMpointcutMap specialize the UCMmap class whereas PointcutStub and AspectStub specialize the Stub class. Joinpoint is a new class associated with PathNode since each path node can be a joinpoint. To be exact, this is not true for path nodes such as direction arrows which only serve as visual aids. Therefore, the association between PathNode and Joinpoint is optional (0..1).

The association between PathNode and Joinpoint indicates an additional relationship, showing that path nodes on pointcut maps are matched against joinpoints in the base model. Note that Joinpoint instances and their associations are created only at run time and are therefore not part of a URN source model.

Finally, the AspectStub is required for visualizing the composed system (see Sect. 4.2) and there is an association between aspects to capture any precedence relationships. This is required for conflict resolution of aspects trying to insert behavior at the same insertion point (see Sect. 4.4).

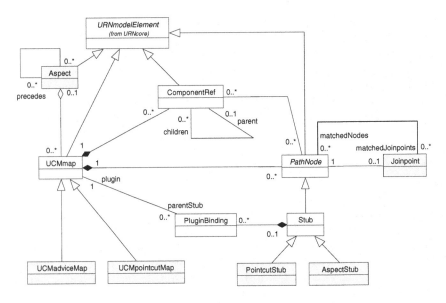

Fig. 15. Extended URN metamodel

With the help of these new classes in the URN metamodel, an aspect can now be defined. An Aspect contains zero or more UCMmaps, some of which are UCMadviceMaps. Only UCMadviceMaps contain zero or more PointcutStubs. A UCMpointcutMap plugs only into a PointcutStub. An AspectStub contains only one or more UCMadviceMaps. Finally, only the PathNodes of a UCMpointcutMap match zero or more Joinpoints. These constraints could be expressed with OCL in the aspect-oriented URN metamodel.

4   Algorithms for Tool Support

Current URN tool support with jUCMNav allows advice maps, pointcut maps, and pointcut stubs including the binding to pointcut maps to be defined in the UCM model. This does not require any additional features to be implemented as the standard features of jUCMNav are sufficient (anything discussed in Sect. 3 can be done with jUCMNav right now).

Full support for AoUCM, however, requires additional features in order to facilitate the matching of pointcut maps to other maps in the UCM model, to indicate on base maps whether a path node is advised, to indicate on advice maps which base maps are being advised by the aspect, to compose aspect maps and base maps into a complete view of the system, and to switch back and forth between the visualization of the base system with aspects and the composed system. Algorithms for these additional features have been implemented and tested to verify the feasibility of this approach and will be released soon into the official version of jUCMNav.

4.1 Matching Algorithm

The matching algorithm compares the static structure of a pointcut map with all other maps in the UCM model except for other pointcut maps. The matching algorithm establishes a mapping from each path node on the pointcut map to path nodes in the UCM model. A successful match requires a mapping of each path node on the pointcut map to exactly one path node in the UCM model. As the pointcut map may be matched several times by the UCM model, the result contains a list of mappings for each matched instance of the pattern described by the pointcut map. Several path node types such as direction arrows as well as stubs including the start and end points of its plug-ins are not relevant to the matching algorithm and are therefore not mapped. These path node types are called map "white space".

The matching algorithm is a recursive algorithm that begins at a start point of the pointcut map and at each step scans the next relevant path node following the current path node on the pointcut map (i.e., map "white space" is skipped). If multiple branches leave or enter the current path node, all branches are considered in one step. The following step will then continue to consider all branches at once. If the matching algorithm finds a matching path node in the UCM model for the initial path node of the pointcut map, the matching algorithm scans the base UCM model and the pointcut map in parallel. At each step, the algorithm tries to match all next path nodes of the pointcut map against all next path nodes in the UCM model. This match requires all possible permutations to be considered. For example, let us assume that the matching algorithm has mapped an OR-fork from the pointcut map to an OR-fork in the UCM model and both OR-forks have two branches. Then, the first branch of the OR-fork on the pointcut map can be matched either against the first or second branch of the OR-fork in the UCM model. The same applies to the second branch. If more than one permutation can be matched against the path nodes on the pointcut map, the matching algorithm will continue to explore recursively each matched permutation as an individual match candidate.

At each step, new mappings are added to the result if the matching is successful. If the matching is not successful, the mappings established for the current match candidate are discarded and the candidate is not pursued further. The matching, however, continues with all other still valid permutations and their corresponding mappings. Matching may not be successful in one of the following cases:

- The next path node of the pointcut map cannot be matched against the next path node in the base UCM model (in case only one branch and therefore only one next path node has to be considered).
- The set of next path nodes of the point cut map cannot be matched against the set of next path nodes in the base UCM model (in case several branches have to be considered).
- The next path node or set of path nodes can be matched but a new mapping contradicts the already established mappings.

Finally, the matching algorithm takes cycles on the pointcut maps into account in order to avoid infinite loops by not further considering an already visited path node on the pointcut map. See Appendix A for more details on the matching algorithm.

The following criteria are taken into account to decide whether a path node in the pointcut map matches another path node. The names and types of the path nodes must match. The component names of the path nodes must match as well as the location of the path node in the component (first, last, or any path node in the component). Furthermore, the names of conditions have to be matched and the type of branch (e.g., timeout branch) has to be matched.

When matching a set of next path nodes on the pointcut map against another set of next path nodes, each matching pair of path nodes must fulfill the criteria listed in the previous paragraph. In addition, the current implementation requires the number of path nodes to be the same in each set for the match to be successful. Alternatively, the matching algorithm could provide an option to relax this requirement for any path node with multiple outgoing or incoming branches by allowing the set corresponding to a path node on the pointcut map to be smaller than the other set. For example, this would allow matching an OR-fork with two branches on the pointcut map against an OR-fork with two or more branches in the UCM model as long as two of these branches can be matched.

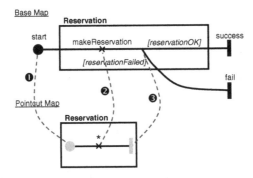

Fig. 16. Example of a mapping between pointcut map and base map

Figure 16 shows an example of a mapping that was established by the matching algorithm. The responsibilities are mapped to each other since the wildcard matches any name. Mappings 1 and 3 contain unnamed start and end points. In terms of the matching algorithm, one can think of unnamed start and end points as free matches. They can be matched with anything as long as they are matched to the path nodes that are closest to the other mappings.

While the mapping of the actual pointcut expression (in this case only the responsibility — see mapping 2) ensures that the pattern described by the pointcut map exists in the base map, the other two mappings (1 and 3) turn out to be the most useful in terms of providing the additional features mentioned at

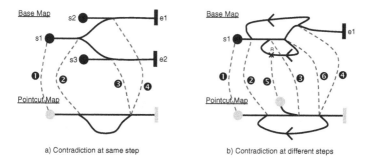

Fig. 17. Contradictory mappings

the beginning of Sect. 4 and discussed in greater detail in Sect. 4.2 and 4.4. Mappings 1 and 3 are so important because they help determine the joinpoints and insertion points associated with the joinpoints. The joinpoint in Fig. 16 is the responsibility in the base map.

As mentioned earlier in the bulleted list, contradictory mappings are the third reason for unsuccessful matches. One such case is illustrated in Fig. 17a. After matching the start point in the pointcut map to s1 in the base map (see mapping 1) and the OR-fork in the pointcut map to the OR-fork in the base map (see mapping 2), the next step attempts to match the successors of the OR-fork in the pointcut map with the successors of the OR-fork in the base map. In both cases, the successors are OR-joins (note that the OR-fork in the pointcut map also has two successors — one for each branch, but the two successors happen to be the same OR-join). For each successor individually, a match is possible (see mappings 3 and 4), but these two mappings contradict each other since the same path node in the pointcut map cannot be mapped to two different path nodes in the base map (or vice versa). Figure 17a shows a contradiction occurring at the same step. Figure 17b, on the other hand, shows a similar contradiction that appears at different steps of the matching algorithm (i.e., the new mapping 6 contradicts mapping 4 established by a previous step of the matching algorithm).

Note that the mappings of one pointcut map to a base map may overlap with mappings established for another pointcut map. Overlapping mappings, however, do not conflict with or contradict each other. See Sect. 4.4 for more details.

4.2 Composition Algorithm

Now that the joinpoints have been identified, the composition strategy for an AoUCM model is fairly straightforward. Given joinpoints, base maps, advice maps, pointcut maps, and plug-in bindings, the composed system is realized by adding *aspect stubs* to the base maps. One such stub links to the appropriate part of an advice map. The insertion points for the static stubs on the base maps are defined by the mappings of the joinpoints found by the matching algorithm. The plug-in bindings for the inserted stubs are also derived from the mappings of the joinpoints.

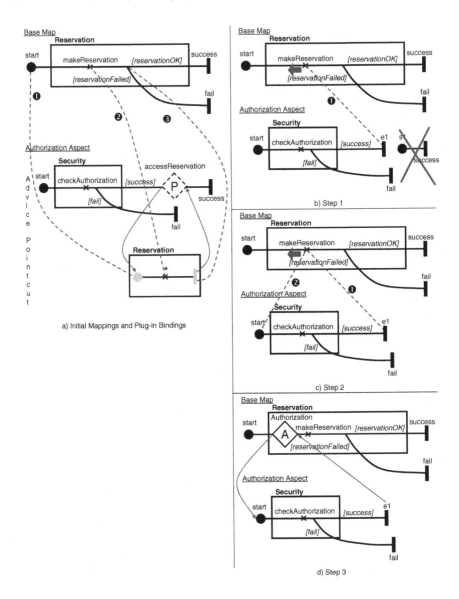

Fig. 18. Composition of aspect and base map

For an example of the composition algorithm, recall the authorization aspect from Fig. 14 and the mappings from Fig. 16 (repeated in Fig. 18a). Note the joinpoint (the responsibility in the base map). The right side of Fig. 18 shows the three steps involved in composing the system.

Step 1 removes the pointcut stub from the advice map while retaining the mappings to the base map. The removal of the pointcut requires new start and end points to be inserted into the advice map (s1 and e1 in Fig. 18b). Empty paths on the advice map are then removed from the advice map (see crossed out path in Fig. 18b) because no new behavior is added by empty paths. In this example advice is only added before the pointcut and therefore only one disjoint path exists after all empty paths are removed. If advice is added before and after the pointcut, then several disjoint paths exist after removing all empty paths.

An in-path of the pointcut stub turns into a new end point. The mapping for a new end point is found by following the plug-in binding of its associated in-path to the start point on the pointcut map. The mapping of the path node after this start point is retained (see mapping 2 in Fig. 18a and mapping 1 in Fig. 18b). An out-path of the pointcut stub turns into a new start point. The mapping for a new start point is found by following the plug-in binding of its associated out-path to the end point on the pointcut map. The mapping of the path node before this end point is retained. Note that if a pointcut stub contains multiple pointcut maps, several mappings are retained.

In addition, the direction towards the next closest mapping is also retained (see the large arrow called the *closest-mapping arrow* in Fig. 18b). The closest-mapping arrow points towards the path node in the base model identified by the mapping from the unnamed start or end point on the pointcut map (depending on which plug-in binding was followed from the pointcut stub). This is especially important for path nodes in the base map that can have more than one path node as successor or predecessor as the following or preceding mapping clearly identifies the successor or predecessor, respectively.

Step 2 scans the path on the advice map to find a corresponding start point for each new end point and a corresponding end point for each new start point. If no or more than one such start or end point can be found, the advice map is malformed and composition cannot proceed. The path is scanned backwards for new end points and forward for new start points. Once a start or end point is found, the same mapping as for the corresponding new end point or new start point, respectively, is created (see mapping 2 in Fig. 18c).

All that is left to do in step 3 is to insert the stub in the base map. The insertion point is the one associated with the joinpoint and the one towards which the closest-mapping arrow identified in step 1 is pointing. The inserted stub is bound to the same component as the joinpoint (in the example in Fig. 18, this path node is identified by the mapping in Step 1). Note that it is possible to specify with the UCM notation whether components on a plug-in map are contained in the component of the corresponding stub. In all presented examples, the components on a plug-in map are not contained in the component of the stub. Finally, the mappings are converted into plug-in bindings and thus, the aspect has been woven into the base map. Several stubs may have to be inserted for one advice map (e.g., if the same pointcut expression is matched successfully against many base maps or if one pointcut stub contains multiple pointcut maps that cause multiple successful matches). See Appendix B for more details on the composition algorithm.

There are a number of special cases that have to be taken into account by the composition algorithm: (a) insertion points before a start point or after an end point and (b) around advice. Figure 7 shows that insertion points exist before a start point or after an end point. These insertion points are required for named start or end points on a pointcut map which are matched against start or end points in the base map, respectively. At step 1 of the composition algorithm, named start points or named end points in pointcut maps receive special treatment when establishing the closest-mapping arrow. The closest-mapping arrow of a start point in the base map that is mapped to a named start point in the pointcut map always points to the insertion point before the start point. The closest-mapping arrow of an end point in the base map that is mapped to a named end point in the pointcut map always points to the insertion point after the end point. Consequently, a stub has to be inserted in the base map either before the mapped start point or after the mapped end point. A stub, however, cannot be simply inserted before a start point or after an end point. Additional start and end points are required as illustrated in Fig. 19 (see s1, e1, s2, and e2). Note that any plug-in bindings of the mapped start or end point have to be transferred to the new start or end point, respectively (e.g., from abc to s1 or xyz to e2 in Fig. 19).

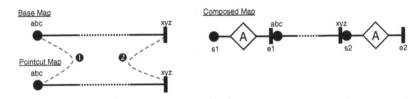

Fig. 19. Composition with named start and end points

The second special case involves around advice. Figure 20 introduces a new feature for the reservation example. Instead of using a waiting list, a reservation at a partner hotel is attempted and the reservation is added to the waiting list only if the reservation at the partner hotel also fails. In terms of the composition algorithm, the only differences to the example in Fig. 18 occur at steps 1 and 3. In step 1, the composition algorithm notices that both, a new start point and a new end point, exist in one path on the advice map (see s1 and e1 in Fig. 20b). This indicates around advice. Because of that, the stubs inserted into the base map in step 3 are marked with A↓ and A↑ in order to highlight that the path segment between the two stubs may be skipped. In the example in Fig. 20, this occurs if the reservation at the partner hotel is successful. The stubs A↓ and A↑ represent the entrance and exit of a tunnel underneath the base map that can be used to circumvent the path segment between the two stubs.

The around advice in Fig. 20 is a weak kind of around advice as the base behavior is not overridden all the time by the aspect. Strong around advice can be indicated even more clearly. Let us assume that the book with hotel partner feature is replacing the waiting list behavior. This is certainly not good customer service but let us ignore this for one moment for the sake of this example. Then,

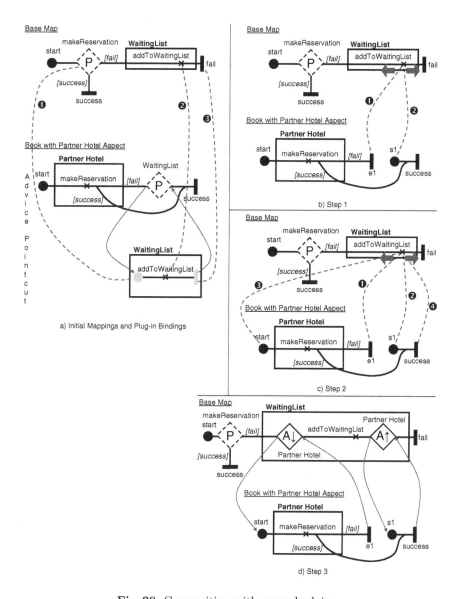

Fig. 20. Composition with around advice

the aspect could be described as in Fig. 21a. The [true] branch is always taken regardless of whether the reservation at the partner hotel was successful or not. The [false] branch is never taken, therefore causing the waiting list behavior to be replaced. The resulting composed system uses stubs without in-paths or out-paths as in Fig. 21b to highlight that the behavior between the stubs is replaced by the aspect. The difference for the composition algorithm lies in step 1 where, in addition to identifying new start and end points on the same path

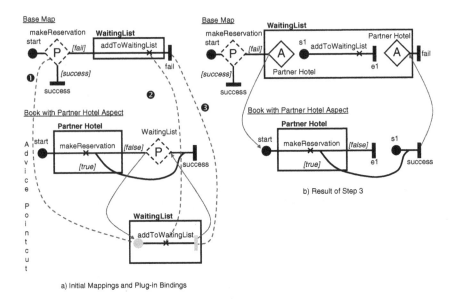

Fig. 21. Composition with strong around advice

on the advice map, the algorithm also performs a scan of the advice map that reveals the existence of a [false] branch leading directly to the pointcut stub. This indicates a strong around advice. In step 3, the stubs without in-paths or out-paths are used and additional start and end points have to be added for the path segment between the two **Partner Hotel** stubs (s1 and e1 in the base map of Fig. 21b.

Note that the replaced path between the **Partner Hotel** stubs in Fig. 21b can optionally be deleted from the base map by the composition algorithm as the path does not serve any purpose in the composed system anymore. It is also possible to merge the two **Partner Hotel** stubs into one stub. This, however, can only be done if the stubs are on the same map. The example in Fig. 21 shows the general case where the two stubs could be on different maps and merging is not possible.

Besides illustrating around advice, this example also shows that aspects can be defined on other aspects because the base map in Fig. 20 is an advice map and is only a base map relative to the book with hotel partner aspect.

4.3   Complete Example of Composed System

The complete composed system is shown in Fig. 22. It is very similar to the non-aspectual UCM model in Fig. 5 except that no root maps are used but the impact of other concerns is shown directly on the maps for making and canceling a reservation. Multiple disjoint plug-in maps for making or canceling a reservation are therefore avoided. The authorization stubs appear in making and canceling a reservation but they are added automatically by the composition algorithm.

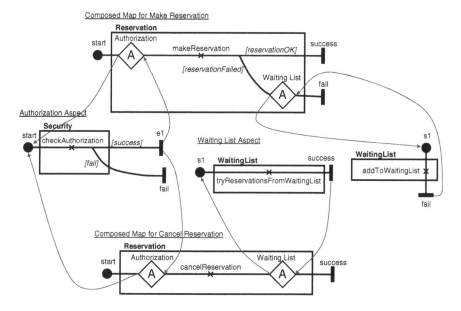

Fig. 22. Composed system

Therefore, they are less of a concern in terms of scalability and maintainability of the model.

4.4 Beyond Matching and Composition

The joinpoints and mappings identified as a result of the matching algorithm are the base of further functionality besides composition. For example, it is possible now

a. to easily indicate on UCMs whether a path node is advised,
b. to easily indicate on advice maps which path nodes on which UCMs are being advised by the aspect,
c. to warn the requirements engineer if multiple aspects are advising the same path node (A simple way of indicating this is to add a dynamic stub to the base map instead of the static stub shown in the examples. The dynamic stub contains a plug-in map for each aspect and a conflict resolution mechanism based on simple precedence rules is used. A precedence rule states that aspect A has to precede aspect B. If no precedence rule is specified, the order is chosen randomly.), and
d. to warn the requirements engineer if the same pointcut advises the same path node in multiple ways (For example see Fig. 23, given a pointcut map containing only an OR-fork with two branches, the OR-fork can be matched against all OR-forks in the UCM model in two ways. The first branch of the OR-fork in the UCM model can be mapped to the first or second branch of

the OR-fork on the pointcut map and the second branch of the OR-fork in
the UCM model can be mapped to the second or first branch of the OR-
fork on the pointcut map, respectively. If advice is being added before this
pointcut, then the same advice would be added twice at the same insertion
point — once for each matched permutation of the OR-fork branches. If
multiple matches of the same pointcut map are not desired, the requirements
engineer can use the warning to modify the pointcut map in order to resolve
the multiple matches.).

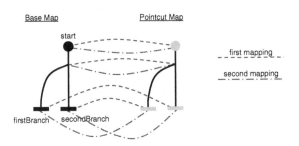

Fig. 23. Multiple mappings of pointcut map

Overlapping mappings from two pointcut maps to a base map do not conflict
with or contradict each other because only the mappings that identify joinpoints
are important. If the latter mappings overlap, then case (c) occurs for which a
conflict resolution mechanism exists.

A phenomenon that is called emergent behavior in the feature interaction
community can also be observed when aspects and the base are composed together, possibly resulting in unexpected behavior. Undesired emergent behavior occurs when an aspect and the base work well individually but not when
combined together. The feature interaction research carried out for UCMs does
apply to AoUCM and can be used to deal with conflicts caused by undesired
emergent behavior. The UCM scenario definitions can be used to describe the
pre-conditions and post-conditions as well as start and expected end points of
aspects and base behavior alike. After composing the system, the scenario definitions can be checked to ensure that no pre-conditions and post-conditions
have been violated and all expected end points are reached. Essentially, UCM
scenarios allow a high-level test suite to be built for the UCM model.

Finally, the descriptions of the matching and composition algorithms in the
previous sections only deal with one pointcut map. In order to compose a UCM
model containing many aspects, one needs to ensure that each pointcut map is
matched against the same base model. When a pointcut map is matched against
the base model, the identified joinpoints can be indicated in the original model
because this does not influence the matching algorithm for the next aspect. Composition, however, does change the structure of the UCM model and therefore
influences the matching algorithm. Therefore, the composition algorithm first
creates a copy of the existing UCM model which can then be safely changed by

the composition algorithm. When the next aspect is added incrementally to the system, the original base model is used to identify the joinpoints for the new aspect. Based on the joinpoints and the original base model, the composition algorithm then makes further changes to the copy of the base model in order to weave the new aspect into the system. The order in which aspects are dealt with, however, is irrelevant for the matching and composition algorithms presented in this paper.

5 Conclusion and Future Work

This paper is the first to discuss in detail AoUCM and algorithms for tool support. It shows how to define aspects with UCMs, presents an algorithm for matching pointcut expressions (defined by pointcut maps) against maps in the UCM model, presents an algorithm for composing and visualizing aspects and the base model together, and extends the URN metamodel with aspect concepts. Compared to other scenario-based approaches to aspect-oriented requirements engineering, AoUCM do not require any new notational concepts, aspects can be modeled unobtrusively, and everything can be modeled visually for an aspect, including parameterized pointcut expressions.

No new notational concepts. AoUCM make use of the same set of modeling elements as traditional UCMs, making it easier to switch from traditional modeling to aspect-oriented modeling. Most significantly, stubs are used to link advice and pointcut expression as well as to visualize the composed system. Jacobson and Ng [25] add the concept of pointcut to use case modeling and change the meaning of extension points. Moreira et al. [12, 28, 29] require several extensions to UML diagrams in order to visualize aspects. Zdun and Strembeck [42] add start and end nodes for aspects. Whittle and Araújo [13, 41], de Bruin and van Vliet [22], as well as Barros and Gomes [15], however, do not require changes to modeling notations (note that stereotyping does not really change the modeling notation).

Modeled unobtrusively. AoUCM allow aspects to be defined without influencing the base model as parameterized pointcut expressions are linked with the base through a matching algorithm. This is a crucial point of aspect-orientation often referred to as obliviousness as the base model must not be polluted by aspect-specific information. Jacobson and Ng violate this point by requiring extension points to be defined in the base. Similarly, de Bruin and van Vliet require Pre and Post stubs to be added to the base model. All other techniques mentioned in the paragraph above, however, model aspects also unobtrusively. Note that the approach by Zdun and Strembeck is not applicable to this category because it is not concerned with defining aspects but visualizing the composed system only.

Visual aspects (including parameterized pointcuts). AoUCM can model visually every part of an aspect including parameterized pointcuts, therefore avoiding a modeling paradigm break. Visual models are usually the preferred choice at higher levels of abstractions. The parameterization is achieved through the use of wildcards but this use of text is minimal. Parameterization of point-cut expressions is important to address scalability issues. Jacobson and Ng use textual expression to define parameterized pointcut expressions. Note that the extend relationship for use case diagrams is a visual representation of a pointcut but does not contain enough information and therefore has to rely on the textual representation. The binding rules used by Whittle and Araújo and composition rules used by Moreira et al. are represented in a textual way. Furthermore, these rules explicitly link one element with another and do not allow parameterized expressions. Barros and Gomes also use a textual representation of pointcuts and also explicitly link nodes in UML activity diagrams, not allowing parameterized expressions. de Bruin and van Vliet define aspects (refinement maps) in a visual way but use limited type matching to merge behavior and structure from the aspect with the base model. Zdun and Strembeck's approach again is not applicable to this category.

In previous work, Mussbacher et al. [31] compared composition techniques of several scenario-based approaches to aspect-oriented requirements engineering and concluded that AoUCM have a **flexible and exhaustive composition technique** with significant advantages over the other approaches mentioned in this section.

In terms of abstraction levels, UCMs are at the same level as the techniques used by Jacobson and Ng, Barros and Gomes, and Zdun and Strembeck. Note that the examples in Barros and Gomes represent rather low-level control flow but that activity diagrams can also be used to describe high-level workflow. UCMs abstract from message and data details. UCMs can therefore be used earlier than message-based behavioral models but also contain more information than UML use case diagrams. Therefore, UCMs are at a **higher level of abstraction** than the work by Whittle and Araújo which is at the message/state machine level. Moreira et al. make use of some models that are at the same and some models that are at a lower level of abstraction than UCMs.

Furthermore, UCMs **model the whole system** making it possible to reason about interactions between various use cases or scenarios. UCMs have already been used not only for scenario interaction detection but also for performance analysis and testing purposes. By applying these research results to the composed UCM model containing the base and aspects, it is possible to achieve greater confidence in the model at a very early stage in the development. This is an advantage over all other techniques mentioned in this section as these techniques model scenarios in isolation.

This paper reports on the first results of a much larger research goal. In the long term, we plan to also extend the GRL part of URN with aspects and synchronize the extensions to the GRL part with the extensions to the UCM part. The matching and composition algorithms have been implemented and tested and will soon be available in an official release of the jUCMNav tool. A case study of a non-trivial e-commerce application is also underway which we hope will further illustrate the benefits of our approach. UCMs have already been used to model systems of significant sizes. Initial results suggest that AoUCM further improve the scalability of UCMs. Finally, some aspects inherently exist in UCMs. As UCMs abstract from message and data details, a simple path going from one component to another may represent a very complex interaction between these two entities, possibly involving multiple message exchanges. Aspects could define such interactions and would allow UCMs to more easily be moved forward to the next abstraction level.

Acknowledgments

This research was supported by the Natural Sciences and Engineering Research Council of Canada, through its programs of Discovery Grants and Postgraduate Scholarships, and by the Ontario Research Network on e-Commerce.

References

[1] Abdelaziz, T., Elammari, M., Unland, R.: Visualizing a Multiagent-Based Medical Diagnosis System Using a Methodology Based on Use Case Maps. In: Lindemann-v. Trzebiatowski, G., Denzinger, J., Timm, I.J., Unland, R. (eds.) MATES 2004. LNCS (LNAI), vol. 3187, pp. 198–212. Springer, Heidelberg (2004)

[2] Alencar, F., Moreira, A., Araújo, J., Castro, J., Silva, C., Mylopoulos J.: Using Aspects to Simplify i* Models. In: 14th IEEE International Requirements Engineering Conference (RE 06), Minneapolis, USA (September 2006)

[3] Amyot, D., Logrippo, L.: Use Case Maps and LOTOS for the Prototyping and Validation of a Mobile Group Call System. Computer Communication 23(12), 1135–1157 (2000)

[4] Amyot, D., Charfi, L., Gorse, N., Gray, T., Logrippo, L., Sincennes, J., Stepien, B., Ware, T.: Feature Description and Feature Interaction Analysis with Use Case Maps and LOTOS. In: Feature Interactions in Telecommunications and Software Systems VI, Glasgow, Scotland, UK, pp. 274–289. IOS Press, Amsterdam (2000)

[5] Amyot, D., Roy, J.-F., Weiss, M.: UCM-Driven Testing of Web Applications. In: Prinz, A., Reed, R., Reed, J. (eds.) SDL 2005. LNCS, vol. 3530, pp. 247–264. Springer, Heidelberg (2005)

[6] Amyot, D., Weiss, M., Logrippo, L.: UCM-Based Generation of Test Purposes. Computer Networks 49(5), 643–660 (2005)

[7] Amyot, D.: Introduction to the User Requirements Notation: Learning by Example. Computer Networks 42(3), 285–301 (2003)

[8] Andrade, R.: Applying Use Case Maps and Formal Methods to the Development of Wireless Mobile ATM Networks. In: Lfm2000: Fifth NASA Langley Formal Methods Workshop, Williamsburg, Virginia, USA, pp. 151–162 (June 2000)

[9] AOSD Community Wiki Research Projects: (accessed February 2007), http://aosd.net/wiki/index.php?title=Research_Projects

[10] AOSD Community Wiki Tools for Developers: (accessed February 2007), http://aosd.net/wiki/index.php?title=Tools_for_Developers

[11] Araújo, J., Coutinho, P.: Identifying Aspectual Use Cases Using a Viewpoint-Oriented Requirements Method. Early Aspects 2003: Aspect-Oriented Requirements Engineering and Architecture Design. In: Workshop of the 2nd International Conference on Aspect-Oriented Software Development (AOSD), Boston, USA (March 2003)

[12] Araújo, J., Moreira, A.: An Aspectual Use Case Driven Approach. VIII Jornadas de Ingeniería de Software y Bases de Datos (JISBD 2003), Alicante, Spain (November 2003)

[13] Araújo, J., Whittle, J., Kim, D.: Modeling and Composing Scenario-Based Requirements with Aspects. In: Proceedings of the 12th IEEE International Requirements Engineering Conference (RE 04), Kyoto, Japan, pp. 58–67. IEEE Computer Society Press, Los Alamitos (September 2004)

[14] AspectJ web site (cited February 2007), http://www.eclipse.org/aspectj/

[15] Barros, J.-P., Gomes, L.: Toward the Support for Crosscutting Concerns in Activity Diagrams: a Graphical Approach. In: Stevens, P., Whittle, J., Booch, G. (eds.) UML 2003 - The Unified Modeling Language. Modeling Languages and Applications. LNCS, vol. 2863, Springer, Heidelberg (2003)

[16] Billard, E.A.: Operating system scenarios as Use Case Maps. In: 4th International Workshop on Software and Performance (WOSP 2004), Redwood Shores, California, USA, pp. 266–277 (January 2004)

[17] Buhr, R.J.A., Casselman, R.S.: Use Case Maps for Object-Oriented Systems. Prentice-Hall, Englewood Cliffs (1995)

[18] Buhr, R.J.A.: A Possible Design Notation for Aspect Oriented Programming. In: Jul, E. (ed.) ECOOP 1998. LNCS, vol. 1445, Springer, Heidelberg (1998)

[19] Buhr, R.J.A.: Use Case Maps as Architectural Entities for Complex Systems. IEEE Transactions on Software Engineering 24(12), 1131–1155 (1998)

[20] Chitchyan, R., et al.: Survey of Analysis and Design Approaches. AOSD-Europe Report ULANC-9 (accessed February 2007) (May 2005), http://www.aosd-europe.net/deliverables/d11.pdf

[21] Clarke, S., Baniassad, E.: Aspect-Oriented Analysis and Design: The Theme Approach. Addison-Wesley, Reading (2005)

[22] de Bruin, H., van Vliet, H.: Quality-Driven Software Architecture Composition. Journal of Systems and Software 66(3), 269–284 (2003)

[23] Elammari, M., Lalonde, W.: An Agent-Oriented Methodology: High-Level View and Intermediate Models. In: 1st International Workshop on Agent-Oriented Information Systems (AOIS), Heidelberg, Germany (June 1999)

[24] Gross, D., Yu, E.: Dealing with System Qualities During Design and Composition of Aspects and Modules: An Agent and Goal-Oriented Approach. In: Proceedings of the 1st International Workshop on Traceability in Emerging Forms of Software Engineering, Automated Software Engineering Conference, Edinburgh, U.K, pp. 1–8 (October 2002)

[25] Jacobson, I., Ng, P.-W.: Aspect-Oriented Software Development with Use Cases. Addison-Wesley, Reading (2005)

[26] Kiczales, G., Lamping, J., Mendhekar, A., Maeda, C., Lopes, C., Loingtier, J.-M., Irwin, J.: Aspect-Oriented Programming. In: Aksit, M., Matsuoka, S. (eds.) ECOOP 1997. LNCS, vol. 1241, pp. 220–242. Springer, Heidelberg (1997)

[27] Miga, A.: Application of Use Case Maps to System Design with Tool Support. MEng thesis, Department of Systems and Computer Engineering, Carleton University, Ottawa, Canada (cited February 2007) (October 1998), http://www.UseCaseMaps.org/tools/ucmnav

[28] Moreira, A., Araújo, J.: Handling Unanticipated Requirements Change with Aspects. In: Proceedings of the 16th International Conference on Software Engineering and Knowledge Engineering (SEKE), Banff, Canada (June 2004)

[29] Moreira, A., Araújo, J., Brito, I.: Crosscutting Quality Attributes for Requirements Engineering. In: Proceedings of the 14th Internatinal Conference on Software Engineering and Knowledge Engineering (SEKE), Ischia, Italy, pp. 167–174. ACM Press, New York (2002)

[30] Mussbacher, G., Amyot, D., Weiss M.: Visualizing Aspect-Oriented Requirements Scenarios with Use Case Maps. In: International Workshop on Requirements Engineering Visualization (REV 2006), Minneapolis, USA (September 11, 2006)

[31] Mussbacher, G., Amyot, D., Whittle, J., Weiss M.: Flexible and Expressive Composition Rules with Aspect-oriented Use Case Maps (AoUCM). In: 10th International Workshop on Early Aspects (EA 2007), Vancouver, Canada (March 13, 2007)

[32] Rashid, A., Moreira, A., Araújo, J.: Modularisation and Composition of Aspectual Requirements. In: Proceedings of the 2nd International Conference on Aspect-Oriented Software Development, Boston, USA, pp. 11–20. ACM Press, New York (2003)

[33] Roy, J.-F., Kealey, J., Amyot, D.: Towards Integrated Tool Support for the User Requirements Notation. In: Gotzhein, R., Reed, R. (eds.) SAM 2006. LNCS, vol. 4320, pp. 183–197. Springer, Heidelberg (May 2006) (accessed February 2007), http://www.softwareengineering.ca/jucmnav

[34] Scratchley, W.C., Woodside, C.M.: Evaluating Concurrency Options in Software Specifications. In: 7th International Symposium on Modeling, Analysis and Simulation of Computer and Telecommunication Systems (MASCOTS), College Park, MD, USA, pp. 330–338 (October 1999)

[35] Siddiqui, K.H., Woodside, C.M.: Performance aware software development (PASD) using resource demand budgets. In: Workshop on Software and Performance (WOSP), Rome, Italy, pp. 275–285 (July 2002)

[36] Tarr, P., Ossher, H., Harrison, W., Sutton, S.M.: N degrees of separation: Multidimensional separation of concerns. In: Proceedings of the 21st International Conference on Software Engineering (ICSE 99), pp. 107–119. ACM press, NewYork (1999)

[37] URN - Goal-oriented Requirement Language (GRL), ITU-T Draft Recommendation Z.151. Geneva, Switzerland (September 2003), (accessed February 2007), http://www.UseCaseMaps.org/urn

[38] URN – Use Case Map Notation (UCM), ITU-T Draft Recommendation Z.152. Geneva, Switzerland (September 2003) (accessed February 2007), http://www.UseCaseMaps.org/urn

[39] User Requirements Notation (URN) Language Requirements and Framework, ITU-T Recommendation Z.150. Geneva, Switzerland (February 2003) (accessed February 2007), http://www.itu.int/ITU-T/publications/recs.html

[40] Weiss, M., Amyot, D.: Business Process Modeling with URN. International Journal of E-Business Research 1(3), 63–90 (2005)

[41] Whittle, J., Araújo, J.: Scenario Modelling with Aspects. IEEE Proceedings Software 151(4), 157–172 (2004)

[42] Zdun, U., Strembeck, M.: Modeling the Evolution of Aspect Configurations using Model Transformations. In: Proceedings of the Linking Aspect Technology and Evolution Workshop (LATE), Bonn, Germany (March 2006)

A   Matching Algorithm

A high level summary of the algorithm follows, showing how one pointcut map is matched against the UCM model. In addition to the two operations matchPointcutMap and match, two more, rather straightforward operations were implemented. The first operation decides, given two path nodes, whether the two path nodes match according to the criteria mentioned in Sect. 4.1. It is used by matchPointcutMap. The second operation finds, given two sets of path nodes, all permutations that match elements in one set against elements in the other. It is used by match. Note that (a) each element in one set has to be matched against exactly one element in the other set and vice versa, and that (b) the second operation makes use of the first to match individual elements.

```
Operation: matchPointcutMap

Input: UCMPointcutMap pointcutMap, UCMmodel baseUCM

Output: MappingsList

Exception: NoMatchFound (if match is unsuccessful)

begin // matchPointcutMap
    MappingsList resultMappingsList = Ø
    PathNode initPointcutNode = pointcutMap.getInitialPathNode()
    foreach PathNode pn in baseUCM
        if initPointcutNode matches pn then
            MappingsList firstMapping = Ø
            add new Mapping(initPointcutNode, pn) to firstMapping
            try
                // Match next path nodes of initPointcutNode against next path nodes of
                // pn and return matchList (which contains firstMapping plus
                // new mappings found by match()).
                MappingsList matchList = match(initPointcutNode, pn, firstMapping)
                add matchList to resultMappingsList
            endtry
            catch NoMatchFound
                // Do nothing and continue for loop (this gives initPointcutNode a
                // chance to be matched against other path nodes in the UCM model).
            endcatch
        endif
    endforeach// PathNode
    if resultMappingsList == Ø then
        throw new NoMatchFound() // No mapping found at all.
    endif
    return resultMappingsList
end // matchPointcutMap


Operation: match

Input: PathNode pointcutNode, PathNode baseNode, MappingsList currentMappings

Output: MappingsList

Exception: NoMatchFound (if match is unsuccessful)

begin // match
    if pointcutNode does not have any next path nodes then
        return currentMappings // Stops recursion.
```

endif
// Else, there are still path nodes to match.
MappingsList finalMappingsList = ∅
// In order to match the next path nodes, all permutations of these path nodes
// have to be considered. Hence the need for the first for loop!
// The resulting permutations contain all possible mappings between all next
// path nodes of pointcutNode and all next path nodes of baseNode.
// These mappings can be accessed with getMappings() for each
// permutation. A match is successful if at least one permutation can be
// matched recursively.
Find all matching permutations of baseNode's next path nodes
foreach permutation p **in** the found permutations
    MappingsList permutationMappings = ∅
    // The following if statement catches an invalid permutation because the
    // mappings for the permutation contradict already established mappings.
    // Therefore, discard this permutation and move on to the next.
    if currentMappings contradict p.getMappings()
        then continue with next loop iteration
    endif
    copy currentMappings **to** permutationMappings
    add p.getMappings() **to** permutationMappings
    try
        MappingsList mergeResult = ∅
        // For each mapping in the current permutation a recursive match has to
        // be attempted. Hence, the need for the second for loop! There are two fail
        // cases: 1) the recursive match cannot find any matching path elements
        // (match() is not successful) or 2) the merging of all mappings causes
        // contradictory mappings (merge is not successful).
        foreach mapping pointcutNode2 to baseNode2 **in** p.getMappings()
            // Match recursively next path nodes of pointcutNode2 against next
            // path nodes of baseNode2 and return mappingsList (which contains
            // permutationMappings plus new mappings found by match()).
            // Match() throws NoMatchFound exception if not successful.
            MappingsList recursionResult = match(pointcutNode2, baseNode2,
                            permutationMappings)
            // At this point, the results need to be merged. This is necessary
            // because in each pass of the for loop a branch is explored recursively
            // and a match is only found if the results from all branches together
            // make sense (i.e. they do not contradict each other). Merge also
            // throws NoMatchFound exception if not successful.
            merge recursionResult **with** mergeResult
        endforeach // mapping
        add mergeResult **to** finalMappingsList
    endtry
    catch NoMatchFound

```
                      // Do nothing and continue for loop (this gives the next permutation a
                      // chance).
                  endcatch
              endforeach // permutation
              if finalMappingsList == ∅ then
                  throw new NoMatchFound()
              endif
              return finalMappingsList
          end // match
```

B   Composition Algorithm

A high level summary of the algorithm follows, showing how one aspect is woven into the base model. The result of the algorithm is a list of UCMs that were changed by the composition of the given aspect. In addition to the operation composeAspect, three more operations were implemented: removePointcutStubs, scan, and insert-Stub. Descriptions of these operations can be found in the comments below.

```
Operation: composeAspect
Input: Aspect aspect, UCMmodel baseUCM, MappingsList mappingsList
Output: UCMmapList
Exception: MalformedAdviceMap, CompositionNotRequired
begin // composeAspect
    UCMmapList updatedMaps = ∅
    foreach UCMadviceMap am of aspect
        // Removing all pointcut stubs from the advice map results in one or more
        // disjoint paths on the advice map. In-paths are replaced by end points.
        // Out-paths are replaced by start points. Empty paths are deleted before
        // proceeding. For each new start and end point on the advice map, the
        // following is created based on mappingsList:
        // a) mapping(s) to the base model
        // b) reference(s) to the closest path node in the base model with a mapping
        // from the pointcut map (not necessary for start/end points mapped to
        // named start/end points on pointcut map)
        // In the simplest case, there is only one mapping and one reference because,
        // there is only one pointcut map that is matched against one base map.
        // However, several mappings and references may have to be established
        // because one pointcut map may be matched against many base maps and
        // also because one pointcut stub may contain several pointcut maps.
        // In addition, a path that contains both (new start and end points) is marked
        // as around advice. An around advice that contains a false branch leading
        // directly to a new end point is marked as strong around advice.
        MappedUCMmap disjointPaths = am.removePointcutStubs(mappingsList)
        // Only consider this advice map if it was possible to match the pointcut
        // expression (in this case a mapping to the base model exists)
        if disjointPaths.getNumberOfMappedPathNodes() > 0 then
```

```
          add disjointPaths to updatedMaps
          foreach mapped PathNode pn of disjointPaths
                    // A mapped path node is either a new start point or a new end point.
                    // Scan disjointPaths to find the corresponding end or start point,
                    // respectively. In case of a new start point, DisjointPath is scanned
                    // forward. In case of a new end point, DisjointPath is scanned
                    // backwards. Scan throws a MalformedAdviceMap exception if no or
                    // more than one corresponding path node is found.
                    PathNode correspondingPathNode = disjointPaths.scan(pn)
                    // Remembering the correspondingPathNode for each pn essentially
                    // duplicates the mapping from pn to the path node in the base model
                    // for the correspondingPathNode.
                    pn.addCorrespondingPathNode(correspondingPathNode)
          endforeach// PathNode
          foreach mapped PathNode pn of disjointPaths
                    // Go through all mappings and references created by
                    // removePointcutStubs
                    foreach Mapping m of pn
                              // Insert a stub at the path node in the base model identified by m
                              // (see (a) above). The insertion point is on the path segment
                              // towards the referenced path node of pn for the mapping m (see
                              // (b) above). Plug-in bindings are also established from the stub to
                              // pn and to pn.getCorrespondingPathNode.
                              // If a stub has already been inserted at the same location, a new
                              // stub is not inserted but the existing stub is made dynamic (if it is
                              // static) and only a new plug-in map is added.
                              // If the path of pn is marked as around advice, then the inserted
                              // stub is labeled with up and down indicators.
                              // If the path of pn is marked as strong around advice, then the out-
                              // path or in-path of the inserted stub is removed (if pn is an end or
                              // start point, respectively). The corresponding plug-in binding is also
                              // removed.
                              UCMmap updatedBaseMap = m.getBaseMap().insertStub(m)
                              add updatedBaseMap to updatedMaps
                    endforeach// Mapping
          endforeach// PathNode
     endif
  endforeach// UCMadviceMap
  if updatedMaps == Ø then
          // No composition occurred because no mappings were established.
          throw new CompositionNotRequired()
  endif
  return updatedMaps
end // composeAspect
```

Handling Conflicts in Aspectual Requirements Compositions

Isabel Sofia Brito[1], Filipe Vieira[2], Ana Moreira[2], and Rita A. Ribeiro[3]

[1] Escola Superior de Tecnologia e Gestão, Instituto Politécnico de Beja, Portugal
isabel.sofia@estig.ipbeja.pt
[2] CITI/Departamento de Informática, Universidade Nova de Lisboa, Portugal
fil.vieira@gmail.com, amm@di.fct.unl.pt
[3] UNINOVA, Portugal
rar@uninova.pt

Abstract. Composing aspectual concerns with base concerns may raise conflicting situations that need to be identified and resolved. A conflict is detected whenever two or more concerns that contribute negatively to each other and have the same importance need to be composed together. This paper discusses the use of Multiple Criteria Decision Making (MCDM) methods to support aspectual conflict management in the context of Aspect-Oriented Requirements Engineering. The final solution relies on the use of the obtained concern rankings to handle unresolved conflicts. An illustrative example is presented to discuss how MCDM methods can be used for aspectual conflict handling.

1 Introduction

Certain specific types of concerns span traditional module boundaries (for example, classes in an object-oriented decomposition). Concerns of this nature, known as *crosscutting concerns* [3, 12], are responsible for producing tangled representations that are difficult to understand and to evolve. A *concern* refers to a matter of interest which addresses a certain problem that is important to one or more stakeholders. Aspect-oriented software development (AOSD) [3, 12] aims at addressing crosscutting concerns by providing means for their systematic identification, separation, representation and composition [18]. Crosscutting concerns are encapsulated in separate modules, known as *aspects* [15], and composition mechanisms are later used to weave them back with other core modules.

This paper is based on our previous work on Aspect-Oriented Requirements Engineering (AORE) [6, 7] focusing on the conflict management problem, also discussed in [17, 18]. In [6] we proposed three main activities to support AORE: identify concerns, specify concerns and compose concerns. In this current paper we concentrate on the composition activity, where conflicting situations may emerge in a given match point. A match point identifies specific locations in the base concerns where other concerns' behavior (crosscutting or non-crosscutting) should be satisfied [7]. In this context, a conflict occurs any time two or more concerns that contribute

A. Rashid and M. Aksit (Eds.): Transactions on AOSD III, LNCS 4620, pp. 144–166, 2007.

negatively to each other, and have the same importance, need to be composed in the same match point. For example, consider the case where a given module, which was conceived to model or implement a given functionality of a system, needs to be secure and to react in a very short period of time. Based on some catalogues, for example the NFR Framework [11], security and response time contribute negatively to each other, i.e. the more secure we want our module to be, the less fast it may become, and vice-versa. This means that the system may not be able to satisfy both concerns with the same degree of importance. Therefore, the satisfaction of these two particular concerns may lead to a number of architecture choices that would serve their needs with varying levels of satisfaction. A discussion about the side effects of this problem can be found in [17]. For this reason, it is important to understand well each concern, study the level of impact that each one may have on others and decide on their relative importance before any solution decision is made. As explained in [17], the optimal architecture is the one that involves architectural choices satisfying each concern within some acceptable limits. These limits are derived from discussion with stakeholders. The work presented in this paper aims at supporting such discussions and subsequent negotiations.

It is worth pointing out that conflict management is a real problem, regardless of whether or not one uses AOSD to handle it. The difference is that in traditional software development methods, such as object-oriented methods, several distinct base modules would need to include security and response time behaviors, while in AOSD, both security and response time behaviors are modularized and each one implemented as a separate aspect. Approaches like [1, 19] identify possible inconsistencies between what is wanted and what is possible to meet. In other words, the selection process encompasses the balancing of conflicting interests between stakeholders.

Considering that Multiple Criteria Decision Making (MCDM) techniques offer the possibility to find, given a set of alternatives and a set of decision criteria, the best alternative, the contribution of this paper is, therefore, to propose the use of MCDM methods to support conflict management resolution. To solve MCDM problems many types of techniques have been proposed (see for instance [25]): direct scoring and ranking methods, trade-off schemes, distance-based methods, value and utility functions, interactive methods. The selected method was the Analytical Hierarchical Process (AHP) [20] with a simpler aggregation process [24]. The main reason why the AHP method was selected is that it allows pairwise comparisons (a kind of trade-off and interactive method), which seems appropriate to handle the kind of problems in hand. Moreover, AHP helps guarantee the logical consistency of many human-based judgments, as well as synthesizing a wide-range of data in a single solution. The end result is a list of concerns ranked according to a set of criteria. This list of ranked concerns will lead the choice of the system's architecture design, as previously mentioned. In addition, we also compare the results obtained with the AHP method with the classical weighted average decision matrix [21] to assess the selected method.

This paper is organized as follows: Sect. 2 introduces an AORE model and briefly introduces how other AORE approaches handle conflicts. Section 3 gives an overview on MCDM. Section 4 discusses our proposal to handle conflicts in AORE, illustrates the main ideas with an example and discusses the obtained results. Section 5 compares the results obtained by the application of the AHP method with those obtained by using the simple weighted average for aggregation. Section 6 discusses some related work and Sect. 7 concludes our work and points directions for future work.

2 Aspect-Oriented Requirements Analysis Approach

From the AORE approaches studied (e.g., [4, 6, 13, 17, 18]), the Aspect-Oriented Requirements Analysis (AORA) approach [6, 7] is the one that collects enough information during requirements to allow a direct use of MCDM techniques. Therefore, this approach was chosen for this work. AORA defines three primary tasks, each one divided into several subtasks, as illustrated in Fig. 1. These tasks can be accomplished iteratively and incrementally.

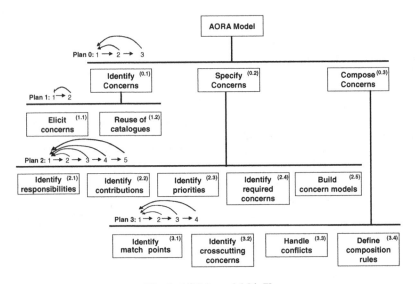

Fig. 1. AORA model [6, 7]

2.1 Identify Concerns

This task aims at identifying the concerns of a system, where a *concern* refers to a matter of interest which addresses a certain problem that is of importance to one or more stakeholders. Such a concern can be defined as a set of coherent requirements, defining a property that the future system must provide. This can be accomplished by analyzing the initial requirements, transcripts of stakeholders' interviews, etc. Good sources for concern identification are the existing catalogues, such as the non-functional requirements catalogue offered by Chung et al. [11].

2.2 Specify Concerns

This task is composed of several subtasks whose main goal is to collect several types of information about a concern, store that information in a template (see Table 1) and build concern visual models (e.g., UML use case, interaction and class diagrams [22]).

Table 1. A template to specify concerns

Concern Elements	Definition
Name	Concern designation.
Description	Short description of the intended behaviour of the concern.
Sources	Source of information, e.g., stakeholders, documents, system's domain, catalogues and business process.
Stakeholders	Entities (person or organization) that have an interest in a particular decision. This includes people who influence a decision, or can influence it, as well as those affected by it.
Decomposition	Concerns can be decomposed into simpler ones based on AND and OR relationships. When all (sub) concerns are needed to achieve the concern, we have an AND relationship. If not all the sub concerns are necessary to achieve the concern, we have an OR relationship.
Classification	Helps the selection of the most appropriate approach to model the concern (e.g. functional, NFR [11]).
Type	This element states if the concern is crosscutting or non-crosscutting. This information is derived based on the "Required Concerns" (below).
List of Responsibilities	
Responsibility #	List of what the concern must perform; knowledge or proprieties the concern must offer.
List of Contributions	
Contribution #	List of concerns that contribute/affect this concern. This contribution can be positive (**+**) or negative (**-**).
List of Importance	
Stakeholders' Importance	Expresses the importance of the concern for a given stakeholder. It can take the values: *Very Important, Important, Medium, Low, Very Low* and *Don't Care.*
List of Required Concerns	
Required Concerns#	List of concerns needed or requested by the concern being described.

The *Name* element is the concern designation, while the element *Description* provides a textual explanation about the concern's objectives and behaviour. The *Sources* element states the origins of the concern, having several possible values, as stakeholder requirements, external catalogues of non-functional requirements (as in [11]), etc.

Non-functional requirements are mapped into non-functional concerns. These might be very coarse-grained, compared with other concerns. Therefore, we suggest the use of Softgoal Interdependency Graphs (SIG) [11] that shows the interdependencies between softgoals (or non-functional requirements). Based on these interdependencies, we identify concern decompositions. This information is added to the *Decomposition* element of the template.[1]

The *Classification* element classifies the concern according to its type, e.g., functional, non-functional. The *Type* element classifies the concern according to its' crosscutting nature. The *Stakeholders* element shows which stakeholders interact with the concern. The *Responsibilities* element lists the operations that the concern should provide, while the *Contributions* element offers a list of positive and negative interactions with other concerns. This element helps detecting conflicts whenever concerns contribute negatively to each other. The *Stakeholders' importance* element assigns priorities to concerns from the stakeholders' perspective, in an attempt to help solving the identified conflicting situations. Finally, the *Required concerns* element acts as a dependency reference to other concerns in the system. This element will be used to identify which concerns are crosscutting.

The information about each concern is collected in a template. These concerns, and their relationships, can be modeled more rigorously using textual or visual representations, such as UML [22].

2.3 Compose Concerns

This task offers the possibility to compose a set of concerns, including crosscutting concerns, incrementally, until the whole system is analyzed. A concern is crosscutting if it is required by more than one other concern. This task is accomplished by taking into account the information in rows *Required concerns* in Table 1.

Each composition takes place in a match point in the form of a composition rule. A match point tells us which concerns (crosscutting or non-crosscutting) should be composed together in a given point (strongly related with a join point in AspectJ [2]). A composition rule shows how a set of concerns can be weaved together by means of some pre-defined operators. In order to accomplish this, we need to identify crosscutting concerns (those that are required by more than one other concern). At this point conflicting situations can be detected — whenever concerns that contribute negatively between them (row *List of contribution* in Table 1), have the same importance (row *List of stakeholders' importance*) and need to be composed in the same match point. These conflicting situations are identified automatically by our AORA tool [5].

2.4 Conflicts Handled by Existing AORE Approaches

Several AORE approaches [6, 7, 17, 18] handle conflicts mostly based on intuitive and very simple reasoning methods that are error prone and do not allow a rigorous engineering approach to the problem. For example, while [6] proposes allocating different priorities to conflicting concerns, in [7] conflict solving is based on the principle of iteratively identifying the dominant candidate aspect, or crosscutting concern, with respect to a set of stakeholders' requirements. This is achieved by importance comparison, which may involve trade-off negotiations with stakeholders. For example, suppose we have four concerns with priority "Very Important" to all

---

[1] Note that other types of concerns can also be decomposed into simpler concerns.

stakeholders; a negotiation is required so that the concerns can be ranked. The process starts by analysing two concerns to identify the dominant one, then take this and analyse it with a third concern and so forth until we have taken into consideration all the concerns. The result is the concern with higher priority between them all. Next the process is repeated to identify the second dominant concern among the remaining concerns, and so forth until we have a dependency hierarchy between all the concerns.

Moreira et al. [17] and Rashid et al. [18] use a similar idea, by assigning weights to those aspects that contribute negatively to each other. Weighting allows them to describe the extent to which an aspect may constrain a base module. The scales used are based on ideas from fuzzy logic. Again, concerns contributing negatively to each other and with the same weight with respect to a given base module require explicit, but informal, negotiations with the stakeholders.

The main limitations of these approaches are:

(1) each concern must be allocated one single different importance using intuition;
(2) conflict handling is based on one criterion, the importance, not considering other parameters that may have an impact on the decision;
(3) different stakeholders may have different interests on the same concern, and the relative importance/power of each one might be different (so their relative position might have to be taken into account);
(4) trade-offs must be negotiated informally with the stakeholders without any rigorous and systematic analysis technique or tool.

It was with these limitations in mind that we started exploring rigorous alternatives that could be used effectively without having to rely so strongly on a single criterion (importance), taking into consideration other possible useful information collected during the application of the methods.

The informal process discussed in the current approaches, may lead to wrong decisions, especially in situations where several different stakeholders have different expectations on the same system and the number of potential conflicting aspects is high. Moreover, there are other criteria that have an impact on the decision and which are not usually considered, as we will discuss in Sect. 4. Therefore, guaranteeing that the solutions being suggested are as good as possible, or finding the combination that better satisfies the stakeholder goals, may turn into a complex process. For example, to increase the number of clients being served simultaneously, to reduce the time of response and to improve the security access, may require a difficult analysis of trade-offs. So that we consciously know how much we are able to give up to get a little more of what we want most, we need rigorous tools that help us deal with these type of problems.

The main goal of this paper is to address this issue, by investigating the advantages of using MCDM methods to help in this difficult process. Given that several factors may have a different, sometimes opposite, impact on the end result, MCDM methods seem adequate for this job because they provide a mathematical framework to handle subjective judgments in conflicting situations.

3   MCDM: An Overview

MCDM (Multiple Criteria Decision Making) models aim at supporting decision makers to solve conflicting situations [21]. The MCDM field is usually divided into multiple-objective decision making (MODM) and multiple attribute decision making (MADM) [27]. In our work we focus on MADM but we will use the more general notation of criteria instead of attribute, i.e., MCDM. MCDM methods use mathematical techniques to help decision makers to choose among a discrete set of alternative decisions. These methods do not try to compute an optimal solution, but to determine, via various ranking procedures, either a ranking of the relevant actions (decision alternatives) that is "optimal" with respect to several criteria, or the "optimal" actions amongst the existing solutions (decisions alternatives) [21].

Two phases are usually needed to rank the alternatives or to select the most desirable one: (i) the aggregation of the degree of satisfaction for all criteria, per decision alternative (rating) and (ii) the ranking of the alternatives with respect to the global aggregated degree of satisfaction [27].

Triantaphyllou [21] warns that there may never be a single MCDM method that guaranties that a solution (derived ranking of alternatives) is the correct one because of the subjective assignment of alternative classifications and weights for criteria. Even within the fuzzy MCDM domain [10] this type of problem remains ill-defined by nature. It is a hard problem to know the best solution, even under perfect knowledge of the input data of a MCDM problem.

There are three parameters in an MCDM problem: the set of alternatives to be ranked; the set of criteria that will be used for classifying (rating) each alternative; and the weights (importance) attributed to each criterion. The weights represent the relative importance of that criterion in relation to others in a decision scenario. The higher the weight, the higher the importance of the criteria is for the decision maker. Usually, decision problems are represented in a decision matrix, as depicted in Table 2.

Table 2. Decision Matrix

	Weight $_1$	Weight $_2$	...	Weight $_j$
	Criteria$_1$	Criteria $_2$	...	Criteria $_j$
Alternative $_1$	x_{11}	x_{12}	...	X_{1j}
...	...	...	...	...
Alternative $_i$	x_{i1}	x_{i2}	...	x_{ij}

The normalized mathematical formulation of a MCDM problem is:

$$D(A_i) = \left[\bigoplus_j (x_{ij} \otimes w_j) \right] / \sum_j w_j \qquad (1)$$

where w_j is relative importance of criteria, x_{ij} rating of the alternative for the respective criteria and $\oplus$, $\otimes$ are appropriate (to be selected) aggregation operators. When we are dealing with a simple weighted average aggregation, the $\otimes$ is the operator multiplication and $\oplus$ is the summation. The best alternative A_i is the one with the highest ranking.

To solve MCDM problems many methods have been proposed [10, 21, 26]: direct scoring and outranking methods, trade-off schemes, distance based methods, value and utility functions, interactive methods. Direct scoring techniques are widely used, particularly the weighted scoring method (also called weighted average method), and this is the reason why we compare it with the approach selected for our work, the AHP. The AHP method [20, 21] was selected because it uses pairwise comparisons for its weighting process (it belongs to the class of trade-off and interactive methods [26]), which allows a direct match for solving our problem, i.e., our conflicts are between each pair of concerns. With this method there is no need (as all other methods require) to have a rating for each criterion per alternative as well as a weight for each criterion.

3.1 An Introduction to the AHP Method

AHP [20] is a decision analysis method that ranks alternatives based on a number of criteria. This method provides a mathematically rigorous process for prioritization and decision-making; by reducing complex decisions to a series of pairwise comparisons and then synthesizing the results, decision-makers arrive at the best decision based on a clear rationale. Based on our specific problem conflict handling characteristics, the AHP is a valid option because:

(a) it offers an interpretation of the problem with low complexity;
(b) it uses deductible and systematic procedures for reducing complexity;
(c) it permits trade-off analysis in conflicting situations;
(d) it provides a way to express preferences (pairwise) between all criteria and between all alternatives;
(e) it calculates the judgements logical consistency;
(f) its final result is based on the synthesis of the different judgements.

The AHP method can be described in five steps, each one described below.

Step 1: Problem Definition: In this step we define the problem goal.
Step 2: Graphical Representation of the Problem: This step is divided into three sub-steps: state the objective (according to goal encountered in step 1), define the criteria and choose the alternatives. Fig. 2 illustrates an example of a hierarchical tree.

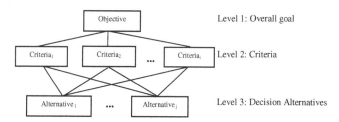

Fig. 2. AHP hierarchical tree

Step 3: Establish Priorities: Pairwise comparisons are used to define the preferences for alternatives over each criterion, as well as the weights of each criterion. To accomplish this, Satty uses the scale [1..9] to rate the relative importance/preference of one criterion over another, and constructs a matrix of the pairwise comparison ratings [20]. The same process applies to the definition of the importance of criteria. If a criterion is less important than other, then the inverse preference is rated in the ratio scale 1/1, 1/2, 1/3, ..., 1/9.

The reason for Satty's scale is based on psychological theories [20] and experiments that points to the use of nine unit scales as a reasonable set that allows humans to perform discrimination between preferences for two items. Each value of the scale can be given a different interpretation allowing a numerical, verbal or graphical interpretation of the values [20]. An example of pairwise priorities assignment for a problem with three alternatives is depicted in Table 3. An example of pairwise comparison to express the relative importance (weights) between two criteria is depicted in Table 4.

Table 3. Example of AHP pairwise classification of alternatives for a criterion

Criterion	Alternative 1	Alternative 2	Alternative 3
Alternative 1	1	3	9
Alternative 2	1/3	1	5
Alternative 3	1/9	1/5	1

The comparative matrices are reciprocal, hence they have to satisfy the property: $a_{ji}=1/a_{ij}$.

Table 4. Example of AHP pairwise assignment of weights (importance) between two criteria

Weights	Criterion 1	Criterion 2
Criterion 1	1	5
Criterion 2	1/5	1

The interpretation of the matrix in Table 3 is: Alternative 1 is *weakly more important* than Alternative 2 and *absolutely more important* than Alternative 3; Alternative 2 is *moderately more important* than Alternative 3. The interpretation for Table 4 is: the weight (importance) of Criterion 1 is *moderately more important* than Criterion 2. Note that the ratios on both matrices (Tables 3, 4) represent the inverse of the mentioned interpretations, the diagonal is always 1 to express neutrality between the same alternative or criterion, and the complete matrices are denoted as reciprocal matrices [20].

Step 4: Synthesis: In this step we calculate the priority of each alternative solution and criteria being compared. Several mathematical procedures can be used for synthesization, such as eigenvalues and eigenvectors [20]. However, here, as mentioned before, we use an averaging method, which provides similar results and is much simpler to apply [24]. The synthesis is determined in two phases:

1.   The process for synthesis follows a bottom-up approach. Hence, starting from the bottom of the hierarchical tree and using the reciprocal matrices as shown in Table 3 they are normalized per column and then we calculate the average per line to obtain a priority vector for each matrix corresponding to each

criterion. The same process is done for the pairwise matrices corresponding to the criteria relative importance (Table 4).

2. Next, the vectors per criterion are combined into a single matrix and this new matrix is multiplied by the priority vector obtained from the criteria importance matrix to obtain the overall objective (i.e., ranking of alternatives).

This process is repeated as many times as needed until the tree root is reached.

Step 5: Consistency: The logical quality of the decisions is guaranteed by computing the consistency ratio (*CR*), which measures the consistency of the pairwise comparison judgments:

$$CR = \frac{CI}{RCI} p \tag{2}$$

where *CI* represents the consistency index and *RCI* is a random consistency index. *RCI* is an pre-defined average random index derived from a sample of size 500 of randomly generated reciprocal matrices [21, p. 59] and depends on the number of elements being compared. *CI* is calculated using:

$$CI = (\lambda_{\max} - n)/(n-1) \tag{3}$$

where *n* is number of items being compared and λ_{max} is obtained from:

$$AW = A * W$$

$$\lambda_{\max} = (\sum_{i}^{n} AW_i / W_i)/n \tag{4}$$

where *A* is pairwise reciprocal matrix, *W* weights vector, index *i* corresponds to each value in the *AW* vector and *n* is again the number of elements.

If the consistency ratio *CR* exceeds 10%, this is indicative of inconsistent logical judgements [20]; in such cases, the decision maker should revise the original values in the respective pairwise comparison matrix [24]. It should be noted that this consistency ratio ensures that the transitive property (if a>b and b>c then a>c) is guaranteed, which means the user pairwise judgements, are logical [20].

In summary, we have chosen the AHP [20] with the simplified aggregation method [24] because: it is a well-known and accepted method; it is appropriate for handling conflicting concerns problems; it has the ability to quantify subjective judgements; it is capable of comparing alternatives in relation to established criteria; it provides the means to establish preferences (pairwise) between all criteria and between alternatives in relation to each criterion; and it provides means to guarantee the logical consistency of the judgements.

4 Applying AHP to the AORA Model

This section starts with a brief background on our preliminary attempts to use AHP for conflict resolution, and then introduces an example to illustrate the proposed application of the AHP method to the selected AORA approach [6, 7].

4.1 Illustrative Example

Let us consider the following illustrative example: to use the subway each client must possess a card in which was credited a certain amount of money. Each card can be bought and credited at selling machines that are available at subway stations. To start a journey, a passenger should use his/her card on an entrance machine. This machine validates the card and allows the owner of a valid title to initiate a trip. In a similar way, when a passenger ends her/his journey, s/he inserts the card in an exit machine. At this moment the price to pay is calculated and debited from card. The price will depend on the distance travelled. If the card does not have enough credit to pay for the trip, then it must be credited at any of the available machines in the subway. The client can request a refund of the money contained in his/her card in a selling machine.

The application of the AORA method to this example results in a list of concerns, each one described using the template in Table 1, and a list of match points with the priorities of each concern given by each stakeholder. Note that the identification of the these concerns, their description in a template, match points and corresponding composition rules is not the aim of this paper. Here we will simply use the results of the application of the method to handle a well identified problem (already motivated in sect. 1 and 2).

The list of concerns we have identified is:

- **Non-functional concerns: Accuracy, Compatibility, Response Time, Multi-Access, Security and Fault tolerance.** Security has been decomposed into Integrity and Availability (based on [11]). These sub-elements can be referenced by using the "." notation, like Security.Integrity or Security.Availability. For simplicity we will use Integrity and Availability instead of Security.Integrity and Security.Availability.
- **Functional concerns.** Enter Subway, Validate Card, Buy Card, Exit Subway, Refund Card and Credit Card.

The list of match points derived from the concerns' templates is: Enter Subway, Exit Subway, Buy Card, Refund Card and Credit Card.

To illustrate the use of the AHP process, we will focus on a single match point, the Enter Subway match point. Table 5 and 6 present the Enter Subway and Response Time descriptions, which concentrates the information regarding the concern to which the match point under study was defined.

Based on existing work, for example [11] and [23] as well as our knowledge of the system, the positive and negative contributions between concerns is identified. For the Enter Subway match point, Fig. 3 illustrates the resulting schema of concern contributions. For example, multi-access contributes negatively to response time (the higher number of passengers the system needs to handle, the faster it needs to be), while response time contributes positively to availability (the faster the system is, the longer it is free to handle more passengers). Note that the contributions specified here are symmetric, but this is not always the case. For example, usability contributes negatively to testability, but testability contributes positively to usability (please see [23] for more information).

Table 5. Enter Subway template

Concern Elements	Definition	
Name	Enter Subway	
Sources	Stakeholders, set of initial requirements, knowledge of the system	
Stakeholders	Passenger, System owner, Developer	
Description	This concern is responsible for handling the beginning of a trip	
Decomposition	<none>	
Classification	Functional	
Type	Non-Crosscutting	
Responsibilities	(1) Register an entrance (2) Return the card to the client	
Contributions	<none>	
Stakeholder	Passenger:	Very Important
Importance	System owner:	Very Important
	Developer:	Very Important
Required Concerns	(1) Response Time (2) Accuracy (3) Integrity (4) Availability (5) Validate Card (6) Multi-Access (7) Fault Tolerance	

Table 6. Response Time template

Concern Elements	Definition	
Name	Response Time	
Sources	Stakeholders, requirements, NFR catalogue, knowledge of the system	
Stakeholders	Passenger, System owner, Developer	
Description	The machine has to react in time when clients and passengers use the system with a card in entering, exiting and buying machines	
Decomposition	<none>	
Classification	Non-functional	
Type	Crosscutting	
Responsibilities	(1) Reacts in-time (<t) when a passenger enters the subway (2) Reacts in-time (<t) when a passenger exits the subway (3) Reacts in-time (<t) when a client buys card (4) Reacts in-time when a client asks for refund (5) Reacts in-time when a client/passenger credits a card	
Contributions	(1) Accuracy (−) (2) Availability (+) (3) Integrity (−) (4) Multi-Access (−)	
Stakeholder	Passenger:	Very Important
Importance	System owner:	Very Important
	Developer:	Very Important
Required Concerns	<none>	

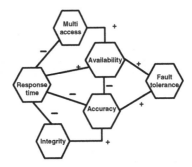

Fig. 3. Contributions between concerns for Enter Subway match point

Note that the identification of the above concerns and their specification in terms of the entries in Tables 5 and 6 is not the aim of this paper. Here we will simply use the results of the application of the AORA method to manage conflicts.

The goal of the rest of this section is to rank all the concerns required by Enter Subway, including those that contribute negatively to each other.

4.2 Applying the AHP Method

As described in Sect. 3.1, the AHP method is composed of five main steps. The result is the ranking of concerns. It should be noted that we developed the whole application in excel, which shows that there is no need for sophisticated tool support to implement this approach.

Step 1: Problem Definition
The goal is to rank the concerns required in a given match point. In our case, as mentioned before, the match point selected is "Enter subway". The alternatives are the different concerns identified in the Enter Subway match point:

A = {Accuracy, Response time, Availability, Integrity, Multi-Access, Validate Card, Fault Tolerance}.

The criteria, also referred to as decision criteria, represent the different dimensions from which the alternatives can be analysed. For our problem, we have two major criteria:

C = {Contribution, Stakeholders_Importance}

By dividing the *Stakeholders_Importance* criterion into sub-criteria it is possible to use individual stakeholder judgments as part of the decision problem. The main reason for the division is that the relation between concerns and its importance is dependent of the judgement of each stakeholder regarding the variables that are influent in her/his perspective of the system. Therefore, the identified *Stakeholders_Importance* sub-criteria are:

$C_{stakeholder\_importance}$ = {Passenger, System owner, Developer}.

Step 2: Graphical Representation of the Problem

With the identified objective, criteria and alternatives we can now build the hierarchical tree for our match point, as depicted in Fig. 4.

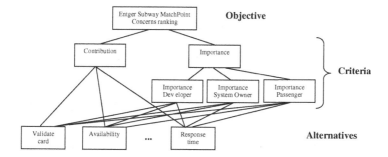

Fig. 4. Graphical representation of the enter subway match point

Step 3: Establish Priorities

As mentioned, AHP uses a pairwise comparison matrix to determine the ratings of judgements and comparisons are quantified by using the AHP [1..9] scale. In our example, the pairwise matrices are shown in Tables 7, 8, 9, 10, 11, and 12.

Table 7. Pairwise comparison matrix for criterion Contribution (4th level of tree)

Contribution	Accuracy	Response Time	Availability	Integrity	Multi-Access	Validate Card	Fault Tolerance
Accuracy	1.000	1.000	0.500	1.000	0.333	0.250	0.333
Response Time	1.000	1.000	0.500	0.333	0.333	0.250	0.333
Availability	2.000	2.000	1.000	0.500	0.500	0.333	0.500
Integrity	1.000	3.000	2.000	1.000	1.000	0.500	1.000
Multi-Access	3.000	3.000	2.000	1.000	1.000	0.500	1.000
Validate Card	4.000	4.000	3.000	2.000	2.000	1.000	2.000
Fault Tolerance	3.000	3.000	2.000	1.000	1.000	0.500	1.000

Table 8. Pairwise comparison matrix for importance of stakeholder Passenger (4th level of tree)

Passenger Importance	Accuracy	Response Time	Availability	Integrity	Multi-Access	Validate Card	Fault Tolerance
Accuracy	1.000	0.143	1.000	1.000	0.500	1.000	5.000
Response Time	7.000	1.000	6.000	6.000	6.000	6.000	7.000
Availability	1.000	0.167	1.000	1.000	2.000	2.000	3.000
Integrity	1.000	0.167	1.000	1.000	0.333	0.333	2.000
Multi-Access	2.000	0.167	0.500	3.000	1.000	2.000	3.000
Validate Card	1.000	0.167	0.500	3.000	0.500	1.000	2.000
Fault Tolerance	0.200	0.143	0.333	0.500	0.333	0.500	1.000

Table 9. Pairwise comparison matrix for importance of stakeholder System Owner (4th level)

System Owner Importance	Accuracy	Response Time	Availability	Integrity	Multi-Access	Validate Card	Fault Tolerance
Accuracy	1.000	1.000	2.000	2.000	1.000	1.000	2.000
Response Time	1.000	1.000	2.000	2.000	1.000	2.000	2.000
Availability	0.500	0.500	1.000	2.000	0.500	2.000	3.000
Integrity	0.500	0.500	0.500	1.000	0.500	0.500	2.000
Multi-Access	1.000	1.000	2.000	2.000	1.000	1.000	2.000
Validate Card	1.000	0.500	0.500	2.000	1.000	1.000	2.000
Fault Tolerance	0.500	0.500	0.333	0.500	0.500	0.500	1.000

Table 10. Pairwise comparison matrix for importance of stakeholder Developer (4th level)

Developer Importance	Accuracy	Response Time	Availability	Integrity	Multi-Access	Validate Card	Fault Tolerance
Accuracy	1.000	1.000	1.000	1.000	1.000	1.000	2.000
Response Time	1.000	1.000	0.500	3.000	0.500	0.500	3.000
Availability	1.000	2.000	1.000	2.000	1.000	1.000	3.000
Integrity	1.000	0.333	0.500	1.000	1.000	1.000	1.000
Multi-Access	1.000	2.000	1.000	1.000	1.000	1.000	3.000
Validate Card	1.000	2.000	1.000	1.000	1.000	1.000	3.000
Fault Tolerance	0.500	0.333	0.333	1.000	0.333	0.333	1.000

Tables 7, 8, 9, and 10 show pairwise priority assignments for the alternatives based on Contribution, Passenger Importance, System Owner Importance, and Developer Importance criteria, respectively. The assigned values are subjective and based on the authors' experience.

Now, we need to establish the relative importance of each stakeholder (level 3 of the tree) as well as the relative importance between the two criteria (level 2 of the tree). Tables 11 and 12 show the relative importance (preferences) of each criteria for both levels of the tree, again attributed by experience.

It should be noted that for large problems the total number of required comparisons is quite time consuming. Nevertheless, there are ways to avoid deriving priorities for

Table 11. Pairwise comparison matrix for Stakeholders Importance criterion (3rd level of tree) and respective Priority Vector (calculated)

Stakeholders Importance	Passenger Importance	System Owner Importance	Developer Importance	Priority Vector
Passenger	1.000	0.333	0.500	0.163
System Owner	3.000	1.000	2.000	0.538
Developer	2.000	0.500	1.000	0.297

Table 12. Paiwise comparison of criteria weights (2nd level of tree) and respective Priority Vector (calculated)

Criteria Weights	Contribution	Stakeholders Importance	Priority Vector
Contribution	1.000	0.500	**0.333**
Stakeholder Importance	2.000	1.000	**0.667**

alternatives by means of pairwise comparisons, for example by deriving relative weights from different comparisons. This would reduce the number of comparisons to *n-1*; however, if an error is introduced in this process, a strong negative impact can be felt in the final result [21, p. 86]. Fortunately, there are commercial tools, such as Expert Choice, Rank Master and Descriptor, to support the AHP process, facilitating its use and speeding up the calculations.

Step 4: Synthesis
After creating all pairwise comparisons it is now possible to calculate the priority of each alternative in terms of each criterion. First we calculate the normalized pairwise comparison matrix by dividing each element of the comparison matrix by the sum of each column. Then we find the estimated relative priorities by calculating the average of each row of the normalized matrix. At the end of this step we have the priority vectors for each pairwise matrix. Second, we collect the priority vectors for the third level of matrix in one matrix and using the importance priority vector (Table 11) we calculate the synthesized value for level 3. Table 12 shows the intermediate collected vectors and the final priority vector for level 3.

Now, to calculate the final ranking, we need to combine, into a single matrix, the final priority vector determined in Table 13 with the final vector resulting from Table 7, and then multiply it by the criteria weights priority vector of level 2 (Table 12). The results are shown in Table 14.

Observe that, in our example, we only have two major criteria at level 2 and three sub-criteria at level 3 (Fig. 4); hence, the final ranking was obtained by first synthesizing level 3 (Table 13) and then synthesizing level 2 (Table 14). As mentioned before, the AHP works with a bottom-up approach.

Table 13. Priority matrix for level 3 plus final Vector

	Passenger Importance	System Owner Importance	Developer Importance	Priority Vector
Accuracy	0.093	0.178	0.146	0.155
Response Time	0.478	0.196	0.146	0.227
Availability	0.114	0.149	0.186	0.154
Integrity	0.067	0.091	0.113	0.093
Multi-Access	0.123	0.178	0.172	0.167
Validate Card	0.088	0.138	0.172	0.1408
Fault Tolerance	0.038	0.071	0.065	0.064

Table 14. Final Ranking (synthesis)

	Contribution	Stakeholders Importance	Final Priorities	Ranking
Accuracy	0.071	0.155	0.127	5th
Response Time	0.058	0.227	0.171	2nd
Availability	0.097	0.154	0.135	4th
Integrity	0.149	0.093	0.112	6th
Multi-Access	0.168	0.167	0.168	3rd
Validate Card	0.288	0.140	0.189	1st
Fault Tolerance	0.168	0.064	0.099	7th

Let us now interpret the final ranking in Table 14 in the context of our Enter Subway match point, where negative contributions were found between several concerns, as shown in Fig. 3. The system can only be used with a valid card, therefore, it is not a surprise that the concern Validate Card appears raked first. Response Time come next in the ranking because we need to do our best to avoid long queues. Third ranking is Multi-Access because it is important to guarantee the use of the system by thousands of passengers at the same moment. Furthermore, Availability needs to be accomplished first than Accuracy and Integrity[2] in order to guarantee that the system is accessible for the passengers and helps Multi-Access and Response Time (this is possible because Availability has positive contribution to Response Time and Multi-Access). Accuracy appears in fifth place because his concern contributes negatively to Response Time and Availability, which have higher preferences for the stakeholders, so Accuracy priority needs to be lower in order to help guaranteeing the stakeholders preferences. Integrity is ranked sixth and Fault Tolerance comes later, in the seventh position. Fault Tolerance contributes positively to Accuracy and Availability so its composition helps the others.

Note that the resulting raking can also be used to guide an incremental development and even to define the composition rule, but this issue in not the focus of this paper.

Step 5: Consistency

The AHP method provides means to evaluate the consistency of the judgements that the decision maker demonstrated during the pairwise comparisons. This reduces any possible error that might have been introduced during the judgement process. Since our example was small we decided to check the consistency for all pairwise matrices instead of just obtaining a final consistency ratio. The results using equations (2), (3) and (4) are shown in Table 15.

The consistency indexes obtained are a good indication that logical consistent judgments were made on all pairwise comparisons, because they are well below the required 10% threshold, as explained in Sect. 3.1.

---

[2] As we said before, Security has been decomposed into Integrity and Availability.

Table 15. Final consistency ratio for all pairwise matrices

Pairwise matrices	Consistency Index (CR)
Table 7 (Contribution)	0.02
Table 8 (Passenger)	0.07
Table 9 (System Owner)	0.04
Table 10 (Developer)	0.05
Table 11 (Stakeholders Importance)	0.01
Table 12 (Criteria Weights)	0.00

4.3   A Summary of Our Initial Experiments with AHP

In our first attempt to use the AHP method to manage conflicts within the AORA approach [6], we tried to handle all the concerns in the whole system at once. However, we soon realised that we needed to first resolve conflicts with respect to particular match points. The very first problem we had to solve was to identify the set of alternatives (based on the problem under study) as well as the list of criteria (from the template in Table 1) that could bring useful information to the conflict resolution process. While the alternatives are the required concerns in a given match point, the criteria are a subset of the fields in the template.

Initially, the fields selected were Sources, Type, Contribution, Classification and Importance (at that time, Importance was stakeholder independent). These experiments led us to change the "Importance" element to be stakeholder dependent, since different stakeholders may have different interests on each concern. This allowed us to be able to differentiate stakeholders' interest on each alternative. Another decision that is worth noting is that Sources, Type and Classification have been identified as having no effect in the solutions obtained. While Sources is a string and it is virtually impossible to associate a degree of trust to it, Type and Classification ranges are crisp binary values and therefore there is no indecision associated with them.

During the process refinement, we realised that the Contribution field, which initially also looked like a binary crisp type, could have an impact on the results obtained. The explanation is that we could "quantify" the strength of the negative contributions. For example, considering two concerns A and B, contributing negatively to each other, we can associate a degree of strength to this relationship of the kind "highly negative", "negative", "not too negative", for example.

After several experiments, the criteria chosen were Importance (one value for each stakeholder) and Contribution.

5   AHP Versus Weighted Average

The AHP approach proved to produce useful information and since it ensures logical consistency, contributes to the developers trust on the results. Moreover, the AHP pairwise structure provides the means to express, easily, preferences between criteria (e.g., passenger is less important than system owner) and as well as between alternatives for each criterion (e.g., response time is much more important than accuracy for passenger). Nevertheless, it is rather cumbersome in terms of requiring pairwise comparisons for all levels of the decision tree and, within each level, to obtain weights for criteria. This makes its application time consuming. In addition, AHP does not deal with the problem of dependencies between more than two concerns because of its pairwise structure.

Hence, we decided to compare the AHP method with a widely known direct scoring method such as the classical weighted average (1), using the same illustrative example. Obviously, with this method we lose the possibility of using pairwise judgment and checking the logical consistency of the judgements made, but we gain in terms of time spent. In addition, with the simple WA we can neither compare the intermediate values nor use direct pairwise judgements to express our preferences between each pair of concerns, since in the classical weighted average method the assigned importance are direct (it is a direct scoring method).

In spite of the drawbacks of using a simple weighted average approach for our type of problem, it is a widely used method and a good candidate for comparison purposes. Furthermore, we will use a classification scale within the interval [0, 1] to enable a direct comparison with the final results of the AHP method. To allow some interpretation of the classification of alternatives we will use a discrete set of values from the interval scale, such as: {Very important: 0.9, Important: 0.75, Medium: 0.5, Low: 0.3, Very low: 0.1}. This classification is based on discrete fuzzy sets, as described in [10]. Table 16 shows the weights (i.e., the relative importance of criteria).

Table 16. Criteria weights

Criteria	Criteria Weights
Contribution	
Developer Importance	
Passenger Importance	
System Owner Importance	0.75

Table 17 shows the classifications for each alternative per criterion, the final priority obtained with Eq. (1), and the respective final ranking.

Table 17. Alternatives classification, final priorities and ranking for Enter Subway match point

EnterSubway Match Point	Contribution	Developer Importance	Passenger Importance	System Owner Importance	Final Priorities	Ranking
Accuracy	0.1	0.5	0.5	0.75	0.529	6th
Response Time	0.9	0.75	0.75	0.3	0.601	3rd
Availability	0.9	0.3	0.75	0.5	0.597	4th
Integrity	0.9	0.5	0.5	0.5	0.570	5th
Multi-Access	0.1	0.3	0.75	0.9	0.623	2nd
Validate Card	0	0.9	0.5	0.9	0.635	1st
Fault Tolerance	0.1	0.5	0.5	0.3	0.35	7th

Comparing the results just obtained (depicted in Table 17) with those obtained by applying the AHP ranking (in Table 14) we can observe that both methods agree in the first concern ranking, Validate Card. The 2nd ranking for AHP is given to Response Time and third to Multi-Access, while classical WA considers Multi-access the 2nd and Response Time the 3rd priority. The two concerns have a high ranking but Response time seems more essential in a system that deals with the public. The 4th place is the same for both approaches. There is an inversion regarding Accuracy and Integrity, respectively 5th and 6th for AHP, versus 6th and 5th for classical WA. Again the results of the AHP seem more appropriate because we need to ensure Accuracy before being worried with Integrity. Fault Tolerance occupies the last position in both methods.

Obviously, the classical WA method (1) is much simpler and provides good enough results; however, it does not allow: using sound logical pairwise comparisons (expressing different actors' preferences); consistency checks; and an easy interpretable hierarchical representation with various levels (Fig. 4). Hence, the choice between using this method or the AHP requires a decision between using a faster and simpler method (although with direct classifications) versus using AHP, which ensures pairwise psychological robustness, logical consistency and interpretability.

To conclude, we should remember that since all MCDM problems are always ill-defined [21] one should ensure that the classifications and weights of criteria reflect, as much as possible, the users and developers opinions. Another problem, common to all MCDM methods, is that big changes in the assigned classifications (both pairwise or direct) may result in different rankings. Hence, the selection of a "good" MCDM method should be done having in mind: the type of problem; the subjective nature of classifications and their dependencies; the need to express preferences between criteria and alternatives; check trade-offs between the advantages/disadvantages of each method for the problem at hand. In this paper we compared two well-known methods and discussed their results and respective advantages and drawbacks.

In summary, we can say that within subjective contexts, as is the case of resolving conflicts in AORE in general, MCDM methods, despite their limitations, are a suitable approach. Moreover, it seems that for resolving conflicts between concerns the AHP method provides more robust and logical sound results, but with an overhead of being a more time consuming method.

6   Related Work

Chung et al. propose a reasoning schema to detect and solve conflicting situations between non-functional concerns [11]. However, this process does not support means for a rigorous consistency checking neither does it offer a systematic trade-off analysis technique. Yen and Tiao [25] presents a formal framework that facilitates the identification and the trade-off analysis of conflicting requirements. This framework describes a systematic approach for analyzing the trade-offs between conflicting requirements using techniques based on fuzzy sets. However, again, there is no check of consistency of priorities in order to minimize the errors during the decision process.

Goal-oriented approaches detect priorities as the base attribute to handle conflicting goals. Formal techniques and heuristics are proposed for detecting conflicts and divergences from specifications of goals/requirements and of domain properties [16]. The major difference with respect to our work is that consistency of judgements is not guaranteed.

In [1] a goal-oriented approach is presented to manage conflicts in COTS-based development. This work aims at developing a selection process of how to identify and manage conflicting interests between costumers and vendors in order to support COTS decision-making. This process demonstrated that conflicts may arise when there is a mismatch between requirements and features. So, they have proposed a set of matching patterns to support the evaluation of how features match requirements. This works differs from ours because it proposes a set of alternative solutions at design level and we propose a ranking of alternatives (concerns) at requirements level.

CORA (Conflict-Oriented Requirements Analysis) incorporates requirement ontology and strategies for restructuring requirements transformations as a mean to reduce or remove conflicts [19]. This work deals with technical inconsistency and stakeholders conflicts, and ours deals with technical conflicts.

In [14] AHP is used to compare requirements pairwise according to relative value and cost where stakeholders are considered as having equal relevance. In our case a ranking process is used to establish stakeholders' degree of importance using the AHP and then we compare this method with the classical weighted average method.

In Win-Win Spiral Model [8], QARCC [9] is an exploratory knowledge-based tool used for identification of potential conflicts among quality attributes. QARCC diverges from ours, e.g.,: (i) instead of a knowledge-based tool we present a mathematical technique; (ii) QARCC fails to provide a method to evaluate quality of stakeholders' judgements. In our case, a consistency index is used to identify inconsistent judgement thus suggesting to the decision maker judgement revision; (iii) QARCC is based on key stakeholders identification; we use stakeholders' priority ranking to identify different degrees of importance among them (for priority criteria). Fewer stakeholders may result in less overhead and inconsistencies but erratic judgements may have more impact in the system.

7 Conclusions and Future Work

A rigorous technique to support conflict management at the AORE level has been presented. The technique uses a particular multi-criteria analysis method, the AHP, to find, given a set of alternatives and a set of decision criteria, the best alternative for a given problem. Such a technique is not only useful in the context we have described here, but it looks very promising as a tool to support architectural choices during the software architecture design.

We also compared the AHP with a classical weighted average method and the results proved that selecting the appropriate MCDM is always a question of trade-offs between advantages of each method. In this work we noticed that AHP ensures more psychological robustness in classifying the concerns, logical consistency and better interpretability at the expense of longer time to formulate and calculate the results. In order to answer the question of trade-offs between MCDM methods we plan to explore other methods from both the crisp and fuzzy multi-criteria domain to assess which method is more appropriate for the AORE conflict management problem. We also plan to explore the use of the AORE template responsibilities given that most of the existing AORE approaches use a similar concept. Finally, we also need to study how the level of granularity and dependency of/between concerns can influence the decision process.

References

[1] Alves, C., Finkelstein, A.: Investigating Conflicts in COTS Decision-Making. International Journal of Software Engineering & Knowledge Engineering 13(5) (2003)

[2] AspectJ Project (2006), http://www.eclipse.org/aspectj/

[3] Aspect-Oriented Software Development (AOSD) web page http://www.aosd.net/

[4] Baniassad, E., Clarke, S.: Theme: An Approach for Aspect-Oriented Analysis and Design, ICSE'04, Edinburgh (2004)

[5] Brito, I., Moreira, A.: Towards an Integrated Approach for Aspectual Requirements. In: 14th IEEE International Requirements Engineering Conference, MI, USA (2006)

[6] Brito, I., Moreira, A.: Integrating the NFR Approach in a RE Model. In: Early Aspects Workshop at AOSD'04. Lancaster, UK (2004)

[7] Brito, I., Moreira A.: Towards a Composition Process for Aspect-Oriented Requirements. In: Early Aspects Workshop at AOSD Conference. Boston, USA (2003)

[8] Boehm, B., Madachy, R.: Using the WinWin Spiral Model: A Case Study. Computer 31(7), 33–44 (1998)

[9] Boehm, B., In, H.: Identifying Quality-Requirement Conflicts. Computer Science Department & Center for Software Engineering, University of Southern California (1996)

[10] Chen, S., Hwang, C.: Fuzzy Multiple Attribute Decision Making: Methods and Application. LNEMS, vol. 375. Springer, Heidelberg (1993)

[11] Chung, L., Nixon, B., Yu, E., Mylopoulos, J.: Non-Functional Requirements in Software Engineering. Kluwer Academic Publishers, Dordrecht (2000)

[12] Elrad, T., Fitman, R.E., Bader, A.: Communications of the ACM: Aspect-Oriented Programming, vol. 44(10). ACM Press, New York (2001)

[13] Jacobson, I., Ng, P.-W.: Aspect-Oriented Software Development with Use Cases. Addison-Wesley, Reading (2004)

[14] Karlsson, J., Ryan, K.: A Cost-Value Approach for Prioritizing Requirements. IEEE Software 14(5) (1997)

[15] Kiczales, G., Lamping, J., Mendhekar, A., Maeda, C., Lopes, C., Loingtier, J.-M., Irwin, J.: Aspect-oriented Programming. In: Aksit, M., Matsuoka, S. (eds.) ECOOP 1997. LNCS, vol. 1241, pp. 220–242. Springer, Heidelberg (1997)

[16] Lamsweerde, A., Darimont, R., Letier, E.: Managing Conflicts in Goal-Driven Requirements Engineering. IEEE Transactions on SE 24(11), 908–926 (1998)

[17] Moreira, A., Rashid, A., Araújo, J.: Multi-Dimensional Separation of Concerns in Requirements Engineering. In: 13th IEEE Internatonal Conference on RE, France, (August 2005)

[18] Rashid, A., Moreira, A., Araújo, J.: Modularization and Composition of Aspectual Requirements. In: International Conference on AOSD, USA, ACM Press, New York (March 2003)

[19] Robinson, W., Volkov S.: Conflict-Oriented Requirements Restructuring. GSU CIS Working Paper 99-5, Georgia State University (1999)

[20] Saaty, T.L.: The Analytic Hierarchy Process, Network. McGraw-Hill, New York (1980)

[21] Triantaphyllou, E.: Multi-Criteria Decision Making Methods: A Comparative Study. Kluwer Academic Publishers, Dordrecht (2000)

[22] Unified Modeling Language – Specification, version 2.0 (2004), http://www.omg.org

[23] Wiegers, K.E.: Software Requirements, 2nd edn. Microsoft Press, Redmond (2003)

[24] Williams, A.S., Sweeny, D.J., Williams, T.A.: Quantitative Methods for Business. South-Western publishing Co (2000)

[25] Yen, J., Tiao, W.A.: A Systematic Tradeoff Analysis for Conflicting Imprecise Requirements. In: 3rd IEEE International Symposium on RE (1997)

[26] Yoon, K.P., Hwang, C.-L.: Multiple Attribute Decision Making. In: Lewis-Beck, M.S. (ed.) Quantitative Applications in the Social Sciences, pp. 7–104. Sage Publications, Thousand Oaks (1995)

[27] Zimmerman, H.J., Gutsche, L.: Multi-Criteria Analysis. Springer, Heidelberg (1991)

Weaving Multiple Aspects in Sequence Diagrams*

Jacques Klein[1], Franck Fleurey[1], and Jean-Marc Jézéquel[2]

[1] IRISA/INRIA, Campus de Beaulieu,
35042 Rennes cedex, France
jacques.klein@irisa.fr,
franck.fleurey@irisa.fr
[2] IRISA/ Université de Rennes 1, Campus de Beaulieu,
35042 Rennes cedex, France
jezequel@irisa.fr

Abstract. Handling aspects within models looks promising for managing crosscutting concerns early in the software life-cycle, up from programming to design, analysis and even requirements. At the modeling level, even complex behavioral aspects can easily be described for instance as pairs of sequence diagrams: one for the pointcut specifying the behavior to detect, and the second one for an advice representing the wanted behavior at the join point. While this is fine for informal documentation purposes, or even intuitive enough when a single aspect has to be woven, a more precise semantics of both join point detection and advice weaving is needed for using these modeling artifacts for Model Driven Engineering activities such as code generation or test synthesis. This paper proposes various interpretations for pointcuts that allow multiple behavioral aspects to be statically woven. The idea is to allow join points to match a pointcut even when some extra-messages occur in between. However, with this new way of specifying join points, the composition of the advice with the detected part cannot any longer be just a replacement of the detected part by the advice. We have to consider the events (or the messages) of the join point, but also the events which occur between them, and merge them with the behavior specified within the advice. We thus also propose a formal definition of a new merge operator, and describe its implementation on the Kermeta platform.

1 Introduction

The idea of encapsulating crosscutting concerns into the notion of aspects looks very promising for complementing the usual notion of modules available in most languages. By localizing these crosscutting concerns, the software engineer can get a better control over variations, either in the product line context or for software evolutions. The need to isolate these crosscutting concerns has been popularized by the AspectJ programming language, but there is a growing interest in

---

* This work has been partially supported by the European Network of Excellence on Aspect-Oriented Software Development (AOSD-Europe), 2004–2008.

A. Rashid and M. Aksit (Eds.): Transactions on AOSD III, LNCS 4620, pp. 167–199, 2007.

also handling them earlier in the software life-cycle, for instance at design time
[6], or during requirements analysis [2,14,24,29] and notably through the Early
Aspect community and the series of Early Aspect workshops[3].

At modeling level, even complex behavioral aspects can easily be described
for instance as pairs of UML 2.0 Sequence Diagrams (SDs), one SD for the pointcut (specification of the behavior to detect), and the second one for an advice
representing the wanted behavior at the join point. This is usually fine enough
for informal documentation purposes, or even intuitive enough when a single
aspect has to be woven. The idea of Model Driven Engineering is however that
it should be possible to use these modeling artifacts beyond mere documentation
purposes, for example for validation purposes (simulation or test case generation)
and also for code generation, including targeting non-aspect-oriented platforms
(e.g. vanilla Java, or real-time embedded systems). A more precise semantics of
both join point detection and advice weaving is then needed.

In this paper, we focus on finite scenarios expressed by means of SDs. We
will call *base scenario* a scenario which describes the concern that determine
the dominant structure of the system, and *behavioral aspect* a pair of scenarios
which describes a concern that crosscuts the base scenario. For join point detection at modeling time, we need to statically find where in the base scenarios are
the join points. The partial order induced by a SD and the hierarchical nature
of UML 2.0 SD (similar to High-Level Message Sequence Charts [13]) makes it
necessary to address the problem at the semantic level [18] with static analysis
techniques such as loop unrolling, etc.

For the composition of the advice into the base SD, when we are weaving
a single aspect into a base SD and when a join point[1] is a strict sequences of
messages, the composition is trivial once the join point has been identified: the
advice SD just replaces the portion of the SD that is matched by the pointcut at
the join point. However weaving multiple aspects at the same join point can be
difficult if a join point is simply defined as a strict sequence of messages, because
aspects previously woven might have inserted messages in between.

The contribution of this paper is to propose a new interpretation for pointcuts expressed as SDs to allow them to be matched by join points where some
messages may occur between the messages specified in the pointcut. However,
with this new way of specifying join points, the composition of the advice with
the detected part cannot any longer be a replacement of the detected part by
the advice. We have to consider the events (or the messages) of the join point
which are not specified within the pointcut and merge them with the behavior
specified within the advice. We thus propose a formal definition of a new merge
operator, called an *amalgamated sum*, and describe its implementation on the
meta-modeling platform Kermeta [19].

---

[1] Note that in this paper, we borrowed the term "join point" from AspectJ terminology.
In contrast to AspectJ, however, we consider "join points" as a representation of an
element or a collection of elements of the language of scenario used rather that as
"well-defined points in the execution of the program" (cf. [16]). The term join point
will be formally defined in Sect. 3.

The rest of the paper is organized as follows. Section 2 formally introduces the scenario language used and the notion of behavioral aspects. Section 3 introduces various interpretations for join points and Sect. 4 describes three detection algorithms for these join points. Section 5 presents our composition operator for sequence diagrams (*amalgamated sum*). Section 6 presents its implementation on the Kermeta platform [19]. Section 7 discusses future works whose aim at overcoming a current limitation of our approach. Section 8 compares our approach with related works, and Sect. 9 concludes this work.

2   Sequence Diagrams and Aspects

2.1   Scenarios: UML 2.0 Sequence Diagrams

Scenario languages are used to describe the behaviors of distributed systems at an abstract level or to represent systems behavioral requirements. They are close to users understanding and they are often used to refine use cases with a clear, graphical and intuitive representation. Several notations have been proposed, among which UML 2.0 SDs [21], Message Sequence Charts (MSCs) [13] or Live Sequence Charts [8]. In this paper, the scenarios will be expressed by UML 2.0 SDs. To define formally SDs in an easier way, we call basic sequence diagrams (bSD), a SD which corresponds to a finite sequence of interactions. We call combined sequence diagrams (cSDs) a SD which composes bSDs (with sequence, alternative and loop operators). In this way, a cSD can define more complex behaviors (even infinite behaviors if the cSD contains loops).

More specifically, bSDs describe a finite number of interactions between a set of objects. They are now considered as collections of events instead of ordered collections of messages in UML 1.x, which introduce concurrency and asynchronism increasing their power of expression. Figure 1 shows several bSDs which describe some interactions between the two objects *customer* and *server*. The vertical lines represent lifelines for the given objects. Interactions between objects are shown as arrows called messages like *log in* and *try again*. Each message is defined by two events: message emission and message reception which induces an ordering between emission and reception. In this paper, we use arrows represented with an open-head that corresponds to asynchronous messages[2] in the UML2.0 standard notation. Asynchronous means that the sending of a message does not occur at the same time as the corresponding reception (but the sending of a message does necessarily precede the corresponding reception). Consequently, in Fig. 2, the event e_3 corresponding to the reception of the first message a and the event e_2 corresponding to the sending of the second message a are not ordered. Events located on the same lifeline are totally ordered from top to bottom (excepted in specific parts of the lifeline called coregions).

We recall that in the UML2.0 specification, the semantics of an Interaction (a Sequence Diagram) is a set of traces, i.e., a set of sequences of events. Consequently, all events are not totally ordered. For instance, in Fig. 2, the bSD M

---

[2] We use asynchronous messages to be more general.

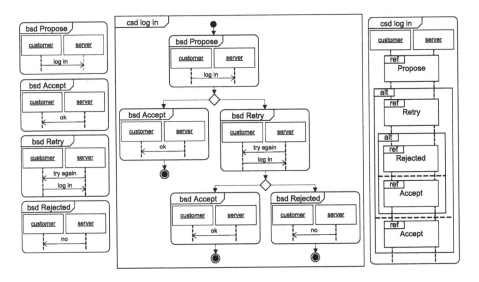

Fig. 1. Examples of bSDs and combined SD

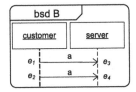

Fig. 2. Example of a bSD

generates two traces: $\{< e_1, e_3, e_2, e_4 >; < e_1, e_2, e_3, e_4 >\}$. These traces imply that the events e_2 and e_3 are not ordered. For this reason, we use the notion of partial order as used in other languages of scenarios as Message Sequence Charts to define formally the notion of bSD:

Definition 1. *A basic sequence diagram is a tuple $B = (I, E, \leq, A, \alpha, \phi, \prec)$ where: I is a set of objects participating to the interaction, E is a finite set of events (message emissions and receptions), $\leq$ is a partial ordering imposed by lifelines and messages, A is a set of actions (message name), and α and ϕ are mappings associating respectively an action name and a location (i.e. an object affected by the event) with an event. $\prec \subseteq E \times E$ is a relation that pairs message emissions and receptions.*

In Definition 1, the sentence "$\leq$ is a partial ordering imposed by lifelines and messages" means that events are totally ordered along a same lifeline (for instance, in Fig. 2 the event e_1 precedes the event e_2, and the event e_3 precedes the event e_4), and a message emission must always precede the corresponding reception (for instance, the event e_1 precedes the event e_3, and the event e_2 precedes the event e_4). Then, by transitivity, the partial order $\leq$ is obtained. Note that the events within an individual lifeline are totally ordered only if each event is unique. To ensure the uniqueness of each event, we use a unique identifier for each event.

We will denote by $T(e)$, the type of an event e. The type of an event indicates whether an event is a send event or a receive event. We will denote by $min(E) = \{e \in E | \forall e' \in E, e' \leq e \Rightarrow e' = e\}$, the set of minimal events of E, i.e., the set of events which have no causal predecessor. We will denote by $pred_{\leq,E}(e) = \{e' \in E | e' \leq e\}$, the set of predecessors of the event e, and by $succ_{\leq,E}(e) = \{e' \in E | e \leq e'\}$, the set of successor of e. These two notations can be used with a subset E' of the set E: $pred_{\leq,E}(E') = \{e \in E | \exists e' \in E', e \leq e'\}$ and $succ_{\leq,E}(E') = \{e \in E | \exists e' \in E', e' \leq e\}$. Slightly misusing the notation, when M' is a bSD which is a "part" of a bSD M, we will denote $pred(M')$ as the set of events of M' plus the set of predecessors of the events of M'. Finally, we will also use, for instance, the notation $pred_{<,E}(e) = \{e' \in E | e' < e\}$ to denote the set of strict predecessors of the event e (order $<$ instead of $\leq$) .

Basic SDs alone do not have sufficient expressive power: they can only define finite behaviors, without real alternatives. For this reason, they can be composed with operators such as sequence, alternative and loop to produce a SD called combined SDs (cSD) (also called UML 2.0 Interaction Overview Diagram). Figure 1 shows two equivalent views of the same cSD called *log in* (one view is more compact). This cSD *log in* represents the specification of a customer log on a server. If the customer makes two bad attempts, then he/she is rejected. Else, he/she is accepted. We can see that the cSD allows an alternative between the bSDs Accept and Retry, and between the bSDs Accept and Rejected. The cSD also composes sequentially the bSDs Propose and Accept (denoted *Propose•Accept*), the bSDs Propose and Retry (denoted *Propose•Retry*), etc... The notion of sequential composition (noted • or *seq* with the UML2 notation) is central to understanding the semantics of cSD. Note that we use the notion of *weak sequential composition* presented in the UML 2.0 specification [21](p 454). Roughly speaking, (weak) sequential composition of two bSDs consists of gluing both diagrams along their common lifelines. Note that the sequence operator only imposes precedence on events located on the same lifeline, but that events located on different lifelines in two bSDs $M1$ and $M2$ can be concurrent in $M1 • M2$. Sequential composition can be formally defined as follows:

Definition 2 (Sequential Composition) [3]
The sequential composition of two bSDs $M_1 = (I_1, E_1, \leq_1, A_1, \alpha_1, \phi_1, \prec_1)$ *and* $M_2 = (I_2, E_2, \leq_2, A_2, \alpha_2, \phi_2, \prec_2)$ *is the bSD* $M_1 • M_2 = (I_1 \cup I_2, E_1 \uplus E_2, \leq_{1•2}, A_1 \cup A_2, \alpha_1 \cup \alpha_2, \phi_1 \cup \phi_2, \prec_1 \uplus \prec_2)$, *where:* $\leq_{1•2} = (\leq_1 \uplus \leq_2 \uplus \{(e_1, e_2) \in E_1 \times E_2 \mid \phi_1(e_1) = \phi_2(e_2)\})^*$.

---

[3] We recall that we use the notion of *weak* sequential composition. It also exists a strong sequential composition. In a strong sequential composition of two bSDs M_1 and M_2, all the events of M_1 have to occur before an event of M_2 can occur.

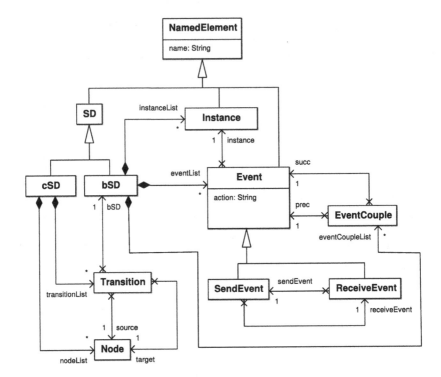

Fig. 3. Metamodel of SD

To calculate the new partial ordering $\leq_{1\bullet2}$, sequential composition consists in ordering events e_1 in bMSC M_1 and e_2 in bMSC M_2 if they are situated on the same lifeline, and then compute the transitive closure of this ordering. In this definition, $\uplus$ is the disjoint union of two multisets, i.e., an usual union operation where common elements of both sets are duplicated. This operator is necessary because even if the two operands have two identical events (events with the same name), the two events have to present in the result. Indeed, for instance imagine we want to make the sequential composition $B \bullet B$, where B is a bSD which contains only one message A. In this case, it is obvious that the two operands contain the same events, but in the result we want that all the events appear. Thus, in the sequential composition we have to copy and rename the identical events and it is made with the disjoint union.

The cSD *log in* can be considered as a generator of a set of behaviors. For instance, the cSD *log in* generates the set of behaviors $\{Propose\bullet Accept, Propose\bullet Retry \bullet Accept, Propose \bullet Retry \bullet Rejected\}$. This set of behaviors can be potentially infinite (as soon as a combined SD contains the operator loop, the set of bSDs generated is infinite), but in this paper we will only consider finite SDs.

Figure 3 depicts the sequence diagram metamodel used to implement the weaving process presented in this paper (the implementation is described in Sect. 6). We present this metamodel in this section to show that it fits very well with the previous definitions of bSD and cSD. In Fig. 3, we can note that cSD has an automata structure, in that a cSD contains a set of nodes and a set of transitions which are linked to bSDs. In this way, cSD can compose bSDs through sequences, alternatives and loops. We can also note that a bSD contains a set of objects (class Instance), a set of events (class Event) and a partial order on the events. The partial order is built with the class EventCouple which orders two events: the event "prec" precedes the event "succ". A set of pairs of events ($prec, succ$) forms the partial order. The class Event is linked to the class Instance. In this way, we obtain the mapping ϕ of Definition 1. Finally, the class Event contains an attribute "action" which represents the message name (with this attribute, we easily obtain the mapping α of Definition 1).

2.2 Behavioral Aspects

We define a *behavioral aspect* as a pair $A = (P, Ad)$ of bSDs. P is a pointcut, i.e. a bSD interpreted as a predicate over the semantics of a base model satisfied by all join points. Ad is an advice, i.e. the new behavior that should replace the base behavior when it is matched by P. Similarly to AspectJ, where an aspect can be inserted "around", "before" or "after" a join point, we will show in the next sections that an advice may equally complete the matched behavior, replace it with a new behavior, or remove it entirely.

When we define aspects with sequence diagrams, we keep some advantages related to sequence diagrams. In particular, it is easy to express a pointcut as a sequence of messages. Figure 4 shows three behavioral aspects. The first allows the persistence of exchanges between the customer and the server. In the definition of the pointcut, we use regular expressions to easily express three kinds of exchanges that we want to save (the message *log in* followed by either the message *ok*, the message *try again*, or the message *no*). The second aspect allows the identification of a log in which fails. The third aspect allows the addition of a display and its update.

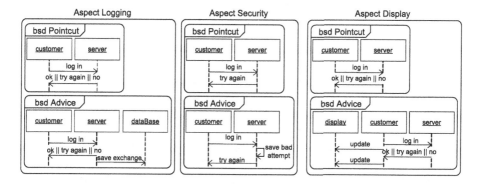

Fig. 4. Three behavioral aspects

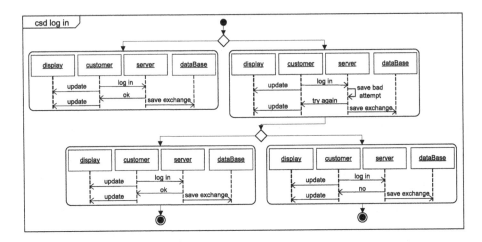

Fig. 5. Result of the weaving

In Fig. 1, the cSD *log in* represents a customer log in on a server. The customer tries to log in and either he succeeds, or he fails. In this last case, the customer can try again to log in, and either he succeeds, or the server answers "no". The expected weaving of the three aspects depicted in Fig. 4 into the cSD *log in* is represented by the cSD in Fig. 5.

3   Various Definitions of Join Points

As mentioned in the introduction, weaving multiple aspects at the same join point can be difficult if a join point is simply defined as a strict sequence of messages, because aspects previously woven might have inserted messages in between. In this case, the only way to support multiple static weaving is to define each aspect in function of the other aspects, which is clearly not acceptable.

The weaving of the three aspects depicted in Fig. 4 allows us to better explain the problem. If the join points are defined as the strict sequence of messages corresponding to those specified in the pointcut, the weaving of these three aspects is impossible. Indeed, when the aspect *security* is woven, a message *save bad attempt* is added between the two messages *log in* and *try again*. Since the pointcut detects only a strict sequence of messages, after the weaving of the aspect *security*, the aspect *display* cannot be woven anymore. We obtain the same problem if we weave the aspect *display* first and the aspect *security* afterwards.

To solve this problem of multiple weaving, we introduce new formal definitions of join points which make possible the detection of join points where some events can occur between the events specified in the pointcut. In this way, when the aspect *security* is woven, the pointcut of the aspect *display* will allow the detection of the join point formed by the messages *log in* and *try again*, even if the message *save bad attempt* has been added.

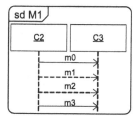

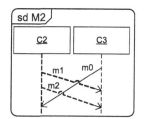

The messages m1 and m2 form a
general part, a safe part, an enclosed
part and a strict part of M1

The messages m1 and m2 form a
general part, a safe part, an enclosed
part of M1 but not a strict part

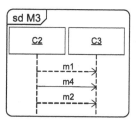

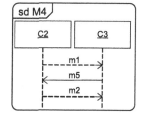

The messages m1 and m2 form a
general part and a safe part of M1, but
neither an enclosed part nor a strict part

The messages m1 and m2 only
form a general part of M1

Fig. 6. Illustration of the notions of parts

In our approach, the definition of join point will rely on a notion of *part of a
bSD*. A join point will be defined as a part of the base bSD such that this part
corresponds to the pointcut. To define the notion of correspondence between a
part and a pointcut, in Sect. 3.2, we introduce the notion of isomorphism between
bSD. To define in a rigorous way the notion of join point, we also have to formally
define the notion of part of a bSD. In Sect. 3.1, we propose four definitions for
parts of a bSD, some of which allow the multiple weaving of aspects.

3.1   Notion of Part of a bSD

We propose four definitions of parts of a bSD which allow the definition of four
different types of join points. These definitions of parts will be called: *strict
part, general part, safe part* and *enclosed part*. Before introducing formally the
definitions of parts, we use Fig. 6 to give a first intuitive idea of these parts.

Let us imagine we want to detect a message $m1$ followed by a message $m2$
from $C2$ to $C3$ in the bSDs in Fig. 6. Firstly, it is clear that the messages $m1$
and $m2$ form a join point in the bSD $M1$, but it is not obvious that these two
messages form a join point in the other bSDs because there is either a message
which "surrounds" $m1$ and $m2$ (in $M2$), or a message between $m1$ and $m2$ (in
$M3$ and $M4$).

We propose a first definition of part called *strict part* which only allows the detection of the message $m1$ and $m2$ in the bSD $M1$. This definition is the most restrictive, because with this definition, the wanted behavior can be presented in a bSD without to be detected when, for instance, it is surrounded by a message or when another message is present between the messages forming the wanted behavior.

Conversely, we propose a definition of part called *general part* which allows the detection of the message $m1$ and $m2$ in all the bSDs. This definition is the less restrictive. Some messages can be present between the messages forming the wanted behavior.

We also propose one variant of strict part called *enclosed part*, and one variant of general part called *safe part*. An enclosed part allows the detection of the message $m1$ and $m2$ in the bSDs $M1$ and $M2$. As a strict part, an enclosed part allows the detection of a strict sequence of messages, but in addition, the sequence of messages can be surrounded by others messages as in the bSD $M2$. A safe part allows the detection of the message $m1$ and $m2$ in the bSDs $M1$, $M2$ and $M3$, i.e., a safe part allows the detection of a sequence of messages which is not necessarily a strict sequence of message, but unlike general part, the order on the events specified in a pointcut have to be preserved in a safe part (this last remark will be detailed afterwards).

Now, we formally introduce the four definition of parts. A strict part characterizing a strict sequence of messages can be defined by:

Definition 3 (Strict Part). *Let M be a bSD. We will say that M' is a strict part of M if there exist two bSDs X and Y such that $M = X \bullet M' \bullet Y$, $\bullet$ being the operator of sequential composition*[4].

In Fig. 6, the messages $m1$ and $m2$ form a strict part only into the bSD $M1$.

A general part, characterizing a part which can be "surrounded" by messages and where some messages can occur between the messages of the part, can be defined by:

Definition 4 (General Part). *Let $M = (I, E, \leq, A, \alpha, \phi, \prec)$ be a bSD. We will say that $M' = (I', E', \leq', A', \alpha', \phi', \prec')$ is a general part of M if:*

$$- \ I' \subseteq I, \quad E' \subseteq E, \quad A' \subseteq A, \quad \alpha' = \alpha_{|E'}, \quad \phi' = \phi_{|E'};$$
$$- \ \leq' \subseteq \leq_{|E'}, \quad \prec' = \prec_{|E'}, \quad \forall (e, f) \in \prec, e \in E' \Leftrightarrow f \in E'.$$

In Fig. 6, the messages $m1$ and $m2$ form a general part into all the bSDs.

A safe part allows the characterization of a join point where some events can occur between the events specified in the pointcut, if and only if the order of the events specified in the pointcut is preserved in the join points. A safe part can be formally defined by:

Definition 5 (Safe Part). *Let $M = (I, E, \leq, A, \alpha, \phi, \prec)$ be a bSD. We will say that $M' = (I', E', \leq', A', \alpha', \phi', \prec')$ is a safe part of M if:*

---

[4] Note that according to Definition 2, the sequential composition of two bSDs provides a bSD.

- M' is a general part of M;
- $\leq' = \leq_{|E'}$.

In Fig. 6, the messages $m1$ and $m2$ form a safe part into the bSDs $M1$, $M2$ and $M3$. The order of the events of a safe part is the same as the order of the events of the initial bSD restricted to the events of the safe part ($\leq' = \leq_{|E'}$). That is why the messages $m1$ and $m2$ do not form a safe part into $M4$, because with only the messages $m1$ and $m2$, the receiving of the message $m1$ and the sending of the message $m2$ are not ordered whereas in the bSD $M4$, these two events are ordered (by transitivity) because of the message $m5$.

Finally, an enclosed part defines a strict sequence of messages but this sequence can be "surrounded" by others messages. More formally:

Definition 6 (Enclosed Part). *Let $M = (I, E, \leq, A, \alpha, \phi, \prec)$ be a bSD. We will say that $M' = (I', E', \leq', A', \alpha', \phi', \prec')$ is an enclosed part of M if:*

- *M' is a safe part of M;*
- *$pred_{\leq,E}(E') \cap succ_{\leq,E}(E') = E'$.*

In Figure 6, the messages $m1$ and $m2$ form an enclosed part into the bSDs $M1$ and $M2$. Since an enclosed part is a part where no event can be present between the events forming the enclosed part, the message $m1$ and $m2$ do not form an enclosed part into $M3$.

The set $pred_{\leq,E}(E') \cap succ_{\leq,E}(E')$, which represents the intersection between the set of predecessors of E' and the set of successors of E', [5], indicates the presence of events "between" the events of E'. Indeed, if an event $e \notin E'$ come between two events e' and e'' of M' ($e' \leq e \leq e''$ and $\phi(e') = \phi(e) = \phi(e'')$), then e belongs to $pred_{\leq,E}(E')$ and to $succ_{\leq,E}(E')$. Therefore $pred_{\leq,E} E' \cap succ_{\leq,E}(E') \neq E'$

Let us note that for the four proposed definitions of part of a bSD, the definitions are based on the semantics of the language of scenarios used, since we take account of the message names, but also of the partial order induced by the pointcut.

3.2   Join Point

Roughly speaking, a join point is defined as a part of the base bSD such that this part corresponds to the pointcut. Since we have defined four notions for parts of a bSD, we have four corresponding strategies for detecting join points. It remains to define the notion of correspondence between the pointcut and the part. To do so, we introduce the notions of morphisms and isomorphisms between bSDs.

Definition 7 (bSD Morphism). *Let $M = (I, E, \leq, A, \alpha, \phi, \prec)$ and $M' = (I', E', \leq', A', \alpha', \phi', \prec')$ be two bSDs. A bSD morphism from M to M' is a triple $\mu = < \mu_0, \mu_1, \mu_2 >$ of morphisms, where $\mu_0 : I \to I'$, $\mu_1 : E \to E'$, $\mu_2 : A \to A'$ and:*

---

[5] Let us note that E' is necessarily inclued in $pred_{\leq,E}(E')$ and in $succ_{\leq,E}(E')$ because each event of E' is its own predecessor and its own successor ($e \leq e$, $\leq$ being reflexive by definition).

(i) $\forall (e, f) \in E^2, e \le f \Rightarrow \mu_1(e) \le' \mu_1(f)$
(ii) $\forall (e, f) \in E^2, e \prec f \Rightarrow \mu_1(e) \prec' \mu_1(f)$
(iii) $\mu_0 \circ \phi = \phi' \circ \mu_1$
(iv) $\mu_2 \circ \alpha = \alpha' \circ \mu_1$

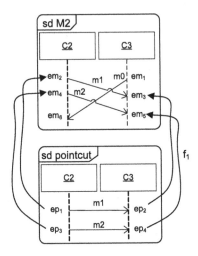

Fig. 7. Illustration of the notion morphism

Note that properties (i) and (ii) mean that by a bSD morphism the order and the type of the events are preserved (the type of an event is preserved means that, for instance, a sending event of M will be always associated with a sending event of M'). Note that property (iii) also means that all events located on a single lifeline of M are sent by μ_1 on a single lifeline of M'. Figure 7 shows a bSD morphism $f = < f_0, f_1, f_2 >: pointcut \rightarrow M2$ where only the morphism f_1 associating the events is represented (for instance, the event ep_1 which represents the sending of the message $m1$ is associated with the event em_2). Note that since each event of a bSD is unique, a bSD morphism f from a bSD M to a bSD M' always defines a unique part of M'.

Definition 8 (bSD isomorphism). *A bSD morphism* $\mu = (\mu_0, \mu_1, \mu_2)$ *from a bSD* M *to a bSD* M' *is an isomorphism if the three morphisms* μ_0, μ_1, *and* μ_2 *are isomorphic and if the converse morphism* $\mu^{-1} = (\mu_0^{-1}, \mu_1^{-1}, \mu_2^{-1})$ *is also a bSD morphism.*

With this definition of isomorphism, we can define the notion of join point in a general way:

Definition 9 (join point). *Let* M *be a bSD and* P *be a pointcut. Let* M' *be a part of* M. *We will say that* M' *is a join point if and only if there exists a bSD isomorphism* $\mu = (\mu_0, \mu_1, \mu_2)$ *from* P *to* M' *where the morphisms* μ_0 *and* μ_2 *are identity morphisms (P and M' have the same objects and action names).*

In a nutshell, for each definition of *a part of a bSD*, there is a corresponding definition of join point. In Fig. 7, if we consider the *pointcut* depicted, it is easy to see that the messages $m1$ and $m2$ are a join point if we take the enclosed part, the safe part or the general part as definition of part of a bSD, because there exists a bSD isomorphism between the pointcut and an enclosed part, a safe part or a general part of $M2$.

3.3   Successive Join Points

To define the notion of successive join points the simple definition of join point is not precise enough. Indeed, in Fig. 8, the pointcut $P1$ matches two different parts of $M1$, but these parts become entangled. Let us consider now the pointcut $P2$ and the bSD $M2$. If we take the definition of general part as the definition of part, there are four possible join points. Indeed, the first message a and the first message b can form a join point, as can the second message a and the second message b, but the first message a with the second message b or the second message a with the first message b can also form join points.

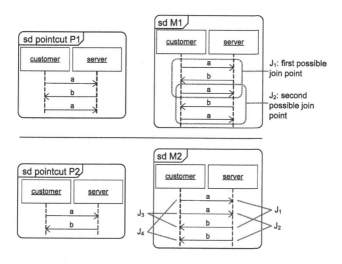

Fig. 8. Multiple possible matching

These multiple conflicting join points pose a problem. Among the conflicting join points, which should be chosen? Considering all these potential join points might not make sense from the point of view of someone using aspect weaving tools. In practice, we can reasonably expect that when a join point is detected, no elements of this join point can be used to form another join point. Roughly speaking, we can define successive join points as a set of disjoint join points taken in sequence.

The advantage of this definition is that it is safe in the sense that the weaving of the advice at a join point cannot conflict with the weaving of the advice at another join point. For instance, let us imagine that a weaving of an aspect removes a join point. If we weave this aspect into the bSD $M2$ in Fig. 8, and if $J1$ is the first detected join point, then the messages a and b forming $J1$ are removed. In this case, the conflicting join points $J3$ and $J4$ have no meaning anymore since one of its constituent messages no longer exists.

However, this answer is debatable. In the proposed example, $J1$ and $J2$ can form a join point because they don't share the same messages. The ideal solution is perhaps to give the choice to the user by proposing several semantics of notion of successive join points. Nevertheless, in the sequel of this paper, we will only give a definition of the notion of successive join points which is (in an informal way) a sequence of disjoint join points. Other semantics of successive join points could be considered as interesting future work.

To define this sequence of disjoint join points, firstly we propose a way to order the parts of a bSD which are isomorphic to a pointcut in order to find the first join point matched by the pointcut. Then we show the first join point is always unique, because the order defined on the parts is a lattice. Secondly, we define successive join points in an inductive way by considering the first join point J which appears in a bSD M, and by continuing with M minus J.

Definition 10 (ordered parts). *Let* $M = (I_M, E_M, \leq_M, A_M, \alpha_M, \phi_M, \prec_M)$ *be a bSD and* $P = (I_P, E_P, \leq_P, A_P, \alpha_P, \phi_P, \prec_P)$ *be a pointcut. Let* J_1 *and* J_2 *be two parts of* M *such that there exist two bSD isomorphisms* $f = <f_0, f_1, f_2>$: $P \to J_1$ *and* $g = <g_0, g_1, g_2>$: $P \to J_2$. *We will say that* J_1 *precedes* J_2 *(or that* J_2 *succeeds* J_1), *denoted* $J_1 \ll J_2$, *if and only if:*

$$\forall e \in E_P \text{ such that } T(e) = send, f_1(e) \leq_M g_1(e).$$

In Fig. 8, with this order we can say that the part J_1 precedes J_2 in bSD $M1$. We can also say that the part formed by the first message a and the first message b in the bSD $M2$ precedes all the other parts formed by a message a and a message b.

Afterwards, we will be especially interested in the *minimum* part of the order $\ll$, that is to say the part which precedes all the other parts. For a set $\mathcal{J}_{P,M}$ of all the parts of a bSD M isomorphic to a pointcut P, we will denote by $min(\mathcal{J}_{P,M})$ the minimum part. In the same way, if $\mathcal{J}_{P,M}$ is the set of all the join points of P in M, we will call the *minimum join point* the join point equal to $min(\mathcal{J}_{P,M})$. However, $\ll$ does not define a total order. For instance, in Fig. 8, $J3$ and $J4$ are not ordered by $\ll$. Therefore, it is not obvious that $min(\mathcal{J}_{P,M})$ is unique. To demonstrate the uniqueness of $min(\mathcal{J}_{P,M})$, we show that $\ll$ is a lattice.

Theorem 1. *Let* $\mathcal{J}_{P,M}$ *be the set of join points of a bSD* M *corresponding to a pointcut* P *and let* $\ll$ *be the order on these join points as defined by Definition 10, then* $(\mathcal{J}_{P,M}, \ll)$ *is a lattice.*

The proof of this theorem is given in Appendix.

Now, we can inductively define successive join points as follows:

Definition 11 (Successive Join Points). *Let M be a bSD and P be a point-cut. Let $J_1, J_2, \ldots, J_k$ be k parts of M isomorphic to P. These k parts are successive join points of P in M if:*

1. *J_1 is the minimum join point of P in M ;*
2. *$\forall i \in \{2 \ldots, k\}$, J_i is the minimum join point of P in M', M' being the bSD which contains the events of M minus the events of J_{i-1} and all the events which precede the events of J_{i-1}, so $M' = M - pred(J_{i-1})$.*

Taking the minimum join point every time guarantees the uniqueness of the successive join points. Roughly speaking, successive join points are detected in sequence at the earliest position where they appear in a bSD.

However, the result $M' = M - pred(J_{i-1})$ is not always a well-formed bSD. Indeed, in Fig. 9, the minimum join point J_1 of P in M is formed by the two first messages a and b. When we remove the events $pred(J_1)$ (the events of J_1 and the events which precede J_1), we have to remove the event corresponding to the sending of the message c. Therefore, the result $M' = M - pred(J_1)$ is only formed by the two last messages a and b, and the event corresponding to the reception of the message c. This is not really a problem because the algorithms proposed afterwards can be applied even if a bSD is of the kind of M'.

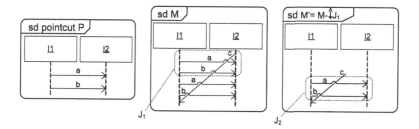

Fig. 9. Example of a not well-formed bSD

3.4   Which Detection Stategies Should Be Chosen?

Each definition of part of a bSD presented in the previous sub-section leads to a specific join point detection strategy. This sub-section discusses some arguments for and against these strategies.

First, it is important to note that for the four proposed definitions of part of a bSD (so the four strategies), the definitions are based on the semantics of the language of scenarios used, since we take account of the message names, but also of the partial order induced by the pointcut.

The definition of strict part is the most restrictive, because with this definition, the wanted behavior can be presented in a bSD without being detected when, for instance, it is surrounded by a message. On the other hand, this definition is easy: we only search a decomposition of a base bSD M such that $M = M_1 \bullet J \bullet M_2$ (J being the join point). In [18], we have showed that this simplicity allows the achieving of good decidability results for join point detection in infinite scenarios.

Conversely, the definition of general part is the least restrictive. Some messages can be present between the messages forming the wanted behavior. This fact can imply the detection of join points interleaved with behaviors not expected by the user. Moreover, the partial order defined by the pointcut is not necessarily preserved in the detected join point. The major advantage of a join point defined as a general part remains the property to easily weave several aspects at the same join point.

The definitions of enclosed part and safe part combine the advantages and the drawbacks of a strict part and a general part. An enclosed part looks like a strict part, but it can be surrounded by some messages. Therefore, if we want to look for a strict sequence of messages in a certain way, this definition seems to be appropriate. However, an enclosed part has the drawback that it does not tolerate the weaving of multiple aspects at the same join point. If we want to weave several aspects at the same join point, while the partial order defined by the pointcut is preserved, the definition of safe part seems to be appropriate. However, a safe part has the drawback for the detection of join points interleaved with behaviors not expected by the user, because some messages can be present between the messages of the join points.

Despite this short discussion on the advantage and the drawbacks of each definition, the main interest of the proposed approach is that a user can choose as he/she wishes the semantics of the weaving in finite scenarios. The user is free to choose the definition of part which suits him/her the better by adapting the algorithm of detection according to the chosen definition. We will show how this flexibility can be easily implemented with the Kermeta environment in Sect. 6.

4   Join Point Detection

In [18], Klein et al. propose an algorithm to detect a strict part, i.e. a strict sequence of messages. In this paper we propose three new algorithms to detect join points defined as an *enclosed part*, a *general part*, or a *safe part* of a bSD.

Firstly, in Sect. 4.1, we introduce a general algorithm which contains two "abstract functions" *findSetsOfEvent* and *min*. Secondly, in Sect. 4.2, we show how these functions can be specialized for each notion of join points to obtain the three new algorithms.

4.1   General Algorithm

Algorithm 1 allows the construction of an isomorphism $\mu = (\mu_0, \mu_1, \mu_2)$ from a pointcut P to a part M' of a bSD M, such that μ_0 and μ_2 are identity morphisms. In this way, the isomorphism indicates the first join point M' in M. We denote by $\pi_i(M) \subseteq E_M$ the projection of a bSD M on an object i of M and by $\pi_E(M)$ the restriction of a bSD M to a subset $E \subseteq E_M$. Moreover, we use a function

β_E which, for an event e of E, gives the position of e on the object containing e. More specifically, the position of an event on an object is defined by the number of events which precede it on this object: $\forall e \in E, \beta_E(e) = card(\{e' \in E | \phi(e) = \phi(e') \wedge e' \leq e\})$. Finally, we introduce the function $\Gamma_{E,o}(n)$ which gives the event of E localized on the nth position on the object o ($\Gamma_{E,o}(n) = e$ such that $\beta_E(e) = n \wedge \phi(e) = o$).

For all objects of a pointcut P, the first part of the algorithm (line 1–4) allows the construction of the sets of events of M localized on the same object, such that the actions related to these events are the same as the actions related to the events of P. The variable w_i represents a word of all events on an object i of the base bSD M. With the function $findSetsOfEvent$, we take, for each object i, all the set of (strict or non-strict) sequence of events of M which have the same action names as the events of P on the object i. Since the decision to take a strict sequence of events or a non-strict sequence of events depends on the definition of parts, the function $findSetsOfEvent$ has to be detailed for each definition of parts.

The second part of the algorithm (line 5–13) allows the construction of a part M' of M when it is possible. After the first part of the algorithm, with the function min, we take the first (or minimum) set of events forming a part. Since we propose four definitions of parts, this function min has to be specified for each definition of parts. The notion of minimum set of events or minimum parts is the one defined in the previous section (related to the definition of ordered parts, Definition 10).

An example of how the algorithm works in a practical way is given in the following sub-section.

Algorithm 1. Abstract Algorithm of Join Point Detection (P,M)

---

input: pointcut $P = (I_P, E_P, \leq_P, , A_P, \alpha_P, \phi_P, \prec_P)$,
 bSD $M = (I_M, E_M, \leq_M, A_M, \alpha_M, \phi_M, \prec_M)$
output: $\mu = (\mu_0, \mu_1, \mu_2) : P \rightarrow M', M' = (I_{M'}, E_{M'}, \leq_{M'}, A_{M'}, \alpha_{M'}, \phi_{M'}, \prec_{M'})$ join point of M

1: For each $i \in I_P$ do
2:    $w_i = \pi_i(M)$ /* a word of all events on the object i */
3:    $V_i = findSetsOfEvent(w_i, \pi_i(P))$
4: End For
5: $E_{M'} = min(\cup_{i \in I_P} V_i)$
6: If ($E_{M'} = \emptyset$) then
7:    return($null$)
8: Else
9:    μ_0 is the identity isomorphism from I_P to $\phi_M(E_{M'})$,
10:    μ_2 is the identity isomorphism from A_P to $\alpha_M(E_{M'})$,
11:    μ_1 is the isomorphism from E_P to $E_{M'}$ such that $\forall e \in E_P$,
      $\mu_1(e) = \Gamma_{v_{\phi(e)}, \phi(e)} \circ \beta_{E_P}(e)$ /* for each object o of I_p, μ_1 is built
   by associating with the event of o in the ith position, the event
   belonging to $E_{M'}$ on o in the ith position.*/
12:    return($\mu = (\mu_0, \mu_1, \mu_2)$)
13: End If

Note that to detect successive join points in a base bSD M, we start to apply Algorithm 1 on M to obtain the first join point, which we denote J_1 (more precisely, we obtain an isomorphism $\mu = (\mu_0, \mu_1, \mu_2)$ which defines J_1). Secondly, we apply Algorithm 1 on $M' = M - pred(J_1)$ to obtain the second join point J_2, and then we continue in this way as long as the last join point obtained is not null.

4.2 Specialization of the Abstract Algorithm

Enclosed Part Detection
For the detection of enclosed part, the function $findSetsOfEvent$ is equivalent to $V_i = \{v \in E_M^* \mid \exists u, w, w_i = u.v.w \wedge \alpha(v) = \alpha(\pi_i(P))\}$. For a word of events w_i on the object i, the function $findSetsOfEvent$ returns a set V_i where each element v of V_i is a strict sequence of events which have the same action names as the events of P on the object i.

With the function min, it remains to check if the order of the events of P is the same as the order of the events associated to M'. For that, we check if for all pairs of sending-reception of events of P, the events of M' at the same position also form a pair of sending-reception of events. Then, we take the first (or minimum) set of events satisfying the properties. More formally, the function min can be rewritten by:

$$min\Big\{ v_1, \ldots, v_{|I_P|} \in V_1 \times \cdots \times V_{|I_P|} \Big|$$

$$\forall (e, f) \in \prec_P, \big(\Gamma_{v_{\phi(e)}, \phi(e)} \circ \beta_{E_P}(e), \Gamma_{v_{\phi(f)}, \phi(f)} \circ \beta_{E_P}(f)\big) \in \prec_M \Big\}$$

In Fig. 10, with the pointcut P and the bSD M, we are going to show how Algorithm 1 works in a practical way if the function $findSetsOfEvent$ and min are defined as above. The table in Fig. 10 represents the values of some variables used in the algorithm. The two first variables $\alpha(\pi_{I1}(P))$ and $\alpha(\pi_{I2}(P))$ (used in line 3 of the algorithm) represent, respectively, the label of the projection of P on the objects $I1$ and $I2$. These two labels are equal to ab. The two next variables w_{I1} and w_{I2} (in Fig. 10, in table) represent the projection of M on respectively the objects $I1$ and $I2$ (computed in line 2 of the algorithm). Then, for I_1, with the function $findSetsOfEvent$, the algorithm computes the sets of successive events of w_{I1} which have the same action names (or labels) as $\alpha(\pi_{I1}(P))$. We obtain $V_{I1} = \{e_5'e_6'; e_7'e_8'\}$ since the labels of $e_5'e_6'$ and $e_7'e_8'$ are equal to ab. We do the same for I_2 and we obtain $V_{I2} = \{e_{11}'e_{12}'; e_{14}'e_{15}'; e_{17}'e_{18}'\}$. At line 5, with the function min, the algorithm computes the first (or minimum) set of events which form an enclosed part. The first set of events is $\{v_{I1} = e_5'e_6'; v_{I2} = e_{11}'e_{12}'\}$, but it does not satisfy the properties of line 5. Indeed,

$$\forall (e_1, e_3) \in \prec_P, \big(\Gamma_{v_{\phi(e_1)}, \phi(e_1)} \circ \beta_{E_P}(e_1), \Gamma_{v_{\phi(e_3)}, \phi(e_3)} \circ \beta_{E_P}(e_3)\big) =$$
$$\big(\Gamma_{v_{I1}, I1}(1), \Gamma_{v_{I2}, I2}(1)\big) = (e_5', e_{11}') \notin \prec_M.$$

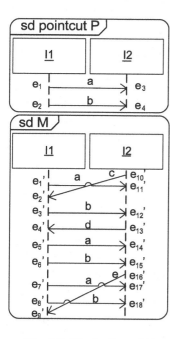

variable	value
$\alpha(\pi_{I1}(P))$	$\alpha(e_1 e_2) = ab$
$\alpha(\pi_{I2}(P))$	$\alpha(e_3 e_4) = ab$
w_{I1}	$e_1{}' e_2{}' e_3{}' e_4{}' e_5{}' e_6{}' e_7{}' e_8{}' e_9{}'$
w_{I2}	$e_{10}{}' e_{11}{}' e_{12}{}' e_{13}{}' e_{14}{}' e_{15}{}' e_{16}{}' e_{17}{}' e_{18}{}'$
V_{I1}	$\{e_5{}' e_6{}' ; e_7{}' e_8{}'\}$
V_{I2}	$\{e_{11}{}' e_{12}{}' ; e_{14}{}' e_{15}{}' ; e_{17}{}' e_{18}{}'\}$
$E_{M'}$	$\{e_5{}' e_6{}' ; e_{14}{}' e_{15}{}'\}$

Fig. 10. Illustration of the general algorithm using the enclosed part strategy

The set of events $\{v_{I1} = e_5'e_6'; v_{I2} = e_{14}'e_{15}'\}$ is the first set which satisfies the properties, so $E_{M'} = \{e_5'e_6'; e_{14}'e_{15}'\}$. The rest of the algorithm builds the isomorphism $\mu = (\mu_0, \mu_1, \mu_2)$ from P to the bSD formed by the events of $E_{M'}$.

Safe Part Detection

For the detection of safe part, the function $findSetsOfEvent$ is equivalent to

$$V_i = \left\{ v = x_1.x_2 \ldots x_k \in E_M^* \mid \exists u_i \in E_M^*, i \in \{1, \ldots, k+1\}, \right.$$

$$\left. w_i = u_1.x_1.u_2.x_2\ldots u_k.x_k.u_{k+1} \wedge \alpha(v) = \alpha(\pi_i(P)) \right\}. \text{ In}$$

this way, we can detect a join point even if there are some events (represented by the u_i) between the events of the join point. Let us note that for $i \in \{1, \ldots, k+1\}$, u_i can contain no event.

The function min looks like the one defined for the detection of enclosed pattern, but in addition, we also have to check if the order of the events of $E_{M'}$ is the same as the order of E_M restricted to the event of $E_{M'}$ (we check if $\leq_{M'} = \leq_{M|E_{M'}}$), because the fact that we allow the presence of other events between the events of a general part can introduce a difference between $\leq_{M'}$ and $\leq_{M|E_{M'}}$. Formally:

$$min\Big\{ v_1, \ldots, v_{|I_P|} \in V_1 \times \cdots \times V_{|I_P|} \big|$$

$$\forall (e,f) \in \prec_P, \big(\Gamma_{v_{\phi(e)}, \phi(e)} \circ \beta_{E_P}(e), \Gamma_{v_{\phi(f)}, \phi(f)} \circ \beta_{E_P}(f)\big) \in \prec_M \wedge \leq_{M'} = \leq_{M|E_{M'}} \Big\}$$

General Part Detection

For the detection of general part, the function $findSetsOfEvent$ is the same as the one used for the detection of safe part.

The function min is similar to the one used for the detection of safe part, except for one difference. According to the definition of a general part, it is not necessary to check whether $\leq_{M'} = \leq_{M|E_{M'}}$. So, in the function min, this checking is not performed (let us note that the property $\leq_{M'} \subseteq \leq_{M|E_{M'}}$ is always verified).

5 Operator of Composition

Now that we can detect join points in a base bSD, it remains to compose the bSD Advice with the join points. In [18], they use the notion of strict part to define the join points. If we note by J the join point and by B the base bSD, by definition, there exist two bSDs B_1 and B_2 such that we can write $B = B_1 \bullet J \bullet B_2$ ($\bullet$ being the operator of sequential composition). If we note Ad the advice representing the expected behavior, all you have to do to compose the advice with the join point is to replace the join point by the advice, and the woven bSD is $B = B_1 \bullet Ad \bullet B_2$.

When we use the notions of general part, safe part or enclosed part to define the join points, the composition of the advice is not so easy. Indeed, with these kinds of join points, some messages can surround a join point or some messages can be present between the messages forming the join point. In these cases, it is not possible to simply replace a join point by an advice because the result cannot be always expressed with the standard operators of composition such as the sequential composition operator. Therefore, we have to define a new operator of composition which takes into account the common parts between a join point and an advice to produce a new bSD which does not contain copies of similar elements of the two operands. We propose an operator of composition for bSDs called *left amalgamated sum*. This sum is inspired by the amalgamated sum proposed in [17]. We add the term *left* because our operator is not commutative, but it imposes a different role on each operand.

Figure 11 shows an example of left amalgamated sum where the two bSDs $base = (I_b, E_b, \leq_b, A_b, \alpha_b, \phi_b, \prec_b)$ and $advice = (I_a, E_a, \leq_a, A_a, \alpha_a, \phi_a, \prec_a)$ are amalgamated. For that, we use a third bSD which we call bSD $pointcut = (I_p, E_p, \leq_p, A_p, \alpha_p, \phi_p, \prec_p)$ and two bSD morphisms $f : pointcut \rightarrow base$ and $g : pointcut \rightarrow advice$ which allow the specification of the common parts of the two bSDs $base$ and $advice$. Moreover, f has to define an enclosed part, a safe part or a general part M' in the bSD $base$ such that f is an isomorphism from the $pointcut$ to M'. We can note that the morphism f is automatically obtained with the process of detection described into the previous section.

The morphism g, which indicates the elements shared by the advice and the pointcut, has to be specified when the aspect is defined. In this way, g allows the specification of abstract or generic advices which are "instantiated" by the morphism. For instance, it is not mandatory that the advice contains objects having the same name as those present in the pointcut. In the three aspects

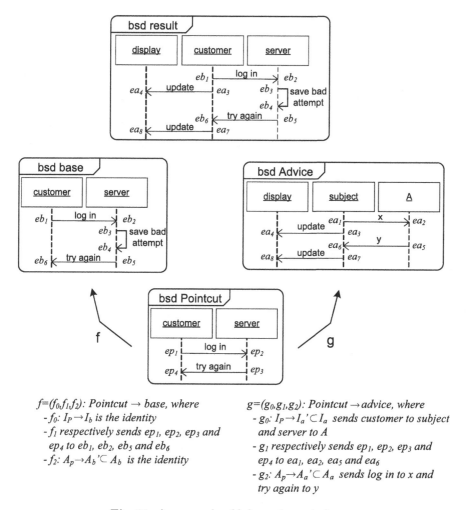

Fig. 11. An example of left amalgamated sum

in Fig. 4, the morphism g is not specified but it is trivial: for each aspect, we associate the objects and the actions having the same names, and the events corresponding to the actions having the same name. The advice of the aspect Display in Fig. 4 could be replaced by the "generic" Advice in Fig. 11. It is the morphism g which indicates that the object *customer* plays the role of the object *subject* and that the object *server* plays the role of the object *A*.

In Fig. 11, the elements of the bSDs *base* and *advice* having the same antecedent by f and g will be considered as identical in the bSD *result*, but they will keep the names specified in the bSD *base*. For instance, the objects *subject* and *A* in the bSD *advice* are replaced by the objects *customer* and *server*. All the elements of the bSD *base* having an antecedent γ by f such that γ has not an image by g in the bSD *advice* are deleted. This case does not appear in the example proposed, but in this way we can delete messages of the bSD *base*. For instance, in an amalgamated sum, if the right operand (the bSD advice in the example) is an empty bSD then the part of the left operand which is isomorphic to the *pointcut* (that is to say the join point), is deleted. Finally, all the elements of the bSDs *base* and *advice* having no antecedent by f and g are kept in the bSD *result*, but the events of the bSD *advice* will always form a "block" around which the events of the bSD *base* will be added. For instance, in Fig. 11, in the bSD *base*, if there were an event e on the object *customer* just after the message *try again*, then this event e would be localized just after the sending of the message *update* (event ea_7) in the woven SD.

Formally, a left amalgamated sum is defined by:

Definition 12 (left amalgamated sum). *Let $M_0 = (I_0, E_0, \leq_0, A_0, \alpha_0, \phi_0, \prec_0)$, $M_1 = (I_1, E_1, \leq_1, A_1, \alpha_1, \phi_1, \prec_1)$ and $M_2 = (I_2, E_2, \leq_2, A_2, \alpha_2, \phi_2, \prec_2)$ be three bSDs. Let $f =< f_0, f_1, f_2 >: M_0 \to M_1$ and $g =< g_0, g_1, g_2 >: M_0 \to M_2$ be two bSDs morphisms such that $f(M_0)$ defines a part M_1' of M_1 and that f is a isomorphism from M_0 to M_1'. The left amalgamated sum of M_1 and M_2 is the bSD $M = M_1 +_{f,g} M_2$ where $M = (I, E, \leq, A, \alpha, \phi, \prec)$ is defined by:*

$$I = I_1 \cup \{i_2 \in I_2 | \nexists i_0 \in I_0, g_0^{-1}(i_2) = i_0\};$$

$$E = \{e_1 \in E_1 | \exists e_0 \in E_0, \exists e_2 \in E_2, f_1^{-1}(e_1) = e_0 \wedge g_1(e_0) = e_2\} \cup \{e_1 \in E_1 | \nexists e_0 \in E_0, f_1^{-1}(e_1) = e_0\} \cup \{e_2 \in E_2 | \nexists e_0 \in E_0, g_1^{-1}(e_2) = e_0\};$$

$$\leq = \begin{pmatrix} \{(e_1, e_2) \in (E_1 \cap E)^2 | e_1 \leq_1 e_2\} \cup \\ \{(e_1, e_2) \in (E_2 \cap E)^2 | e_1 \leq_2 e_2\} \cup \\ \{(e_1, e_2), e_1 \in (f_1(E_0) \cap E), e_2 \in (E_2 \cap E)| \\ \qquad \exists e_2' \in E_2, e_2' = g_1 \circ f_1^{-1}(e_1) \wedge e_2' \leq_2 e_2\} \cup \\ \{(e_1, e_2), e_1 \in (E_2 \cap E), e_2 \in (f_1(E_0) \cap E)| \\ \qquad \exists e_2' \in E_2, e_2' = g_1 \circ f_1^{-1}(e_2) \wedge e_1 \leq_2 e_2'\} \cup \\ \{(e_1, e_2), e_1 \in (pred_{<_1, E_1} f_1(E_0) - f_1(E_0)), e_2 \in (E_2 \cap E)| \\ \qquad\qquad\qquad \phi(e_1) = \phi(e_2)\} \cup \\ \{(e_1, e_2), e_1 \in (E_2 \cap E), e_2 \in (succ_{<_1, E_1} f_1(E_0) - f_1(E_0))| \\ \qquad\qquad\qquad \phi(e_1) = \phi(e_2)\} \end{pmatrix}^*$$

$$\forall e \in E, \alpha(e) = \begin{cases} \alpha_1(e) & \text{if } e \in E_1 \\ \alpha_2(e) & \text{if } e \in E_2 \end{cases};$$

$$\forall e \in E, \phi(e) = \begin{cases} \phi_1(e) & \text{if } e \in E_1 \\ \phi_2(e) & \text{if } e \in E_2 \end{cases};$$

$$A = \alpha(E);$$

$$\prec = (\prec_1 \cup \prec_2) \cap E^2.$$

The first line of the definition of $\leq$ means that each pair of events of E_1 present in E and ordered by $\leq_1$ remains ordered by $\leq$. The second line is equivalent but for the events of E_2. The third line means that an event e_1 of E_1 present in E precedes an event e_2 of E_2 present in E, if there exists an event e_2' of E_2 preceding e_2 and corresponding to e_1 in M_0. The fourth line means that an event e_2 of E_1 present in E succeeds an event e_1 of E_2 present in E, if there exists an event e_2' of E_2 succeeding e_1 and having the same antecedent as e_2 in M_0. Finally, the fifth line means that an event e_1 of E_1 preceding the part detected in M_1, will precede all event e_2 of E_2 if e_1 and e_2 are localized on the same object in M. The last line is equivalent but for the events of E_1 which succeed the detected part.

Let us note that this operator of composition can lead to some situations where there are several possibilities to order the events. For instance, in Fig. 11, let us suppose that the messages *update* in the bSD *advice* are sent by the object A instead of the object *customer*. Then, when we compose the bSD *base* with the bSD *advice*, the sending of the message *update* and the message *save bad attempt* cannot be ordered. In this case, it is the designer who has to specify the expected order.

6   Implementation with Kermeta

To apply the detection and composition algorithms proposed in this paper on practical examples, we have implemented them within the Kermeta environment. This section is divided in three sub-sections. The first one presents the Kermeta environment and details our motivations for using it. The second details how the weaving process is implemented, and the third presents the use of our weaver from a user perspective.

6.1   The Kermeta Environment

Kermeta [19] is an open source meta-modeling language developed by the Triskell team at IRISA. It has been designed as an extension to the EMOF 2.0 to be the core of a meta-modeling platform. Kermeta extends EMOF with an action language that allows specifying semantics and behaviors of metamodels. The action language is imperative and object-oriented. It is used to provide an implementation of operations defined in metamodels. As a result the Kermeta language can, not only be used for the definition of metamodels but also for implementing their semantics, constraints and transformations.

The Kermeta action language has been specially designed to process models. It includes both Object Oriented (OO) features and model specific features. Kermeta includes traditional OO static typing, multiple inheritance and behavior redefinition/selection with a late binding semantics. To make Kermeta suitable for model processing, more specific concepts such as opposite properties (i.e., associations) and handling of object containment have been included. In addition to this, convenient constructions of the Object Constraint Language (OCL), such as closures (e.g., each, collect, select), are also available in Kermeta.

A complete description of the way the language was defined can be found in [19]. It was successfully used for the implementation of a class diagram composition technique in [25] but also as a model transformation language in [20]. To implement the detection and composition techniques proposed in this paper we have chosen to use Kermeta for two reasons. First, the language allows implementing composition by adding the algorithm in the body of the operations defined in the composition metamodel. Second, Kermeta tools are compatible with the Eclipse Modeling Framework (EMF) [5] which allows us to use Eclipse tools to edit, store, and visualize models.

6.2   The Weaving Process as Model Transformations

As detailed previously, the weaving process consists of two steps. Firstly, the detection step uses the pointcut model and the base model to compute a set of join points. Each join point is characterized by a morphism from the pointcut to a corresponding elements in the base model. Secondly, using these morphisms, the advice is composed with each join point in the base model. The first step processes models to extract join points and the second is a model transformation. Fig. 12 details the input and output models of these two steps (each ellipse is a model and the black rectangle on the top left-hand corner indicates its metamodel). Except for morphisms, all models are SDs.

The first step to process or transform models in Kermeta is the definition of the input and output metamodels. Thanks to the compatibility of Kermeta with Eclipse tools, we have used Omondo UML [22] which provides a graphical editor for metamodels in addition to UML editors. Fig. 3 presents the simple metamodels we are using for SDs. We use this sequence diagram metamodel rather than that of UML2.0 for two major reasons. Firstly, as shown in Sect. 2, the metamodel in Fig. 3 fits very well with the formal definitions introduced in this paper. So, the metamodel is relatively small, concise and easy to understand, and the algorithms presented in this paper are easier to write with this metamodel rather than with that of UML2.0. Secondly, it is very simple to write a transformation from the UML2.0 sequence diagram metamodel to the metamodel in Fig. 3 because the concepts are very close. So, we can apply the weaving on a model compliant to the UML2.0 metamodel by performing a transformation from the UML2.0 sequence diagram metamodel to the metamodel in Fig. 3 before the weaving process.

Once the metamodel is defined this way, EMF provides generic tools to create, edit and save instance models. Kermeta allows, on one hand to complete the metamodel with the specification of the bodies of operation and on the other hand to process models created with EMF. We used the same process to define a simple metamodel to represent morphisms. This metamodel contains only one class called Morphism which encapsulates associations between, instances, messages and events of two SDs.

Using the metamodels for SDs and morphisms, we have designed and implemented the complete weaving process. For the detection transformation we have defined a Kermeta abstract class Detection and three sub-classes to implement the different detection strategies. The composition is implemented in a single Kermeta class.

Both the implementation of detection algorithms and the implementation of the composition operator were used to validate the techniques proposed in this paper. The composition was implemented first and tested by providing test cases composed of a base scenario, a pointcut scenario, an aspect scenario, and the morphisms between the pointcut and the advice and between the pointcut and the base scenario. We chose the set of test cases to intuitively cover the

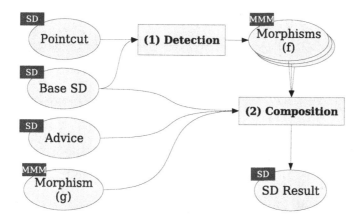

Fig. 12. Transformation of Models

structures of sequence diagrams such as messages between two instances, messages on a single instance, crossing messages or cSD with alternatives, etc. For all test cases, we checked manually that the composed models correspond to the expected models. The implementation of the detection algorithms was tested using various simple scenarios corresponding to detection and non-detection cases. We especially had to test the detection algorithms in situations where several potential matches could be chosen. In addition to the testing of each step of the weaving, we applied our prototype tool on several small academic examples.

6.3   Using the Prototype Tool

This goal of this section is to present the use of our weaving technique from a user perspective.

First, the developer has to model the base scenario of his/her application. To do so we use the UML 2.0 sequence diagram editor available in the TopCaseD eclipse plugin [27]. Figure 13 presents a screenshot of this editor with a base model. The base model consists of an interaction between two instances names *user* and *server*. Figure 14 presents the two scenarios of a behavioral aspect to weave in the base model. The pointcut and advice are presented respectively at the top and at the bottom of the figure. This goal of this aspect is to update a *display* object whenever a *customer* object sends a *log in* message or receives a response from the *server*.

Once the scenarios for both the base model and the behavioral aspect are defined, a wizard can be used to perform the weaving. Figure 15 presents a screenshot of this wizard. To apply our weaving algorithms, the user has to provide the scenarios corresponding to the pointcut and advice and specify in which base models the weaving should be applied. In addition to this, the user can choose the detection strategy to use. If the *strict sequence of messages* is selected then the detection strategy corresponds to the notions of *strict part* and *enclosed part* of a bSD. The check-box *allow surrounding messages* allows

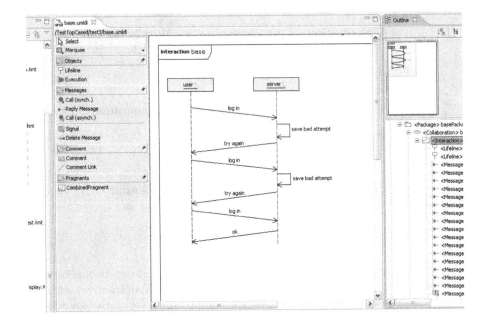

Fig. 13. Screenshot of the base scenario

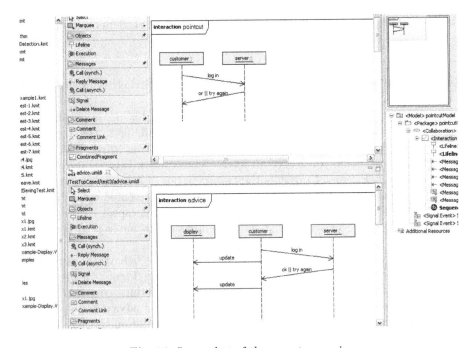

Fig. 14. Screenshot of the aspect scenarios

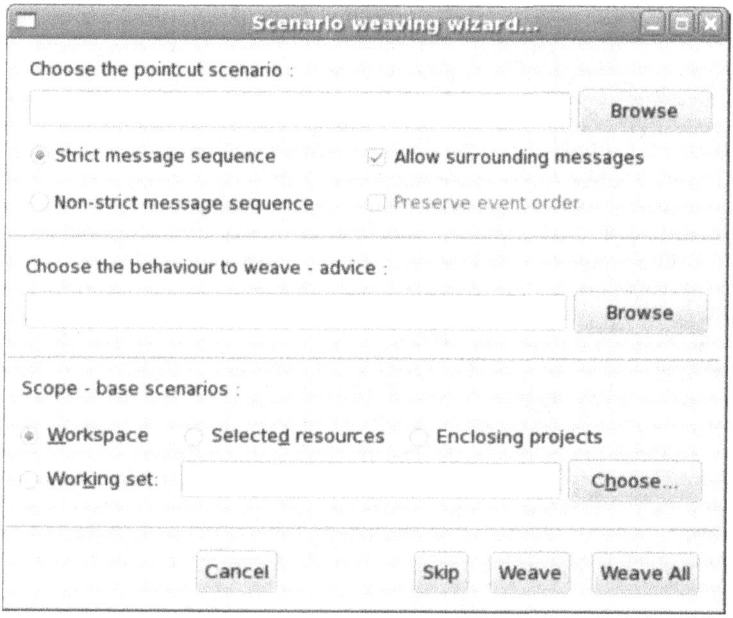

Fig. 15. Screenshot of the weaving wizard

choosing between these two strategies. It the *non-strict sequence of messages* is selected, then the notions of *safe part* and *general part* of a bSD are used. The check box *preserve event order* allows choosing between these two strategies. After choosing the detection strategies, the weaving can be performed at once using the *Weave All* button or interactively using the *Weave* and *Skip* buttons.

Figure 16 presents the result of the weaving of the behavioral aspect in the base model of Fig. 13, with as settings in the wizard, "Non-strict message sequence" and "Preserve event order" selected.

7   Future Works

The algorithms of join point detection proposed in this paper (when the join points are enclosed parts, safe parts or general parts of a bSD) only work for bSDs or combined SDs which generate a finite number of behaviors (cSDs without loop, in this case the weaving can be applied to each bSDs of the set generated by a cSD). When the join points are strict parts of a bSD, the join point detection within infinite behavior is already solved in [18]. More specifically, the detection of join points within infinite behaviors always terminates when the pointcut is connected, i.e., when the pointcut has no parallel component (the pointcut cannot be written as a parallel composition of two other bSDs). However, for the new definitions of join points proposed in this paper, the problem of detection is more complicated. For instance, let us consider the behavioral aspect and the cSD *example* depicted in Fig. 17. When the join points are general parts of a

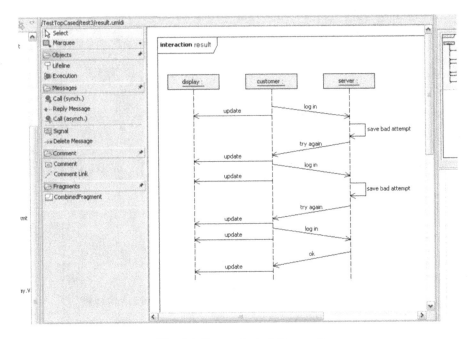

Fig. 16. Screenshot of the result

bSD, the join point formed by the messages a and b is detected in each behavior generated by the cSD *example*. So, the expected behaviors allows any number of messages c between a and b. Since the message d surrounds this potentially infinite number of messages c, the expected behaviors cannot be represented with SDs (we cannot isolate anymore the message c in a loop).

When we consider the join points as general parts, safe part or enclosed part, our future works are to identify the cases for which our static weaving is always possible, even if the base scenario generates an infinite number of behaviors.

In the paper we have chosen to limit the approach to simple name matching. However, in future work, our approach could be extended with more powerful matching mechanisms such as roles or wildcards on object names.

8   Related Works

Clarke and Baniassad [7] use the *Theme/UML approach* to define aspects. Theme/UML introduces a theme module that can be used to represent a concern at the modeling level. Themes are declaratively complete units of modularization, in which any of the diagrams available in the UML can be used to model one view of the structure and behavior the concern requires to execute. In Theme/UML, a class diagram and sequence diagrams are typically used to describe the structure and behaviors of the concern being modeled. The question addressed by their work is more the specification of aspects than the weaving process into non-aspectual models, but our definitions and detection of join point, and our

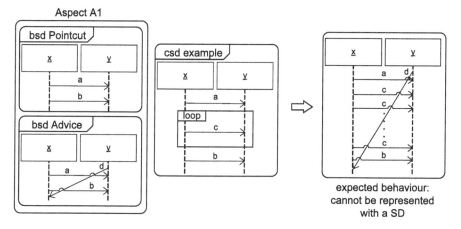

Fig. 17. Impossible weaving

operator of composition can easily be adapted to the Theme approach to keep the advantages of the two approaches.

Similarly to our approach, Whittle and Araujo ([29] and [2]) represent behavioral aspects with scenarios. Aspectual scenarios are modeled as interaction pattern specifications (IPSs introduced in [12]) and are composed with specification scenarios. The weaving process defined in [29] composes scenarios with instantiation and ad-hoc composition operators. The weaving process proposed by [2] is performed in two steps. The first step is to generate state machines from the aspects and from the specification. The weaving process is then a composition of these state machines. However, in these two approaches, the detection of join points is not automated: users have to specify them with a binding relation between an aspect and a specification. Moreover, their composition operator for SDs is not defined formally.

In [26], Stein et al. introduce a way to express various conceptual models of pointcuts in aspect-oriented design. But, they do not provide a way to detect the join points specified by these pointcuts. By contrast, in our approach the detection of the join points and their composition is automatic.

More generally, in [10] and [11], Douence et al. are interested in event pattern matching, which is close to our approach. A significant difference is that they use a monitor to perform event pattern matching at runtime on a program execution, whereas our weaving is made statically at a modeling level. Similar to Douence et al., Walker and Viggers [28] have proposed *declarative event patterns* as a means to specify patterns of events to detect sequence of events in the execution of a system based on a context-free-language-based pattern matching, while Allan et al. [1] have proposed a new history-based language feature called *tracematches* that enables the programmer to trigger the execution of extra code by specifying a regular pattern of events in a computation trace. Our approach differs from both in that we allow the entire pattern (join point) to be replaced or completed, rather than just the final event in the pattern. We can do that because our weaving is static. We do not perform the weaving during the execution of the sequence diagram, but we transform a sequence diagram into another sequence diagram where the aspect is woven.

Still at a programming level, recently Bockisch et al. [4] have proposed a novel implementation of the mechanism of cflow present in AspectJ for which the efficiency of join point detection for dynamic weaving is improved. However, it is only applicable for the detection of sequence of messages in the control flow of a method, whereas with our approach, we can detect any interactions. Moreover, since our weaving is static, performance is not a primary issue.

The aspect model and in particular the mechanism to identify join points plays a critical role in the applicability of the aspect-oriented methodology. According to Kiczales [15], the pointcuts definition language probably has the most relevant role in the success of the aspect-oriented technology but most of the solutions proposed so far are too tied to the syntax of the programs manipulated.

Ostermann et al. [23] try to address this problem by proposing a static joint point model that exploits information from different models of program semantics. They show that this model of joint points increases the abstraction level and the modularity of pointcuts.

9   Conclusion

In this paper we have proposed a technique to statically weave behavioral aspects into sequence diagrams. Our weaving process is automated, and takes into account the semantics of the model used, i.e., the partial order that a SD induces.

To enable the weaving of multiple aspects, we have proposed a new interpretation for pointcuts to allow join points to match them more flexibly. However, with this new way of specifying join points, the composition of the advice with the detected part could not any longer be a replacement of the detected part by the advice. We thus had to consider the events (or the messages) of the join point which are not specified within the pointcut and merge them with the behavior specified within the advice. We proposed a formal definition for such a merge operator, and described its implementation on the Kermeta platform. Moreover, we have presented the use of our weaving technique from a user perspective.

However, our approach suffers from limitations: our algorithms for join point detection only work for bSDs or combined SDs which generate a finite number of behaviors. This has to be considered for further research.

References

1. Allan, C., Avgustinov, P., Christensen, A.S., Hendren, L., Kuzins, S., Lhotak, O., de Moor, O., Sereni, D., Sittampalam, G., Tibble, J.: Adding trace matching with free variables to aspect. In: OOPSLA '05. Proceedings of the 20th annual ACM SIGPLAN conference on Object oriented programming, systems, languages, and applications, vol. 40, pp. 345–364. ACM Press, New York (2005)
2. Araujo, J., Whittle, J., Kim.: Modeling and composing scenario-based requirements with aspects. In: Proceedings of RE 2004, Kyoto, Japan (September 2004)

3. Early Aspects.net (2006), http://www.early-aspects.net/
4. Bockisch, C., Kanthak, S., Haupt, M., Arnold, M., Mezini, M.: Efficient control flow quantification. In: OOPSLA '06. Proceedings of the 21th annual ACM SIGPLAN conference on Object oriented programming, systems, languages, and applications, vol. 41, pp. 125–138. ACM Press, New York (2006)
5. Budinsky, F., Steinberg, D., Merks, E., Ellersick, R., Grose, T.: Eclipse Modeling Framework. The Eclipse Series. Addison Wesley Professional, Reading (2003)
6. Clarke, S.: Composition of Object-Oriented Software Design Models. PhD thesis, Dublin City University (2001)
7. Clarke, S., Baniassad, E.: Aspect-Oriented Analysis and Design: The Theme Approach. Addison-Wesley, Reading (2005)
8. Damm, W., Harel, D.: LSCs: Breathing life into message sequence charts. vol. 19, pp. 45–80 (2001)
9. Davey, B.A., Priestley, H.A.: Introduction to Lattices and Order. Cambridge Mathematical Textbooks (1990)
10. Douence, R., Fradet, P., Südholt, M.: A framework for the detection and resolution of aspect interactions. In: Batory, D., Consel, C., Taha, W. (eds.) GPCE 2002. LNCS, vol. 2487, Springer, Heidelberg (2002)
11. Douence, R., Motelet, O., Südholt, M.: A formal definition of crosscuts. In: Yonezawa, A., Matsuoka, S. (eds.) Metalevel Architectures and Separation of Crosscutting Concerns. LNCS, vol. 2192, pp. 170–186. Springer, Heidelberg (2001)
12. France, R.B., Kim, D.-K., Ghosh, S., Song, E.: A uml-based pattern specification technique. IEEE TSE 30(3), 193–206 (2004)
13. ITU-TS. ITU-TS Recommendation Z.120: Message Sequence Chart (MSC). ITU-TS, Geneva (September 1999)
14. Jacobson, I., Ng, P.-W.: Aspect-Oriented Software Development with Use Cases. Addison-Wesley, Reading (2004)
15. Kiczales, G.: The fun has just begun. Keynote of AOSD'03 (2003)
16. Kiczales, G., Hilsdale, E., Hugunin, J., Kersten, M., Palm, J., Griswold, W.G.: An overview of AspectJ. In: Knudsen, J.L. (ed.) ECOOP 2001. LNCS, vol. 2072, pp. 327–355. Springer, Heidelberg (2001)
17. Klein, J., Caillaud, B., Hélouët, L.: Merging scenarios. In: Workshop on FMICS, pp. 209–226, Linz, Austria (September 2004)
18. Klein, J., Helouet, L., Jézéquel, J.-M.: Semantic-based weaving of scenarios. In: AOSD, Bonn, Germany, March 2006, ACM Press, New York (2006)
19. Muller, P.-A., Fleurey, F., Jézéquel, J.-M.: Weaving executability into object-oriented meta-languages. In: Briand, L.C., Williams, C. (eds.) MoDELS 2005. LNCS, vol. 3713, pp. 264–278. Springer, Heidelberg (2005)
20. Muller, P.-A., Fleurey, F., Vojtisek, D., Drey, Z., Pollet, D., Fondement, F., Studer, P., Jézéquel, J.-M.: On executable meta-languages applied to model transformations. In: Model Transformatios in Practice Workshop, Jamaica (2005)
21. OMG. Uml superstructure, v2.0. OMG Document number formal/05-07-04 (2005)
22. Omondo (2006), http://www.omondo.com
23. Ostermann, K., Mezini, M., Bockisch, C.: Expressive pointcuts for increased modularity. In: Black, A.P. (ed.) ECOOP 2005. LNCS, vol. 3586, Springer, Heidelberg (2005)
24. Rashid, A., Moreira, A.M.D., Araújo, J.: Modularisation and composition of aspectual requirements. In: Proceedings of AOSD'03, pp. 11–20 (2003)
25. Reddy, R., France, R., Ghosh, S., Fleurey, F., Baudry, B.: Model composition - a signature-based approach. In: AOM Workshop, Montego Bay (October 2005)

26. Stein, D., Hanenberg, S., Unland, R.: Expressing different conceptual models of join point selection in aspect-oriented design. In: Proceedings of AOSD 2006 (2006)
27. TopCaseD, (2006), `http://www.topcased.org/`
28. Walker, R.J., Viggers, K.: Implementing protocols via declarative event patterns. In: ACM Sigsoft International Symposium on Foundations of Software Engineering (FSE-12). 29(6), 159–169, (2004)
29. Whittle, J., Araújo, J.: Scenario modelling with aspects. IEE Proceedings - Software 151(4), 157–172 (2004)

Appendix

This appendix contains the proof of Theorem 1.

Proof:
To demonstrate Theorem 1, we assume that two overtaking messages cannot have the same name and we use the following lemma which can be found in the book *"Introduction to Lattices and Order"* [9](p.110):

Lemma 1. *Let $(L, \vee, \wedge)$ be a triple where L is a non-empty set equipped with two binary operations $\vee$ and $\wedge$ which satisfy for all $a, b, c \in L$:*

(1) $a \vee a = a$ *and* $a \wedge a = a$ *(idempotency laws);*
(2) $a \vee b = b \vee a$ *and* $a \wedge b = b \wedge a$ *(commutative laws);*
(3) $(a \vee b) \vee c = a \vee (b \vee c)$ *et* $(a \wedge b) \wedge c = a \wedge (b \wedge c)$ *(associative laws);*
(4) $a \vee (a \wedge b) = a$ *et* $a \wedge (a \vee b) = a$ *(absorption laws).*

then:

(i) $\forall a, b \in L, a \vee b = b \Leftrightarrow a \wedge b = a$;
(ii) *If we define* $\leq$ *by* $a \leq b$ *if* $a \vee b = b$, *then* $\leq$ *is an order relation;*
(iii) *With* $\leq$ *as in* (ii), $(L, \leq)$ *is a lattice such that* $\forall a, b \in L, a \vee b = sup\{a, b\}$ *and* $a \wedge b = inf\{a, b\}$.
∎

We will show that $\mathcal{J}_{P,M}$ can be equipped with two binary operations $\vee$ and $\wedge$ which verify the properties 1–4 of the lemma.

Let $\mathcal{J}_{P,M}$ be the set of join points corresponding to a pointcut $P = (I_P, E_P, \leq_P, A_P, \alpha_P, \phi_P, \prec_P)$ in a bSD $M = (I, E, \leq, A, \alpha, \phi, \prec)$. Let $\vee$ and $\wedge$ be the operators defined for each J_i, J_j of $\mathcal{J}_{P,M}$ by:

$$J_i \vee J_j = \{e, f \in J_i | e \prec f, \exists e' \in E_P, e = \mu_{i_1}(e'), \mu_{j_1}(e') \leq e\} \cup$$
$$\{e, f \in J_j | e \prec f, \exists e' \in E_P, e = \mu_{j_1}(e'), \mu_{i_1}(e') \leq e\}$$

$$J_i \wedge J_j = \{e, f \in J_i | e \prec f, \exists e' \in E_P, e = \mu_{i_1}(e'), e \leq \mu_{j_1}(e')\} \cup$$
$$\{e, f \in J_j | e \prec f, \exists e' \in E_P, e = \mu_{j_1}(e'), e \leq \mu_{i_1}(e')\}$$

$\mu_i = < \mu_{i_0}, \mu_{i_1}, \mu_{i_2} >$ and $\mu_j = < \mu_{j_0}, \mu_{j_1}, \mu_{j_2} >$ being the isomorphisms associating P to the respective join points J_i and J_j.

For $(\mathcal{J}_{P,M}, \vee, \wedge)$, the properties (1) and (2) of the lemma are verified (trivial). Let J_i, J_j and J_k be three join points and $\mu_i =< \mu_{i_0}, \mu_{i_1}, \mu_{i_2} >$, $\mu_j =< \mu_{j_0}, \mu_{j_1}, \mu_{j_2} >$ and $\mu_k =< \mu_{k_0}, \mu_{k_1}, \mu_{k_2} >$ the three isomorphisms associating respectively P to J_i, J_j and J_k. Let e and f be two events of M such that $e \prec f$. If e and f belong to J_i and $(J_i \vee J_j) \vee J_k$, let e' be the corresponding event in P such that $e = \mu_{i_1}(e')$, then according to the definition of $\vee$, e succeeds to $\mu_{j_1}(e')$ and $\mu_{k_1}(e')$. Therefore, e and f also belong to $J_i \vee (J_j \vee J_k)$. In this way, we easily show that $(J_i \vee J_j) \vee J_k = J_i \vee (J_j \vee J_k)$. In the same way, we also show that $(J_i \wedge J_j) \wedge J_k = J_i \wedge (J_j \wedge J_k)$. Finally, to prove the property (4), let us consider the two join points J_i and J_j and their associated morphisms μ_i and μ_j. Let e_2 and f_2 be two events belonging to J_j and $J_i \vee (J_i \wedge J_j)$ (and consequently to $J_i \wedge J_j$) but not to J_i. Let us note e' the event belonging to P such that $e_2 = \mu_{j_1}(e')$. If $e_1 = \mu_{i_1}(e')$, then since e_2 belongs to $J_i \wedge J_j$, $e_2 \leq e_1$, and since e_2 belongs to $J_i \vee (J_i \wedge J_j)$, $e_1 \leq e_2$. Impossible, therefore all the events of $J_i \vee (J_i \wedge J_j)$ belong to J_i.

According to the lemma, $(\mathcal{J}_{P,M}, \ll')$, with $\ll'$ defined by $J_i \ll' J_j$ if $J_i \vee J_j = J_j$, is a lattice. Moreover $\ll'$ is equivalent to the order $\ll$ of Definition 10. The equivalence is easy to demonstrate. Let J_i and J_j be two join points, and μ_i and μ_j their associated isomorphisms to P. If $J_i \ll' J_j$, by definition $J_i \vee J_j = J_j$, and thus all the message send events of J_j succeed those of J_i. The converse is trivial. $\qquad\boxed{\cdot}$

Author Index

Lecture Notes in Computer Science

Sublibrary 2: Programming and Software Engineering

Vol. 4536: G. Concas, E. Damiani, M. Scotto, G. Succi (Eds.), Agile Processes in Software Engineering and Extreme Programming. XV, 276 pages. 2007.

Vol. 4530: D.H. Akehurst, R. Vogel, R.F. Paige (Eds.), Model Driven Architecture - Foundations and Applications. X, 219 pages. 2007.

Vol. 4523: Y.-H. Lee, H.-N. Kim, J. Kim, Y.W. Park, L.T. Yang, S.W. Kim (Eds.), Embedded Software and Systems. XIX, 829 pages. 2007.

Vol. 4498: N. Abdennahder, F. Kordon (Eds.), Reliable Software Technologies - Ada-Europe 2007. XII, 247 pages. 2007.

Vol. 4486: M. Bernardo, J. Hillston (Eds.), Formal Methods for Performance Evaluation. VII, 469 pages. 2007.

Vol. 4470: Q. Wang, D. Pfahl, D.M. Raffo (Eds.), Software Process Dynamics and Agility. XI, 346 pages. 2007.

Vol. 4468: M.M. Bonsangue, E.B. Johnsen (Eds.), Formal Methods for Open Object-Based Distributed Systems. X, 317 pages. 2007.

Vol. 4467: A.L. Murphy, J. Vitek (Eds.), Coordination Models and Languages. X, 325 pages. 2007.

Vol. 4454: Y. Gurevich, B. Meyer (Eds.), Tests and Proofs. IX, 217 pages. 2007.

Vol. 4444: T. Reps, M. Sagiv, J. Bauer (Eds.), Program Analysis and Compilation, Theory and Practice. X, 361 pages. 2007.

Vol. 4440: B. Liblit, Cooperative Bug Isolation. XV, 101 pages. 2007.

Vol. 4408: R. Choren, A. Garcia, H. Giese, H.-f. Leung, C. Lucena, A. Romanovsky (Eds.), Software Engineering for Multi-Agent Systems V. XII, 233 pages. 2007.

Vol. 4406: W. De Meuter (Ed.), Advances in Smalltalk. VII, 157 pages. 2007.

Vol. 4405: L. Padgham, F. Zambonelli (Eds.), Agent-Oriented Software Engineering VII. XII, 225 pages. 2007.

Vol. 4401: N. Guelfi, D. Buchs (Eds.), Rapid Integration of Software Engineering Techniques. IX, 177 pages. 2007.

Vol. 4385: K. Coninx, K. Luyten, K.A. Schneider (Eds.), Task Models and Diagrams for Users Interface Design. XI, 355 pages. 2007.

Vol. 4383: E. Bin, A. Ziv, S. Ur (Eds.), Hardware and Software, Verification and Testing. XII, 235 pages. 2007.

Vol. 4379: M. Südholt, C. Consel (Eds.), Object-Oriented Technology. VIII, 157 pages. 2007.

Vol. 4364: T. Kühne (Ed.), Models in Software Engineering. XI, 332 pages. 2007.

Vol. 4355: J. Julliand, O. Kouchnarenko (Eds.), B 2007: Formal Specification and Development in B. XIII, 293 pages. 2006.

Vol. 4354: M. Hanus (Ed.), Practical Aspects of Declarative Languages. X, 335 pages. 2006.

Vol. 4350: M. Clavel, F. Durán, S. Eker, P. Lincoln, N. Martí-Oliet, J. Meseguer, C. Talcott, All About Maude - A High-Performance Logical Framework. XXII, 797 pages. 2007.

Vol. 4348: S. Tucker Taft, R.A. Duff, R.L. Brukardt, E. Plödereder, P. Leroy, Ada 2005 Reference Manual. XXII, 765 pages. 2006.

Vol. 4346: L. Brim, B.R. Haverkort, M. Leucker, J. van de Pol (Eds.), Formal Methods: Applications and Technology. X, 363 pages. 2007.

Vol. 4344: V. Gruhn, F. Oquendo (Eds.), Software Architecture. X, 245 pages. 2006.

Vol. 4340: R. Prodan, T. Fahringer, Grid Computing. XXIII, 317 pages. 2007.

Vol. 4336: V.R. Basili, H.D. Rombach, K. Schneider, B. Kitchenham, D. Pfahl, R.W. Selby (Eds.), Empirical Software Engineering Issues. XVII, 193 pages. 2007.

Vol. 4326: S. Göbel, R. Malkewitz, I. Iurgel (Eds.), Technologies for Interactive Digital Storytelling and Entertainment. X, 384 pages. 2006.

Vol. 4323: G. Doherty, A. Blandford (Eds.), Interactive Systems. XI, 269 pages. 2007.

Vol. 4322: F. Kordon, J. Sztipanovits (Eds.), Reliable Systems on Unreliable Networked Platforms. XIV, 317 pages. 2007.

Vol. 4309: P. Inverardi, M. Jazayeri (Eds.), Software Engineering Education in the Modern Age. VIII, 207 pages. 2006.

Vol. 4294: A. Dan, W. Lamersdorf (Eds.), Service-Oriented Computing – ICSOC 2006. XIX, 653 pages. 2006.

Vol. 4290: M. van Steen, M. Henning (Eds.), Middleware 2006. XIII, 425 pages. 2006.

Vol. 4279: N. Kobayashi (Ed.), Programming Languages and Systems. XI, 423 pages. 2006.

Vol. 4262: K. Havelund, M. Núñez, G. Roşu, B. Wolff (Eds.), Formal Approaches to Software Testing and Runtime Verification. VIII, 255 pages. 2006.

Vol. 4260: Z. Liu, J. He (Eds.), Formal Methods and Software Engineering. XII, 778 pages. 2006.

Vol. 4257: I. Richardson, P. Runeson, R. Messnarz (Eds.), Software Process Improvement. XI, 219 pages. 2006.

Vol. 4242: A. Rashid, M. Aksit (Eds.), Transactions on Aspect-Oriented Software Development II. IX, 289 pages. 2006.

Vol. 4229: E. Najm, J.-F. Pradat-Peyre, V.V. Donzeau-Gouge (Eds.), Formal Techniques for Networked and Distributed Systems - FORTE 2006. X, 486 pages. 2006.

Vol. 4227: W. Nejdl, K. Tochtermann (Eds.), Innovative Approaches for Learning and Knowledge Sharing. XVII, 721 pages. 2006.

Vol. 4218: S. Graf, W. Zhang (Eds.), Automated Technology for Verification and Analysis. XIV, 540 pages. 2006.

Vol. 4214: C. Hofmeister, I. Crnković, R. Reussner (Eds.), Quality of Software Architectures. X, 215 pages. 2006.

Vol. 4204: F. Benhamou (Ed.), Principles and Practice of Constraint Programming - CP 2006. XVIII, 774 pages. 2006.

Printed in the United States
By Bookmasters